Malory and Christianity

Medieval Institute Publications is a program of
The Medieval Institute, College of Arts and Sciences

 WESTERN MICHIGAN UNIVERSITY

Malory and Christianity: Essays on Sir Thomas Malory's *Morte Darthur*

Edited by D. Thomas Hanks, Jr., and Janet Jesmok

Studies in Medieval Culture LI

MEDIEVAL INSTITUTE PUBLICATIONS
Western Michigan University
Kalamazoo

Library of Congress Cataloging-in-Publication Data

Malory and Christianity : essays on Sir Thomas Malory's Morte d'Arthur / edited by D. Thomas Hanks, Jr., and Janet Jesmok.
    pages cm -- (Studies in medieval culture ; 51)
  Includes bibliographical references and index.
  ISBN 978-1-58044-175-9 (clothbound : alk. paper) -- ISBN 978-1-58044-176-6 (pbk : alk. paper)
  1. Malory, Thomas, Sir, 15th cent. Morte d'Arthur. 2. Christianity in literature. 3. Arthurian romances--History and criticism. 4. Romances, English--History and criticism. 5. Knights and knighthood in literature. 6. Kings and rulers in literature. I. Hanks, Dorrel Thomas, editior of compilation. II. Jesmok, Janet, editior of compilation.
  PR2045.M73 2013
  823'.2--dc23

                                                          2012047041

Manufactured in the United States of America
This book is printed on acid-free paper.
5 4 3 2 1 C P 5 4 3 2 1

Contents

Prefatory Note

In 1985, Medieval Institute Publications published *Studies in Malory*, edited by James W. Spisak. All the contributors to this volume have read and learned from that outstanding collection; it became a model for us. Although The Medieval Institute does not publish series on any authors, we the editors have come to think of this book as *Studies in Malory: II*. We salute the authors and editor of that earlier text.

This collection of essays grew out of a series of sessions on Malory and Christianity organized by D. Thomas Hanks, Jr., at the International Congress on Medieval Studies, Western Michigan University, Kalamazoo, Michigan (May 2005 and 2006). He was assisted in this endeavor by a Visiting Fellowship for Spring 2006 granted by The Medieval Institute of Western Michigan University.

Introduction

Less than a century after the death of Sir Thomas Malory, Roger Ascham wrote in *The Scholemaster* that the "whole pleasure" of Malory's *Morte Darthur* "standeth in two speciall poyntes, in open mans slaughter, and bold bawdrye: In which booke those be counted the noblest Knightes, that do kill most men without any quarell and commit fowlest aduoulteries by sutlest shiftes: as Sir Launcelote, with the wife of king Arthure his master."[1] Though perhaps few would agree with Ascham's dismissive evaluation of the *Morte*'s "speciall poyntes," most readers nonetheless recall most vividly the elements he names: the Round Table knights' many battles and the adulterous love affair between Lancelot and Guinevere. And to be sure, pursuing opponents and pursuing love move the *Morte*'s narrative, but the work's richness comes from its romance and tragic elements: the human quest for maturity and fulfillment and those uncontrollable forces that undermine the quest and destroy the dream. Malory's use of myth and magic to explore these themes has received extensive scholarly attention, but his views on and thematic use of Christianity have long needed a closer look. This volume aims to address that need.

Christianity is omnipresent in the *Morte*, from the second page where King Uther swears "upon the four Evangelistes" to reward Merlin richly if only Merlin will help him to fulfill his desire for Igrayne (1:8.40)[2] to the last line of the work, where the reader learns that after Lancelot's death, four of his companions do battle against the "Turkes" and die "uppon a Good Fryday for Goddes sake" (3:1260.15.) But Eugène Vinaver early sidelined the topic, arguing that Malory, uninterested in Christianity, minimized its importance by paring down or deleting Christian references in the explicitly Christian Grail section. Over time, Vinaver's persuasive view influenced critical reading of the whole *Morte*, overshadowing the views of others like C. S. Lewis, who argued that Malory's text deals seriously with Christian themes and motifs.

Reopening this discussion first requires attempting to define what "Christianity" meant for Malory's time and estate. Malory died just forty years before Henry VIII's accession. Was his Christian world still that of medieval Roman

Catholicism or were the seeds of Protestantism and the Reformation already affecting daily religious practice and belief? In 1929, E. K. Chambers, commenting on Malory's alleged assaults upon Combe Abbey, simply stated as fact that "there was a strong Lollard feeling against religious houses," thus associating Malory with Lollardy.[3] More recently, Christina Hardyment asserted that Lollardy was not a notable force in England in Malory's time. Hardyment places Malory squarely in the traditional religious context of medieval English gentry from his baptism on. Although some contemporary gentry sympathized with the Lollards, Hardyment sees Malory's family, with its connections to the Order of St. John of Jerusalem and the Knights Hospitallers, as "a conventionally pious one."[4] Those connections were strong ones; as P. J. C. Field points out, Malory's uncle was Sir Robert Malory, prior of the Hospital of St. John of Jerusalem in England from 1432 to 1439/40, "one of the greatest magnates of the kingdom and a professional crusader."[5] Speculating on Sir Robert's possible influence upon his nephew, Field points out Malory's "apparent indifference [in the *Morte Darthur*] to ceremony and conspicuous consumption, his dislike of courtly love, and his presentation of knighthood itself as an 'order' with a moral purpose and a religious justification." He adds, "crusades and the defence of Christendom against Islam are more conspicuous in the *Morte Darthur* than in Malory's sources or in most other English Arthurian romances." The pious deaths of Lancelot's final companions noted earlier also support this view for Field.[6]

Scholars are divided concerning religious attitudes in Malory's time; no one perspective dominates the scholarly conversation. The late fifteenth century was a period of transition, a pre-Reformation time with currents tending to Protestantism contending against opposing currents of traditional Roman Catholicism. The issue of just how strong either current may have been has been occupying historians for the last several decades, as Alec Ryrie has pointed out.[7] Moreover, identifying Malory's social class does not help to identify his religious perspective. Seeing him as a member of the gentry class, which follows from Field's widely accepted view that the Malory who wrote the *Morte Darthur* is Sir Thomas Malory of Newbold Revel,[8] offers little information. Historians do not agree on the degree or kind of gentry devotion in medieval England, which has led Catherine Batt to write that "there are problems with extrapolating a theological position for Malory by reconstructing his religious environment, especially as historians of fifteenth-century gentry piety do not agree on mapping its parameters." She notes the two poles of opinion regarding those parameters: "whereas Colin Richmond argues for gentry religion as an increasingly individual and privatized experience, with this class taking ever less interest in parish affairs, Eamon Duffy sees an actively and publicly pious laity much involved in the work of the Church."[9] She continues: "The evidence suggests the gentry might carve out for themselves religious experiences of greater or lesser intensity and engagement, so one cannot

make a priori assumptions about Malory's religion on the basis of social placing."[10] Her conclusion has been contested by Christine Carpenter, who suggests
that the majority of the gentry of Malory's time were educated in and practiced
an "extremely conventional" Catholic piety. Carpenter's review of current work in
this area supports the idea of strongly orthodox views among the greater part of
the late medieval gentry class.[11]

　　As historians continue the debate on pre-Reformation Christianity in
England, it is clear that neither the intensity nor the nature of Sir Thomas Malory's individual religious life is discernible at this distance in time; what is clear
is that religious observances such as tithes, baptisms, marriages, and death rites
would have been central to his daily life.[12] Even as Malory was writing the *Morte*
in Newgate prison, his days would have been punctuated by the bells of Greyfriars
Church just across the way from the prison—a church where he was eventually
buried and where his dust now lies under a rose garden.

　　It is also clear that Malory was a knight, and a decidedly armigerous knight,
bearing not only a coat of arms but the edged weapons implied by that sigil.
Both Chaucer's *Parson's Tale* and William Langland's *Piers Plowman* suggested,
roughly a century before Malory wrote his *Morte*, that one of a knight's duties
was to fight for Holy Church;[13] moreover, Maurice Keen, in his classic *Chivalry*, writes that the knightly vocation was unified with a Christian vocation from
at least 1250, when the anonymous *Ordene de chevalrie* outlined the pious ritual
by which knighthood was conferred.[14] In 1484, the year before he published the
Morte, Caxton himself published his own translation of Ramon Llull's continu-
ously Christian *Libro del ordre de cavayleria* or (as Caxton translated it) *The Book
of the Ordre of Chyvalry or Knyghthode*.[15] The many later accounts of the prayerful
vigil observed prior to the knighting ceremony suggest that Malory, coming from
a lineage of knights, would have seen his vocation as armed godliness, related in
kind to the Crusades.[16] *Le Morte Darthur* affirms that Malory's idea of chivalry
was imbued with Christianity, both conventional and literary. But how deeply and
to what extent? This volume reintroduces into Malory scholarship an extended
discussion on the importance of Christianity in Malory's work. Its contributors
will test many critical assumptions, exploring aspects of this rich text to come to
their own conclusions and to open the door to further study.

Introduction to the Essays

D. Thomas Hanks, Jr., initiates the discussion of Malory and Christianity in "'All
maner of good love comyth of God': Malory, God's Grace, and Noble Love,"
which counters Eugène Vinaver's assertion that Malory minimized and subordi-
nated Christian concerns. Vinaver's edition of Malory's *Works* established seminal
guidelines for reading the *Morte Darthur*. But for Hanks, one such guide was and

is fallacious. Vinaver writes that whereas Malory is perfectly serious about nobility and chivalry, he is not at all "concerned with the yet higher law which cuts across the courtly world in the Grail books" (Malory, *Works*, 1:xc). Hanks argues that this view of Malory's Grail section has colored the rest of the *Morte*, leading many scholars to see Malory's work as a reflection of only the most conventional Christianity of his time. But in fact Malory emphasizes a more-than-conventional Christian concern in several of his explicits, in a prayer for Tristram to which he affixes his own name, and in Christian references appearing throughout the *Morte* (some of them original to him, like the story of Sir Urry). Malory's addition of these Christian elements influences the *Morte's* genre, reframing the tragedy of worldly loss within a comedy of salvation. Further, it develops a theme not found in his sources, that love (and, especially, noble love) comes from God, that it can be irresistible, that it can be sinful, and that it can be forgiven. In the cases of Guinevere and Lancelot, it is forgiven and, indeed, redemptive.

Continuing this view, Corey Olsen argues for a balance of orthodox Christianity with earthly values in "Adulterated Love: The Tragedy of Malory's Lancelot and Guinevere." In the *Morte*, Malory presents Lancelot and Guinevere's love as the paramount example of virtuous love, yet he also depicts the lovers as repenting their relationship and turning to God. Olsen contends that Malory, conscious of this apparent contradiction, embraces both of these readings. Olsen traces patterns of development of "trew" and natural love from Elaine of Astolat through the *Morte's* end, focusing on the most troubling passages, to argue that Malory purposefully explores and enhances the contradiction to show the reformative and even redemptive quality of virtuous love. Through his nuanced and sensitive portrayal of Lancelot and Guinevere, Malory represents the tragedy of a relationship that was virtuous and yet adulterated beyond healing, a relationship that could not be saved and yet led both of its participants to salvation.

"Endless Virtue and Trinitarian Prayer in Lancelot's Healing of Urry," Sue Ellen Holbrook's probing discussion of this key episode, reinforces both Hanks's and Olsen's theses, that Malory was indeed concerned with religious values, values that finally sequester his lovers from condemnation and bring them to salvation. Holbrook argues that when Lancelot heals Urry by the ritual handling of his wounds after praying to the Trinity, Malory locates chivalric communal morality within a Christian paradigm and links this morality, exemplified by Lancelot, to a sacred mystery central to the Christian belief system: the doctrine of the Trinity, in which the Father, the Son, and the Holy Ghost are three in number but one in substance. In comparison with the *Morte's* other healing scenes and prayers, the healing of Urry has the most public setting, succeeds without medical intervention, and involves the only prayer to the Trinity in the whole book. Holbrook argues that the prayer's efficacy springs from its intercessory form, Lancelot's posture of sacrifice, and the virtues he exhibits during this healing event: humility, obedience, sorrow, and *caritas*. These virtues and the *charism* of healing granted Lancelot are tied to the belief that although Christians may harm their souls by wrongful acts, they can refortify their souls through repentance nourished with divine grace. Holbrook considers fifteenth-century history, iconography, morality, and Trinitarian worship to conclude that Lancelot's prayer is definitively Christian and, like other Trinitarian prayers in Malory's cultural context, both rare and potent.

In "Christian Rituals in Malory: The Evidence of Funerals," Karen Cherewatuk emphasizes the *Morte*'s Christian orthodoxy by assessing Malory's engagement with Christianity through the evidence of deathbed ministration and funeral practice. She first acquaints the modern reader with details of late medieval deathbed and funeral practices that a fifteenth-century audience would have immediately grasped. Then she demonstrates that Malory consistently treats the dying to final rites—including confession, anointing, and final Eucharist—and the deceased to all due ceremony, from the tripartite funeral service of vespers, matins, and Mass, to postburial recitation of prayers for the deceased's soul. Through the "dolorous deaths and departings" of Gawain, Guinevere, and Lancelot, Malory develops the theme of repentance. Even the final glimpse of King Arthur, whose passing is the most clearly pagan death scene in the whole book, blends the sacred and the secular. These funerary details show Malory's concern to address a series of Christian beliefs: the immortality of the soul; the efficacy of prayer; the practice of deathbed ministration and acts of penitence preceding death; and, most important, heavenly reward for those who have atoned. The deaths of Gawain, Guinevere, Lancelot, and Arthur reveal the medieval Christian's final struggle for atonement.

Janet Jesmok sees less orthodoxy in the *Morte*, arguing in "Rhetoric, Ritual, and Religious Impulse in Malory's Book 8" that Malory's religious rhetoric sometimes obscures the strong secular underpinning of the last book. Thoughts of the afterlife indeed dominate Malory's last book—Guinevere becomes a nun and an abbess, Lancelot becomes a priest, and his faithful followers take on religious habits—but do these actions and Malory's highly charged religious rhetoric suggest that the characters have found salvation within a conventional Christian context? Jesmok sees a mixed message. Although Queen Guinevere reveals a clear understanding of sin and salvation, Malory's knights' pursuit of the religious life seems to reinforce their secular homosocial bonds. Yet Guinevere's movement toward God finally moves them all—Lancelot and his followers—to at least the *ritual* of religious life and to clear salvation for Lancelot. Although his Christianity is not always persuasive, Malory weaves religion, myth, courtly service, and secular chivalry into an artistically satisfying dénouement for his long, complex work.

Where Jesmok views Malory's last book as an aesthetic resolution of religious and secular themes, Dorsey Armstrong suggests ongoing tension in "Christianity and Social Instability: Malory's Galahad, Palomides, and Lancelot." The outward signs of conventional Christianity are present, but the Round Table's basic principles, including the Pentecostal Oath, evolve from secular chivalry. Furthermore, romantic love, not Christian charity, forms the identities of Arthur's greatest knights. The *Morte*, especially in the formative stages of Arthur's community, demonstrates little of the religious piety or devotion found in other late medieval chivalric works. Furthermore, a close analysis of Sir Galahad, the saintly Grail knight, and Sir Palomides, the Saracen who would be a Christian, reveals that both characters threaten the Arthurian community from opposite poles. As the outsider who seeks acceptance, a figure of otherness who aspires to sameness and inclusion, Palomides challenges the idealized homogeneity of knightly Arthurian ideals. But Galahad, in his strident Christianity, is also disruptive, casting a shadow on Arthur's court. His advent coincides with the announcement of the Grail Quest, where the rules of knighthood that served the community so well prove insufficient or inappropriate. Finally it is Sir Lancelot, the thematic and dramatic crucible, who best demonstrates this struggle between chivalric and religious ideals to which Galahad and Palomides have called attention. Examining these three figures reveals the crisis of conflicting ideals always haunting the *Morte Darthur*.

In "Slouching towards Bethlehem: Secularized Salvation in *Le Morte Darthur*," Fiona Tolhurst argues that the terms "Christian" and "secular" are inadequate means of defining Malory's theological position, given the interpretive challenges posed by both key passages and the explicits. She further demonstrates that Eugène Vinaver's characterization of Malory as a secularizer of *La Queste del Saint Graal* oversimplifies and misleads. She offers the term "secularized salvation" as a more useful way to describe Malory's theological compromise. Malory's Perceval and his aunt, Bors, and Galahad are more earthly than their Vulgate counterparts while his Lancelot is worthier of salvation. Malory compresses *La Queste*'s spiritual hierarchy, raising the status of Perceval, Bors, Gawain, and Lancelot while lowering that of Galahad. Malory's Galahad becomes less a second Christ and more an earthly knight, while Lancelot grows in worthiness to join Perceval, Bors, and Galahad as a member of the spiritual elite. Malory's secularized salvation explains Lancelot's roles as prophet, miracle-worker, and pseudosaint and his eventual salvation; both in the Grail Quest sequence and throughout his "hoole book," it embodies and reflects Malory's historical moment, as Caxton clearly expresses in his preface. In her definitive comparison of Malory's Grail Quest with its French sources, Tolhurst concludes that *Le Morte Darthur* presents a version of practical Christianity that embraces its hero, Lancelot, the greatest of sinful men, and holds him up as a model for contemporary chivalric society. Leading Lancelot to a spiritual Bethlehem, Malory, despite his sins, becomes a spiritual guide in his own right.

In "Malory's Secular Arthuriad," K. S. Whetter challenges Charles Moorman, C. S. Lewis, and some contributors to this collection in arguing that throughout the *Morte* Malory focuses on the secular themes of chivalry, fellowship, and the Round Table's tragic destruction. For Whetter, Malory neither promotes contempt for the world nor highlights the Round Table's sinful failures. Rather, Malory valorizes and eulogizes the earthly deeds and worship of the secular, noble fellowship. Even in the Grail Quest, Malory favors secular concerns over a reverently Christian theme. Carefully analyzing explicits and narrative commentary and providing close readings of key scenes such as Arthur's farewell to the Grail knights, the healing of Sir Urry, the final conversion of the central characters, and Ector's threnody, Whetter concludes that Malory's conception of chivalric companionship celebrates worldly deeds, feelings, and values. The *Morte*'s ending then, rather than a celebration of Christian redemption, is a tableau of irreversible and tragic loss.

Finally Felicia Nimue Ackerman takes a distinctly modern approach in "'In my harte I am [not] crystynde': What Can Malory Offer the Nonreligious Reader?" She discusses elements of the *Morte*'s outlook—attitudes toward honor and shame, one's own death, the deaths of loved ones, and extreme emotionality—that have a compelling secular interest, independent of religion or Christianity. She uses the Malorian views of shame and death to examine contemporary attitudes toward the severely disabled and terminally ill, exploring clichés like "life at any price" and "death with dignity." Ackerman also analyzes contemporary views of emotional expression through the lens of the *Morte Darthur*. Malory's heroic knights are men of lavish emotionality. Far from being strong, silent, stoic types, they are continually experiencing and sometimes succumbing to deep emotion, leading modern readers to see them as childish or effeminate. In the *Morte*, however, lavish emotionality shows not weakness but strength, revealing a great knight's potential for feeling and suffering, and, in fact, manifesting his greatness. Ackerman's reading suggests that the *Morte* is not just a quaint, historical tale but one with modern relevance and wisdom.

NOTES

1. The text of *The Scholemaster* appears on the World Wide Web at https://scholarsbank.uoregon.edu (Renascence Editions, University of Oregon). Ascham's comment on the *Morte* appears toward the end of book 1, easily locatable by electronic search.

2. Malory, *Works*, 3rd rev. ed. Here and throughout, all quotations from Malory's text come from this edition and will be noted parenthetically by volume, page, and line numbers.

3. Chambers, review of *Sir Thomas Malory: His Turbulent Career*, p. 466.

4. Hardyment, *Malory*, pp. 50–52, 66.

5. Field, *Life and Times*, p. 68.

6. Field, *Life and Times*, pp. 80–82.

7. See Ryrie's survey chapter, "Britain and Ireland."

8. Field, *Life and Times*.

9. Batt, *Malory's "Morte Darthur,"* pp. 133–34, citing both Richmond's "Religion and the Fifteenth-Century English Gentleman" and Duffy's *Stripping of the Altars* (1992).

10. Batt, *Malory's "Morte Darthur,"* p. 134.

11. Carpenter, "Religion," pp. 139, 146. We are indebted to Karen Cherewatuk for the reference to Carpenter's essay.

12. For an earlier view of the day-to-day nature of medieval Christianity, see John Van Engen's review of the topic in "The Christian Middle Ages as an Historiographical Problem."

13. Passus VI.23–28 of the B-text, in William Langland, *The Vision of Piers Plowman*, p. 96. For Chaucer, see the Parson's comment that "the swerd that men yeven first to a knyght, whan he is newe dubbed, signifieth that he sholde deffenden holy churche, and nat robben it nor pilen it; and whoso dooth is traitour to Crist" (*Parson's Tale*, in Chaucer, *Riverside Chaucer*, p. 314, line 766).

14. Keen, *Chivalry*, pp. 6–7.

15. Llull, *Book of the Ordre of Chyvalry or Knyghthode*, available in facsimile under this title. The facsimile reproduces the British Library copy of the book, shelfmark IA.55071.

16. For a brief survey of the three modes of creating knights—two of which were imbued with Christian elements to a greater or lesser degree—see Laing and Laing, *Medieval Britain*, p. 27. Their summary comments do not cite a source, but see Dugdale, *Antiquities*: "[A]ntiently," Dugdale reports, "ecclesiastick persons" were allowed to make knights. He adds that the ceremonies of conferring knighthood were both "sacred and courtly" (2:772).

"All maner of good love comyth of God": Malory, God's Grace, and Noble Love

D. Thomas Hanks, Jr.

Introduction

As Janet Jesmok and I note in the introduction to this volume, one of the earliest critics of Sir Thomas Malory's *Morte Darthur*, Roger Ascham, condemned it on the grounds of immorality. He found in it only "open mans slaughter, and bold bawdrye" as opposed to "honestie and godliness." As the latter phrase suggests, Ascham found religious grounds for his argument, writing that he had seen the Bible banished from the royal court when the *Morte* was welcomed there. Arguing against what he saw as the pernicious influence of "Papistes," Ascham maintains that books like the *Morte* ought not be read by (Protestant) Christians.[1] He saw the *Morte* as virulently anti-Christian. I shall argue here that less sectarian eyes will find in it not only battle, adultery, and other human failing but also regular reminders of a Godly grace to be accorded even imperfect humans.

A more modern critic of the *Morte Darthur* than Ascham, Eugène Vinaver, has heavily influenced readers' approach to the *Morte*. From its appearance in 1947, Vinaver's Oxford edition has been considered the definitive *Morte*. And rightly so: Vinaver laid the scholarly groundwork of comparing Malory's *Morte* with its French sources, and he provided a highly readable text much nearer to Malory's original than earlier editions.

All Malorians, then, must be grateful to Vinaver. At the same time, he set directions that still restrict us. For example—and it is the only restriction discussed in this essay—Vinaver followed in Ascham's footsteps when he wrote at length in various places in his edition, and thus influenced generations of scholars, that Malory was either uninterested in or incapable of understanding the Christian element in the Grail story (and by extension throughout the *Morte*). In fact, Vinaver wrote in the introductions to his 1947, 1967, and posthumous 1990 editions that whereas Malory is perfectly serious about nobility and chivalry, he is not at all "concerned with the yet higher law which cuts across the courtly world in the Grail books" (1:xc).[2] He adds that Malory has instead replaced the "sens" (the sense) of the French *Queste* with "a mere pageant of picturesque visions" (1:xc).

9

He writes of Malory's close to the Grail book, which features Lancelot though the French source does not, that "[t]his, like most of Malory's additions, contradicts both the letter and the spirit of the French [source]" (1:xcii). He argues that Malory's "one desire seems to be to secularize the Grail theme as much as the story will allow" (3:1535). In his earlier *Malory* he is as clear as he is censorious: "Malory's *Quest* is . . . a confused and almost pointless story . . . deprived of its spiritual foundation, of its doctrine, and of its direct object."[3]

Scholars have responded to Vinaver over the years, some challenging him and many simply accepting his view. C. S. Lewis was an early challenger. In 1963, well prior to Vinaver's 1967 second edition, he argued that "[the *Morte*'s] handling of the Grail story *sounds* deeply religious, and we have the sense that it is somehow profoundly connected with the final tragedy."[4] Lewis's carefully reasoned argument led Vinaver to qualified agreement. He responds—in the same 1963 volume in which Lewis's essay appeared—that though Malory "tries to cut down the religious exposition and even substitute the worldly for the divine, he produces a work which nonetheless makes a more deeply religious impression on one's mind than the strictly orthodox original upon which it is based."[5] Though he conceded Lewis's point, Vinaver did not alter his comments in his second edition of *Works*, comments that persist in P. J. C. Field's revised third edition of 1990. Judging by his editions alone, then, the great editor of Malory maintained his view that Malory was uninterested in the Christian doctrine of the Grail Quest.

Vinaver's view of Malory's approach to the Grail material has influenced virtually every discussion of Christianity not only in the Grail Quest but throughout the *Morte*. This essay extends Lewis's challenge. I follow Lewis in this debate not to detract from Vinaver's work but because the issue, as Lewis suggested before me, affects the way one reads the entire *Morte*. Owing to his view of Malory's approach to the Grail story's Christianity, Vinaver reads the entire *Morte* as a tragedy, "a tragic tale of human greatness," as he puts it in the last sentence of his closing essay in commentary (3:1626). If, however, one realizes the redemptive effects of the Christian theme, one reads it as a comedy, albeit a comedy with tragic undertones. The Christian theme is clearly evident throughout the *Morte*: Malory not only identifies himself as a Christian in six of his explicits and in a major narrative comment inside the *Morte* but also adds to his source material many original-to-him Christian elements and shadings. Through his changes, Malory gives the narrative a new religious dimension, finally transforming his tale of chivalry and noble love into one of God's grace and Christian redemption.

Explicitly Christian: The Explicits and the Tristram Prayer

The most obviously Christian element Malory adds throughout his *Morte* is not, strictly speaking, part of the *Morte*—or rather, not part of the story proper. This element appears in Malory's section endings, the explicits. Explicits appear often throughout the work, as one would expect in a medieval manuscript containing many episodes. Most of them read much like the first: "Thus endith the tale of Balyn and Balan, two brethirne that were borne in Northhumbirlonde, that were two passynge good knyghtes as ever were in tho dayes" (1:92.16–20).[6] This first explicit straightforwardly announces the end of the tale of Balyn and Balan and gives their backgrounds, then the scribe writes "Explicit" below the bottom line. No surprises here: this is what one expects. Narrative involvement is minimal. A similar explicit ends "The Weddyng of Kyng Arthur" (1:120.28). Six of the work's many explicits, however, scattered throughout the manuscript and always follow-ing major sections, present more than just section endings. In these six explicits, Malory signals his own presence as author, and moreover his presence as a Chris-tian author engaging in a Christian act.

That practice begins in the third explicit, which presents a new narrative voice—in fact, an authorial voice. As appears below, the last lines of the explicit reflect more than the perfunctory closing words of an episode:

> Here endyth this tale, as the Freynshe booke seyth, fro the maryage of kynge Uther unto kyng Arthure that regned aftir hym & ded many batayles.
> And this booke endyth whereas sir Launcelot and sir Trys-trams com to courte. Who that woll make ony more lette hym seke other bookis of kynge Arthure or of Sir Launcelot or Sir Trystrams; for this was drawyn by a knyght presoner, sir Thomas Malleorré, that God sende hym good recover. Amen.
> Explicit (1:180.15–25)

Here, Malory refers to himself as a "knyght presoner," names himself, and asks "that God sende hym good recover. Amen." This sets the tone for most of the major section breaks appearing in the remainder of the manuscript. Although many simple reports of "explicit" or "Heere endyth" this tale or "here begynnyth" this other tale appear in the body of the manuscript, six of the more noticeable section breaks give Malory's name as author and ask for God's deliverance.[7]

Because the last few folios of the Winchester Manuscript have been lost, the last of the Christian explicits, and Malory's last word in his book, appear only in Caxton's 1485 printing (and subsequent printings by Wynkyn de Worde), where again one finds Malory writing

> I praye you all jentylmen and jentylwymmen . . . , praye for me whyle I am on lyve that God sende me good delyveraunce. And whan I am deed, I praye you all praye for my soule.
> For this book was ended the ninth yere of the reygne of Kyng

Edward the Fourth, by Syr Thomas Maleoré, knyght, as Jesu helpe hym for Hys grete myght, as he is the servaunt of Jesu bothe day and nyght.[8]   (3:1260.20–29)

This is the only explicit personal to Malory that Caxton printed in his 1485 edition of *The Morte Darthur*. Wynkyn de Worde, in his 1498 and 1529 printings, followed Caxton's practice. Thus it was that the five other explicits referring specifically to Sir Thomas Malory vanished for centuries, to reappear only after Walter F. Oakeshott looked at the old manuscript at Winchester College in 1934.[9] As in the recovered explicits, the final one addresses Christian concerns. Malory asks his readers to pray for his deliverance (from prison, one assumes), and for his soul. He then closes with a pious request for Jesus to help him, as he is the servant of Jesus at all times. He wrote this explicit in what would be 1468/69, when he was evidently still in Newgate Prison.[10]

Another narrative interjection, the narrator's introduction of Sir Tristram of Cornwall, underscores Malory's Christian concerns: "And every day sir Trystram wolde go ryde an-huntynge . . . . and of hym we had fyrst all the . . . blastis that longed to all maner of game: fyrste to the uncoupelynge, to the sekynge . . . to the flyght, to the deth . . . and many other blastis and termys, that all maner jantylmen hath cause to the worldes ende to prayse sir Trystram and to pray for his soule. Amen, sayde Sir Thomas Malleorré" (2:682.25–683.4). One immediately sees Malory's breach of narrative decorum: seemingly carried away by narratorial enthusiasm, he breaks into his story to add his "Amen" to his narrator's prayer for Tristram's soul. He sees Tristram as an analogue to himself, a knight for whom the prayers of others can be useful, and he adds his own comment to that effect.

In short, Malory inserts throughout his text personal comments that emphasize his Christian understanding of his world. Reading the explicits and the "Amen" addendum as Malory's personal comments changes how one views his text. These are not standard narrative comments, like the first explicit in the Balin story, but instead carefully written appeals to God, appeals so worded that the act of reading them becomes a prayer for Malory's soul[11]—or, oddly, for Tristram's.

Enhanced and Original Christian Elements

The explicits, and Malory's "Amen," are the most obvious Christian elements he adds to his retelling, personalized with his own name. He has likewise added or enhanced Christian elements that are less intrusive, beginning with Merlin's early direction of events. Following that, Malory has changed or added elements or entire episodes in the stories of Elaine of Astolat, the Grail Quest, the lengthy May passage, the Urry story, the ambush in Guinevere's chambers, and climactically in the deaths of Arthur, Guinevere, and Lancelot.

The first of Malory's enhancements appears when Merlin's famous "sword in the stone"—in the *Morte* a sword in an anvil mounted on a stone—is provided by a miracle that, as Merlin states, comes from Jesus. This Christian element is not original to Malory: it appears in his French source as well. Malory enhances the Christian element, however; his Merlin, unlike the Merlin of the French source, counsels the archbishop of Canterbury "to sende for all the lordes of the reame . . . that they shold to London come by Cristmas upon payne of cursynge, and for this cause, that Jesu, that was borne on that nyghte, that He wold of His grete mercy shewe some miracle, . . . who shold be rightwys kynge of this reame" (1:12.15–21). This material, original to Malory, shows Jesus certifying Arthur's kingship; Malory writes that Arthur will rule by divine right. God limits Arthur's rule, also, or so Merlin informs him when after the battle of Bedegraine he tells the young king, with asperity, that he must end his pursuit of the defeated forces of King Lot and his allies: "hit ys tyme to sey 'Who!' for God ys wroth with the for thou wolt never have done" (1:36.28–29). Merlin's claim to know what God desires is also original to Malory (3:1294, n. 36.24–37); Arthur meekly follows Merlin's bidding and ends the battle. In short, Malory carefully aligns Merlin—a major shaper of events early in the *Morte*—with God, both by making Merlin the apparent facilitator of the Godly miracle of the sword in the anvil and by putting into Merlin's mouth advice apparently coming directly from God.[12]

In addition to Merlin's Godliness, consider also the changes in the most straightforwardly Christian part of the *Morte*, the Grail Quest. It was concerning this part of the work that Vinaver first began the debate on Malory's approach to Christianity. The *locus classicus* for his views on Malory's treatment of the Grail story is the "Commentary" in volume 3 of his edition. He devotes nine pages to introducing his textual notes on the Grail section of the *Morte* (3:1534–42); his overall view appears in his comment that the "attitude may be described without much risk of over-simplification as that of a man to whom the quest of the Grail was primarily an *Arthurian* adventure and who regarded the intrusion of the Grail upon Arthur's kingdom not as a means of contrasting earthly and divine chivalry and condemning the former, but as an opportunity offered to the knights of the Round Table to achieve still greater glory in *this* world" (3:1535; Vinaver's emphasis). Vinaver then cites several instances in which he suggests that otherworldly significance has been sacrificed to secular, chivalric interests (3:1535–36).

Vinaver's view of Malory's work becomes clear; either it must "[contrast] earthly and divine chivalry and [condemn] the former" or it must be focused on this world. Vinaver oversimplifies; as appears throughout this essay, I argue that Malory not only values both "earthly and divine chivalry" but that he even suggests in Ector's closing eulogy that the two qualities meet in Lancelot, "hede of al Crysten knyghtes" (3:1259.9–10).

The Grail Quest overall deserves a more extended treatment than I present here; Fiona Tolhurst, in a companion essay in this volume, has given it that treatment. I add to her discussion only one argument: Lancelot becomes a different character in Malory from the one Vinaver writes that he finds in the French source. My colleague Janet Jesmok has even suggested in an ongoing conversation on this topic that Malory converts his Grail Quest to a form of Pilgrim's Progress, with Lancelot as the pilgrim. I offer one observation in support of this argument that I have not seen used by the many other scholars who have commented on Lancelot's role.[13] Recall that in the final days of his quest for the Grail Lancelot enters Castle Corbenic and approaches a room in which he sees the Mass being celebrated and the Eucharist being offered. Although warned by a mystical voice not to enter the room, he sees the priest struggling under his heavy burden and moves to aid him. Struck down at the door for his presumption, he lies unconscious for twenty-four days, during which he sees "grete mervayles," as he tells those who awaken him (2:1017.11). That passage is in the French source.

What Vinaver evidently did not find in Malory's French source is the statement by the curious crowd gathered around Lancelot at this point: "[T]he queste of the Sankgreall ys encheved now ryght in you" (2:1017.30–1018.1). Vinaver, in his note on this passage, reads the parallel passage in the French *Queste* as indicating that the bystanders do not say that the Grail Quest is achieved in Lancelot. According to Vinaver's translation they tell Lancelot instead that his part in the quest is finished, so he need no longer wear his penitential hair shirt. The French passage as Vinaver reproduces it, however, reads "e vous povés bien laissier la haire car vostre queste est achievee" [and you may very well leave off your hair shirt, for your quest is *achievee*] (3:1580, n. to 2:1017.30–1018.2). Vinaver translates "achievee" as "at an end"; an at least equally valid translation would be "achieved," but Vinaver does not admit that possibility. I hesitate to challenge the master's translation, but it does seem as if he translated "achievee" in a way most would not—in a way that accords with his theory but not with the more common meaning of "achievee." I must read "achieved" here, as Malory's use of "encheved" suggests that he did.

Vinaver, however, sees in Malory's translation of the passage a misuse of his French source. He comments, "M[alory] certainly did not intend to . . . [say] that it was Lancelot who achieved the Grail" (3:1580, n. to 2:1017.30–1018.2). However, Malory reports that Lancelot did "encheve" the Grail, though to be sure in the limited sense that Lancelot himself notes in the next two lines: "'Now I thanke God,' seyde sir Launcelot, 'for Hys grete Mercy of that I have sene, for hit suffiseth me'" (2:1018.3–4). I conclude that Malory presents a Lancelot who—as his source tells him—does achieve the Grail to a degree, and can therefore be seen as favored by God in spite of his sins.[14] Malory has in several places altered the narrative he found in the French *Queste*, as Tolhurst observes; he has altered it not to lessen or obscure the *sens* of its Christian element, however, but to broaden it. Malory will conclude that one need not be perfect to achieve one's Christian goals, as Galahad is perfect; one need merely receive grace, as did Lancelot.

Following his revision of Lancelot's role in the Grail Quest, Malory opens a major theme to recur throughout the remainder of the *Morte*: he aligns noble love with Godly grace. He begins with Elaine of Astolat. Elaine falls in love with Lancelot and asks him to marry her or take her as a mistress. He refuses; consumed by her love, she neither eats, sleeps, nor drinks, and is soon on the point of death. Here Malory inserts material original to him; a priest counsels Elaine to leave her thoughts of Lancelot. Her response introduces the concept of Godliness combined with earthly love: "Why sholde I leve such thoughtes? Am I nat an erthely woman? And all the whyle the brethe ys in my body I may complayne me, for my belyve ys that I do none offence, though I love an erthely man, unto God, for He fourmed me thereto, and all maner of good love comyth of God. . . . And of myself, Good Lorde, I had no might to withstonde the fervent love, wherefore I have my deth!" (2:1093.3–1094.3). This speech, which as Vinaver notes is entirely Malory's invention (3:1589–91), opens a theme central to the last part of the *Morte*: "all maner of good love comyth of God." Elaine's lengthy speech comes at the approach of death, a solemn time when the priest's counsel was, to most medieval Christians, incontrovertible. Malory, through Elaine, controverts it. A priest controls the all-important last rites; to argue with a priest while at the point of death gives one's remarks great weight. Malory's audience, surely sympathetic to Elaine at this point, will have read or heard these lines with profound attention.[15]

Following his revision of the Elaine story, more of Malory's original comments about "good love" and God appear in the first May passage, the longest narrative interjection in the *Morte* (see Corey Olsen's essay in this collection for a full analysis of the May passage). In it, the narrator concludes that a worshipful man approaches love in Godliness: "Therefore, lyke as May moneth flowryth and floryshyth in every mannes gardyne, so in lyke wyse lat every man of worship florysh hys herte in thys worlde: firste unto God, and nexte unto the joy of them that he promised hys feythe unto; . . . But firste reserve the honoure to God, and secundely thy quarrel muste com of thy lady. And such love I calle vertuouse love" (3:1119.22–30). As Larry D. Benson has pointed out, both Elaine's passage on Godly "good love" and the May passage are original to Malory.[16] One notes that, like Elaine, Malory's narrator here says that good love, or "vertuouse love," must also be Godly. Malory develops this argument in a lyrical passage of blossoming, burgeoning, and flowering that lasts for one and one-third pages in the manuscript. Obviously, it is important to him. Equally obviously, Malory is here connecting "vertuouse love" with Godliness. The precise nature of the connection is not clear in the passage, and perhaps it was not clear to Malory (indeed, C. David Benson suggests that Malory is obscure or even confused in the May passage's comments on virtuous love).[17]

At the least, the May passage links constancy in love and Godliness. Malory first endorses "stabylité" between lovers (3:1119.16), then notes that a lack of such "stabylité" amounts to "fyeblenes of nature and grete disworshyp" (2:1119.20). Next he writes the longer passage quoted above: the man of worship who has been constant to his lover turns first to God, then to his love; "such love I calle vertuouse love," the narrator concludes (3:1119.30). Perhaps confusedly, but nonetheless surely, Malory has written that a nobly stable love is not only virtuous but Godly. One recalls Elaine's comment to her priest: "all maner of good love comyth of God" (2:1093.7). Malory is giving to his most attractive lovers—Elaine, Lancelot, and Guinevere—a love both noble and Godly.

Having begun with Elaine's statement that "all maner of good love comyth of God," then, Malory has now stated in a long narrative interjection his theoretical view of love: if both "stable" and Godly, then it is "vertuous." He has set the stage for the one passage in his *Morte* wherein Lancelot and Guinevere actually make love—in a tower of Melleagaunt's castle, after the feckless Melleagaunt and his men at arms have abducted the queen and taken her and her badly wounded knights to his castle. Lancelot, furious, comes to the rescue and Melleagaunt yields to him; that night, Lancelot goes to his queen. Though many in the *Morte* have said earlier that Lancelot loves the queen, e.g., the four queens who abducted him (1:257.26–28), the physical demonstration of that love has not appeared until this moment. Now, in a passage of only twenty-one lines, Lancelot comes to the queen's window, they "ma[k]e their complayntes eyther to othir of many dyverce thyngis," and he says he "wysshed that he myght have comyn in to her." In the first statement of her love for Lancelot, Guinevere responds to the double entendre through the bars separating them, "Wyte you well . . . I wolde as fayne as ye that ye myght com in to me." Lancelot then tears the bars from the window and the two become one (3:1131.11–32). Malory does not linger, nor is he graphic; though the "stable" love of the two has been consummated, he does not dwell on the consummation. He spends a great deal more narrative time on an event that follows the night of love and the ensuing trial by combat during which Lancelot kills Melleagaunt. That event is the healing of Sir Urry.

Aside from the events of the Grail Quest, Lancelot's healing of Sir Urry is the most straightforwardly Christian event in the *Morte*. Again, it is original to Malory.[18] The episode follows almost immediately upon Malory's noble lovers' actually making love. That has occurred, and Lancelot has killed Melleagaunt in a judicial duel. His sin has been as it were underlined.

In the episode following those events, Sir Urry of Hungary is carried in. He has been wounded; his wounds can be healed only by the "beste knyght of the worlde" (3:1145.19–20).[19] Urry's mother has been looking for aid in lands "crystened" (3:1145.29, 1146.14), leaving England until the last. Coming to Arthur's court at Pentecost,[20] a day celebrating a Christian miracle, she begs Arthur's help

(3:1146.23–24). Arthur and the other knights—110 at Malory's count—all try in vain to heal the wounded knight, during which attempts there appears no mention of God or Jesus. That changes in Arthur's ejaculation, "Mercy Jesu! . . . where ys sir Launcelot?" (3:1150.35–36). As if summoned, Lancelot rides up. He reluctantly accedes to the universal request to make the attempt—he says it will be presumptuous of him to attempt what all have failed—and kneels alongside Urry. He prays, which none of the others have done. His prayer is simple and eloquent: "Now, Blyssed Fadir and Son and Holy Goste, I beseche The of Thy mercy that my symple worship and honesté be saved, and Thou Blyssed Trynyté, Thou mayste yeff me power to hele thys syke knight by the grete vertu and grace of The, but, Good Lorde, never of myself" (3.1152.20–25).[21] C. David Benson ignores the prayer, writing that Lancelot's achievement is "of this world," not a result of any "spiritual union with God."[22] Lancelot's prayer, however, is the sufficient cause of Urry's healing; Lancelot remains "devoutly knelyng" as he touches Urry's wounds (3:1152.27), and the wounds heal immediately. The miracle has occurred; to underscore the Christian nature of the healing, Malory brings in a cast of hundreds:

> Than kynge Arthur and all the kynges and knyghtes kneled downe and gave thankynges and lovynge unto God and unto Hys Blyssed Modir. . . .
> Than kyng Arthure lat ravyshe prystes and clarkes in the moste devoutiste wyse to brynge in sir Urré into Carlyle with syngyng and lovyng to God.   (3:1152.33–1153.3)

As this ceremony of praise is taking place in the background, in the foreground Lancelot, still kneeling, weeps "as he had bene a chylde that had bene beatyn!" (3:1152.36).

Many scholars have commented on the Urry episode, and especially on Lancelot's weeping.[23] Recently Karen Cherewatuk, in her essay in this volume, notes that "in the Christian tradition, tears have long been associated with contrition or compunction of the heart" (n. 31 in her essay). For myself, I assume that the mixture of awe, wonder, gratitude, and relief that Lancelot must feel is explanation enough for his tears. His prayer has been answered, though he has not been vindicated (recall that he has, just a few pages earlier, made love with Guinevere, then killed Melleagaunt). He is fully aware of his sin, and of his sinful nature. Unlike his son Galahad, he has not somehow earned God's grace through his own perfection; like Malory, and like Malory's audience, he has knowingly done wrong. My colleague and co-editor Janet Jesmok has put this better than I: "This is why Lancelot's spiritual journey is so much more moving than Galahad's. We are like him, a part of him and his desire to be better than he is while still hanging on to the earthly things he loves. When God rewards him, we all weep."[24] In spite of his sin, Lancelot has been publicly granted the grace to take part in a miracle. Small wonder that he weeps.

The Urry tale is central to understanding Malory's approach to his Christian theme.[25] By this point, one has repeatedly read that Lancelot is the best knight "of a sinful man" in the world; one now sees that his sin does not preclude God's grace. Grace does not cancel the sin and its consequences, as appears in the remainder of the *Morte*. However, grace can and does offer forgiveness. Malory dramatically illustrates this Christian truism in his original story of Lancelot's healing Urry. As the wording of Lancelot's prayer makes clear, he has not earned a miraculously healing nature, as Galahad did. Instead, Lancelot has asked for and received grace. Related events will soon occur at the close of the *Morte*, as both Guinevere and Lancelot repent and receive forgiveness.

Following the Urry episode, Malory next adds several new Christian references to the episode in which Lancelot is surprised in Guinevere's chamber by Aggravaine, Mordred, and their twelve followers.[26] Malory has greatly modified here what he found in his sources, the French prose *Mort le Roi Artu* and the Middle English *Stanzaic Morte Arthur*.[27] For example, contradicting the French source, Malory refuses to say that his lovers are abed (as opposed to both sources, which put Lancelot into Guinevere's bed immediately).[28] Moreover, Malory's episode is longer than in either of his sources, and many of the added words express his Christian theme. To be sure, the first two expressions are mere exclamation: Lancelot says of the knights shouting outside the door that "I shall sone stynte their malice, by the grace of God!" (3:1165.26–27). Another exclamation soon follows, as Lancelot cries "A, Jesu Mercy! . . . this shamefull . . . noyse I may not suffir" (3:1166.8–9).

Such exclamations are not especially meaningful in themselves; indeed, in the French *Mort* Guinevere has by this point twice called on the name of God in exclamations similar to Lancelot's (she says "se Dex maït" and "se Dex volsist": "so God help me" and "if God wills").[29] In this episode, though, the two exclamations herald a great deal of added God-talk. Thus Lancelot turns to Guinevere and addresses her as "Moste nobelest Crysten quene," then asks that, if he should be slain, she "pray for my soule" (3:1166.13, 17). Both expressions are original to Malory. So is the queen's response; she replies to Lancelot that should he be killed, she "woll take [her] dethe as meekly as ever ded marter take hys dethe for Jesu Crystes sake" (3:1166.27–28). Given the context, one has to find the idea of Guinevere as martyr somewhat startling, but certainly Christian. Discussing this scene, Catherine Batt writes that when Aggravaine "discovers" the couple, Lancelot and Guinevere's language of martyrdom and invocations of Christ's aid bespeaks their innocence and moral integrity. She notes the disjunction that results from blending adultery with the appeal to Christ.[30] In an opposed view, C.

David Benson suggests that Guinevere's "religious language" simply "stresses the heroic public role" she will play from that point on.[31] I argue that their language further marks Malory's addition of Christian elements to his theme of grace.

Further to add a Godly aura to the unfolding events, Malory next has Guinevere say that "*and hit might please God*, I wolde that they wolde take me and . . . suffir you to ascape" (3:1167.1–3; my emphasis). Lancelot's response intensifies the Christian element of their exchange as he rejects Guinevere's idea and comments afresh on his lack of armor: "That shall never be . . . God deffende me frome such a shame! But, Jesu Cryste, be Thou my shylde and myne armoure!" (3:1167.4–6). Malory has thoroughly departed from his sources in the comments he gives the two lovers; he has also begun what I can only call a hallowing process. He turns his sources' highly secular event into a virtually sacred moment, adding the ideas of martyrdom and of Jesus as shield and armor. Indeed, Malory may be alluding here to Paul's admonitions to his fellow Christians in Ephesians 6:11, "induite vos arma Dei" (Vulgate: clothe yourself in the armor of God).

In short, Malory has virtually tidied away the adultery of his noble pair. Recall that Malory's narrator self-consciously excises his sources' comment that the two were abed, saying that he refuses to speculate, for "love that tyme was nat as love ys nowadayes" (3:1165.13). Moreover, as the crowning event in the episode and another of Malory's additions, the two exchange not only kisses but rings as they part (3:1169.1–2). The entire event thus takes on overtones of a wedding, or at least of a betrothal. Overall, Malory has used Christian elements further to ennoble the lovers whom he earlier praised in his May passage. Malory recognizes that the two are adulterous lovers, but he has used Christian elements to lessen his audience's perception of the sinful nature of their relationship.

Finally, in the closing events of the book, Malory transforms the deaths of his three noblest characters. Arthur, Guinevere, and at the last Lancelot all die holy deaths, or (in Arthur's case) not-quite-a-death (though still holy).

First consider Arthur's death. In both the French *Mort le Roi Artu* and the English *Stanzaic Morte Arthur*, Arthur dies and that's an end of him. Girflet, in the French source, or Bedwere in the English one, comes to a chapel and finds a tomb with Arthur's name on it. Neither questions the attribution, nor do the texts; in each case Arthur is dead and gone. Malory changes that, to hint that Arthur still lives, in some mystic stasis, and will return again. Malory could have known this possibility from William of Malmesbury, or from Wace, or from Layamon's *Brut*: the idea appears in each.[32] Or he could have heard the idea in the "ballads" that William mentions and that Layamon hints at. Wherever he might have heard the story of Arthur's survival, none of the above, and no then-extant text that I can find, makes Arthur's death into a somehow-Christian survival. Malory does.

He begins with the story of Arthur's death, as in his sources: Arthur has to threaten Bedivere into throwing Excalibur into the water, then several ladies sail up on a mysterious ship and take him off to Avalon. So far, this is all from the sources, as is Bedivere's then stumbling off sorrowing, at length to find a chapel with a new tomb. He assumes—as in the sources—that Arthur's body lies there (3:1238–1241). But Malory, as narrator, challenges Bedivere's assumption. I reproduce much of his challenge:

> Thus of Arthur I fynde no more wrytten in bokis that bene auctorysed, *nothir more of the verry sertaynté of hy dethe harde I never rede* . . . [then follows the story of the three queens and the ship].
>
> Now more of the deth of kynge Arthur coude I never fynde, but that thes ladyes brought hym to hys grave, and such one was entyred there whych the ermyte bare wytnes that sometyme was Bysshop of Caunturbyry. *But yet the ermyte knew nat in sertayne that he was veryly the body of kynge Arthur.*
>
> For thys tale sir Bedwere, a knyght of the Table Rounde, made hit to be wrytten; *yet som men say in many partys of Inglonde that kynge Arthure ys nat dede, but had by the wyll of Oure Lorde Jesu into another place; and men say that he shall com agayne, and he shall wynne the Holy Crosse.* Yet I woll nat say that this shall be so, but rather I wolde sey: here in thys worlde he chaunged hys lyff. And many men say that there ys wrytten uppon the tumbe thys:
>
> Hic iacet Arthurus, Rex quondam Rexque futurus
>
> And thus leve I here sir Bedyvere with the ermyte.
>
>   (3:1242.3–30; my emphasis)

Malory writes that Arthur is not necessarily dead, and that in fact "som men say" that he was "had by the wyll of Oure Lorde Jesu into another place," whence he will return to "wynne the Holy Crosse" (3:1242.22–25). Malory's narrator takes care neither to confirm nor to deny this part of the story, but it is all Malory's invention, his addition to his sources.[33] When he writes that "nothir more of the verry sertaynté of hys dethe harde I never rede" (3:1242.4–5), he is drawing a very long bow; he has indeed read of the certainty of Arthur's death, in both of his chief sources. He denies that, however. Moreover, Malory adds the will of "Jesu" to his reading of Arthur's death, though he is careful to underscore his lack of certainty: "some men say" this, he reports, and he will not venture to endorse their saying. He will only affirm, "he chaunged hys lyff."[34] My point, of course, is that Malory has worked a profound change on his materials; further, even if he carefully disavows absolute certainty, he is the first to introduce this element of Arthur's being had by Jesus into "another place" from which he will come again to win the Holy Cross. Malory ends Arthur's earthly life on a decidedly hopeful note.

Others have found the passage less hopeful, or not hopeful at all. Most recently, Elizabeth Edwards and Catherine Batt have read the passage as tentative, with Malory refusing to confirm or deny the hearsay he reports.[35] Elizabeth

Pochoda and Eugène Vinaver see no such uncertainty; each considers the death of Arthur to be irremediable tragedy.[36]

As opposed to the views of Edwards, Batt, Pochoda, and Vinaver, I argue that for Malory, Arthur becomes almost a Christ figure: he has "chaunged hys lyff," is no longer visible on earth, and is to come again, at which point a major redemptive event will occur. Moreover, Arthur's death paves the way for the deaths of Lancelot and Guinevere, both of which will take place in more conventionally Christian settings; with these three deaths Malory turns his story from the human tragedy of infidelity, betrayal, and death to the Christian comedy of salvation: "h[ad] by the wyll of oure Lorde Jesu into another place."

Guinevere's is the first of the remaining two noble deaths. She, too, changes her life—not immediately by dying but by retiring to Amesbury convent. There she lives in robes of black and white and in "fastynge, prayers, and almes-dedis, that all maner of people mervayled how vertuously she was chaunged" (3:1143.8–10). As with Arthur, "chaunged" is the key word. Her new life is briefly and movingly interrupted by Lancelot, who finds her and hopes to return her to the world and to life with him. She rejects both him and the world, resolving in the face of this old-new temptation to stay in the convent and earn her salvation: "thorow oure love that we have loved togydir ys my moste noble lorde slayne. Therefore, sir Launcelot, wyte thou well I am sette in suche a plyght to gete my soule hele . . . that aftir my deth I may have a syght of the blyssed face of Cryste Jesu . . . for as synfull as ever I was, now ar seyntes in hevyn. And therefore . . . I requyre the and beseche the hartily, for all the love that ever was betwyxt us, that thou never se me no more in the visayge" (3:1252.10–20). Firmly refusing Lancelot's request for one last kiss, she adds, "absteyne you from suche werkes" (3:1253.27–28).

Lancelot takes her at her word, and more. As she remains in Amesbury convent, he takes himself into the forest, then into a monkish brotherhood he finds there, and eventually into the priesthood. Edward Donald Kennedy points out that Lancelot's holy life copies Guinevere's example, one that leads him to salvation. Kennedy concludes that "Guenevere . . . achieves salvation for herself and enables Lancelot to achieve it." Karen Cherewatuk takes a similar view, arguing that Malory increases "hagiographic details" in his account of Lancelot's last days, thereby paralleling Lancelot's repentance with Guinevere's.[37]

Years pass, Malory tells us, at the close of which Guinevere receives visions from God prior to her death, again an element of the story original to Malory (3:1255.29–35). Lancelot, who has already been following Guinevere's ascetic example, intensifies his penance after he officiates at her funeral. He eats nothing, drinks little, and passes his days praying while lying on the tomb of his king and queen (3:1257.1–11). His bishop-leader chides him; Lancelot, in a response similar to Elaine of Astolat's deathbed retort to her priest, replies that he does no wrong in mourning the passing of his king and queen. As Kate Dosanjh suggests, though Lancelot has needed and carefully heeded the orders and explanations of various hermits during his part of the Grail Quest, he now rejects his bishop's direction to cease his mourning over the tomb of Guinevere and Arthur: "Launcelot now possesses spiritual self-awareness" and is at last ready to enter heaven, as appears in the archbishop's final dream of Lancelot and the angels.[38]

Self-aware or not, Lancelot, again like Guinevere, receives forgiveness; as with his son Galahad (2:1035.14–16), angels lift him directly into heaven (3:1258.7–10). Lancelot's angels appear in both the French *Mort le Roi Artu* and in the English *Stanzaic Morte*;[39] Malory's chief addition to the account of the two noble deaths is simply the change in the order and manner of Guinevere's death. In both of Malory's sources, Lancelot dies first. By instead putting her death just prior to Lancelot's, and by recounting her visions and his angels, Malory makes it clear not only that both receive God's forgiveness but also that both still love one another. The two signals of their love are, first, Guinevere's constant prayer during her dying that she not see Lancelot again with her "worldly eyen" (3:1255.37); there could be no need to pray thus if no feeling for him remained. More obviously, the continuing depth of Lancelot's love appears in his wasting away while lying on the tomb of the royal pair after he has assisted in burying Guinevere there. He did not show this sorrowful devotion when only Arthur's body reposed (or did not repose) in the tomb.[40]

Malory never suggests that Lancelot and Guinevere ought not love one another. He even, delicately, suggests in Elaine's speech that great love cannot be resisted: one recalls her comment to her priest that she "had no myght to withstonde the fervent love" (2:1094.2–3). The great love between Lancelot and Guinevere is adulterous, therefore sinful; it is nonetheless noble, as Malory points out at length in his May passage. In fact, their love seems to emanate from God, if we are to believe both Elaine and the May passage. If it is, as Malory barely hints, irresistible,[41] it is also forgivable. And, thanks to the penance that medieval Christians saw as the essential third step in receiving God's grace, the noble lovers are forgiven.[42]

Christian doctrine insists and Malory's fiction proclaims that human love, even adulterous human love, does not preclude a holy end. The point of Malory's added theme—one central to the *Morte*—is that one may sin in love, and even sin deeply, but grace is available to the repentant sinner. Those in Malory's audience may not have thought that they could go forth and heal wounds, but they knew, from the teachings of church and priest, that they, like Guinevere and Lancelot, could receive grace. That belief was a commonplace of medieval as of modern Christianity; in his version of the story of Arthur, Guinevere, and Lancelot, Malory finds a new way to discuss it and give it fresh life.

Conclusion

Malory inserts into a story that had not before contained them six Christian explicits, an authorial prayer for Tristram, and many significantly altered, or even original, Christian references. Malory's addition of Christian elements into his text converts the tragedy that Caxton called in his colophon "le morte darthur"—the death of King Arthur—into a Christian comedy. Malory has developed a theme not found in his sources: that love (specifically, noble love) comes from God; that it can be irresistible; that it can be sinful; and that it can be forgiven. Malory resolves his work not in "morte," as Caxton's phrase suggests, but in the ascension of his three major characters into "another place" (3:1242.24). God's grace is part of Malory's universe.

Nonetheless, and in spite of the Christian happy ending, Malory is himself an earthly man writing to earthly men and women. He sees clearly the sadness that is lessened but not canceled by the holy deaths of the three main characters. Bedivere weeps when he supposes Arthur dead; for him, Arthur is dead. Lancelot mourns Guinevere's death until his own comes upon him. Lancelot's brother Ector laments his brother's death in one of the most moving threnodies in English literature (3:1259.9–21). And though Lancelot's kinsmen die in the Holy Land in the best of causes, they are nonetheless lost to followers and readers alike. For even the most devout Christian, death brings attendant grief; Christ himself, Christians recall, is "deeply moved" at the sight of the grief of the two sisters over their brother Lazarus's recent death; then, as he is invited to view the tomb, he begins to weep (John 11:33, 35). Grace does not preclude grief; the tears of things, the *lacrimae rerum*, remain.

Given that he spent the last several years of his life in prison, and wrote his *Morte* during his imprisonment, one can see why Malory adds the explicits praying for good recover; one can see, too, given the charges against him, why he might be motivated to develop throughout his long work a theme of grace that says that sin can be forgiven. If he actually committed any of the crimes of which he was accused—and recall that he was never tried, and that the charges were brought by his political enemies[43]—if he committed any of those crimes, then he needed that reassurance.

NOTES

I must begin by noting that the Medieval Institute of Western Michigan University extended a Visiting Fellowship to me for the spring semester of 2006. This paper stems from the uninterrupted research time and funds the Medieval Institute made available to me; I am deeply grateful.

1. Roger Ascham's *Scholemaster* (1570) is widely available on the World Wide Web. Ascham's comments on the *Morte* appear toward the end of book 1, easily locatable by electronic search.

2. From Vinaver's introduction to Malory, *Works*, 3rd rev. ed. In this essay, all quotations from Malory's text come from this edition and will be noted parenthetically by volume, page, and line numbers.

3. Vinaver, *Malory*, p. 84.

4. Lewis, "English Prose *Morte*," p. 7. Charles Moorman also argues that Malory preserves the *sens* of the French *Queste* ("Tale of the Sankgreal," p. 187).

5. Vinaver, "On Art and Nature," p. 32.

6. Vinaver changes the bibliographic text of the explicit by reproducing it entirely in capital letters. As I have done here, I shall silently reduce Vinaver's uppercase intrusions upon the text to normal upper- and lowercase typography throughout this essay.

7. The other five appear at 1:363, 2:845–46, 2:1037, 3:1154, and 3:1260.16–29.

8. Caxton then adds his own explicit as he begins his colophon "Thus endeth thys noble and Ioyous book" (*Works*, 3:1260, note to line 29).

9. Oakeshott, "Finding of the Manuscript," pp. 1–6.

10. Anne Sutton in 1999 discovered a record suggesting that Malory was in Newgate Prison in 1469 ("Malory in Newgate"). The record to which Sutton refers in her article (p. 258) is dated 1469; it appears only on the World Wide Web at Richard Britnell's page of *Colchester Deeds*, from which I downloaded the following text on 10 February 2006:

> *Lettera testimonialis de dictione Thome Mynton iacentis in extremis.*
> Roger Clyfford, keeper off Newgate, *Sir Thomas Mallery, knight*, sir John Draper, priest, . . . and John Cobbam, . . . certify that on 20 April within Newgate they heard Thomas Mynton, gentleman, there lying in sykenesse abyding the mercy of God, say of his own free will on oath that if he should recover he would fulfill all the obligations he had made Sir Thomas Cook, knight, and that he would not subsequently vex Sir Thomas Cook in any respect.
> Date: 21 April, 9 Edward IV [21 April, 1469]
> CARTULARY COPY: fol. 233r–v [emphasis added]

11. Jennifer Boulanger has recently suggested that Malory's final explicit (as found in Caxton's edition), in common with other inscriptions appearing throughout the *Morte*, is a "redemptive exchange between himself and his reader." In asking for prayer, she writes, Malory duplicates other written requests for redemptive acts found, for example, in Elaine's letter to Arthur's court and on medieval tomb inscriptions that ask prayer for the soul of the deceased. She does not cite such a tomb inscription in the *Morte* but notes rather the role of the *Morte*'s tomb inscriptions in "righting" (and "writing") history—in correcting previous mistaken views of the tomb's occupant ("Righting History," p. 30).

12. A more extensive survey of Merlin's alliance with God appears in Hanks, "T. H. White's Merlin."

13. The scholarly conversation about Lancelot has been extensive. D. S. Brewer argues that "[f]or Malory . . . there is no essential incompatibility between the values of Christianity and those of the High Order of Knighthood, of ideal Arthurian chivalry." Lancelot "succeeds . . . because he is brave and good and repents of his sins," ("'[H]oole book,'" p. 58). P. E. Tucker, in "Chivalry in the *Morte*," suggests that "[Malory's] version gains coherence if it is seen as concerned . . . with Lancelot's experience" (p. 83). R. T. Davies, in "The Worshipful Way in Malory," likewise finds Lancelot's role central to the spiritual theme of the Grail Quest. He writes that Lancelot achieves "a kind of vindication" at Corbenic (p. 170).

Arthur B. Ferguson, in *The Indian Summer of English Chivalry*, also notes Lancelot's partial success in the Grail Quest (p. 54).

Larry D. Benson, in his *Malory's "Morte Darthur,"* argues in his chapter on the Tale of the Sancgreal that Malory followed what Benson calls the "chemin de vaillance"—the "worshipful way" of knighthood, personified by Lancelot. Thus "earthly worship remains a positive value"—and one by which a hermit can predict that Lancelot will die "a holy man" (p. 222). Similarly seeing Lancelot's role as crucial, Mary Hynes-Berry writes in "A Tale Breffly Drawyne Oute of Freynshe" that Malory simply could not see the "allegorical" element in the French *Queste*, so instead focused his Grail story on the imperfect and unstable Lancelot, rather than on Galahad (pp. 96–99). Murray J. Evans suggests in his "Camelot or Corbenic?" that Malory's transformation of Lancelot's characterization allows him to endorse both Camelot and Corbenic, but it also allows him to permit his hero to return to Camelot and to forget Corbenic.

Sandra Ness Ihle, in *Malory's Grail Quest*, suggests that Malory's "major interest" is to trace "how earthly knights, with the Christian vocation that knighthood implies, ought to act to be worthy of seeing the Eucharist unveiled in this world." She adds that Lancelot, though not a Grail knight like Galahad, Perceval, or Bors, nonetheless almost completely succeeds in his quest: "Malory has shown what can be accomplished by the best of those who are of this earth, if they take great pain upon themselves" (pp. 113, 156).

Two others who early joined this debate were Stephen C. B. Atkinson and Dhira B. Mahoney. In his essay in *Studies in Malory*, Atkinson writes that overall, Malory has transformed the Lancelot of the French *Queste* into a knight who will persevere in his pursuit of worship but who sees clearly the superior claims of Godly worship and who achieves a great measure thereof ("Malory's Lancelot," pp. 148–49). Mahoney, in the same volume, argues that Lancelot "is the doctrinal pivot," providing in his successes and failures the very definition of the Grail Quest. He does not discard "chevalerie celestial" as the French source suggests; instead, he grows into it during the course of Malory's story ("Truest and Holiest Tale," pp. 118, 123–24). Jill Mann, conversely, sees Lancelot as fractured in his essence; great knight though he be, his relationship with Guinevere produces a fragmentation that can be only partially healed by confession and by his association with Galahad ("Malory and the Grail Legend," pp. 217, 219).

14. Tolhurst points out that Barber also suggests that Lancelot has a qualified success in his quest for the Grail: see her essay in this volume, note 2, and Barber, *Holy Grail*, p. 218.

15. Though C. David Benson suggests that "any moral theologian could find the holes in Elaine's argument," he nonetheless adds that this view obtains throughout the work's close ("Ending of the *Morte Darthur*," p. 225). Davies anticipated part of my argument as he suggested that stability is at the center of Malory's concept of virtuous love and that Elaine appeals to this sort of stability on her death-bed ("Worshipful Way," pp. 163, 166).

16. Larry D. Benson, *Malory's "Morte Darthur,"* p. 231.

17. C. David Benson, "Ending of the *Morte Darthur*," p. 227.

18. Tolhurst points out in her essay in this volume that Robert L. Kelly does not agree about Malory's originality in the Urry episode. See his "Wounds, Healing," pp. 174–75. Vinaver implies, but does not state, its originality to Malory (3:1611, note to 1145.1).

19. Kenneth Hodges suggests that Urry's wounds parallel the seven deadly sins, and that they recall the sinful natures of Lancelot and Guinevere while also presenting Lancelot as a healer ("Haunting Pieties," p. 41).

20. Vinaver's text reads "[nyghe] the feste of Pentecoste" (3:1145.32), supplying "nyghe" from Caxton's 1485 edition, Sig. aa iij, misprinted a iij. The Winchester Manuscript reads

"vnto." The full clause in the manuscript is "And by fortune she com vnto the feste of pente-coste vntyll kynge Arthurs courte" (fol. 445.17–18). "Vnto" can mean "to," as Vinaver twice notes in his glossary (referring to 1:390.25 and 1:430.9). I conclude that the episode takes place during the feast of Pentecost—a time when Arthur traditionally awaits uncommon events, according to the opening lines of the story of Gareth (1:293.7–12). A later com-ment that the Round Table knights "were there at the hyghe feste" supports that conclusion (3:1148.34–49.1).

21. See Sue Ellen Holbrook's essay in this volume for a full treatment of the role of the Trinity in this passage, in the *Morte* overall, and in Malory's time.

22. C. David Benson, "Ending of the *Morte Darthur*," p. 229.

23. As Olsen points out in his essay in this volume, Earl R. Anderson summarizes much of that scholarship in his "'Ein Kind wird geschlagen,'" pp. 45–46; Anderson himself finds that Lancelot's tears "seem problematic and strange" (p. 69). Some studies do not appear in Anderson's 2003 survey: Davies writes that Lancelot's weeping shows a proper response to a "spiritual . . . crisis" and displays his "spiritual virtue" ("Worshipful Way," p. 171). Terence McCarthy writes that Lancelot's tears are tears of relief, humility, and "recognition of what might have been if he had always put God first" (*Introduction to Malory*, p. 99). Mann sug-gests of the juxtaposition of the court's rejoicing and Lancelot's weeping that it "expresses . . . the precariousness and the preciousness of wholeness" ("Malory and the Grail Legend," p. 220). C. David Benson finds the motivation for Lancelot's tears "mysterious," and adds that Lancelot "neither reaches nor attempts any spiritual union with God, and his miracle is purely physical—he cures wounds, not souls" ("Ending of the *Morte Darthur*," p. 229). Beverly Kennedy suggests that Lancelot's weeping is "[a sign] of God's special grace." She adds that Lancelot's tears arise from "the feeling of excessive joy which accompanies the indwelling of the Holy Ghost" in him (*Knighthood*, pp. 301–2, 303). Supplementing Ander-son's helpful list appear comments by Batt and Hodges: recently, Batt has discussed the incident at length, concluding with the ingenious suggestion that Lancelot's weeping like a child is "the signal of, and means to, authorial and reader creativity." That is, this simile requires readers themselves to determine why Lancelot weeps (*Malory's "Morte Darthur,"* p. 158). Hodges writes that "Launcelot weeps . . . in recognition of . . . grace" ("Haunting Pieties," p. 42). Hodges adds in another essay that Lancelot's tears provide "one of the most poignant recognitions of the mingled glory and shame of his love" (*Forging Chivalric Com-munities*, p. 59).

24. Janet Jesmok to author, private communication.

25. Others have discussed the importance of the Urry story to the closing pages of the *Morte*, though they have not agreed on why it is important, or even on how important it might be. Robert L. Kelly argues that "the episode of the Cart" cannot be reconciled with the miraculous healing. The point of the Urry story, he suggests, "is to focus on [Lancelot's] humility" and on his standing as "the best knight of the world" ("Wounds, Healing," pp. 191, 177). Davies suggests that Lancelot's healing of Urry shows that God has not aban-doned Lancelot in spite of his sin ("Worshipful Way," p. 171). Larry D. Benson writes "[t]hat Lancelot . . . should achieve this healing after reestablishing his faithful love of Guenevere seems a sign of divine approval. It is surely a sign that Malory did not make a simple equation between the sin of lust and the fall of the Round Table" (*Malory's "Morte Darthur,"* p. 228). Judson Allen goes further: "what happens when Sir Urry is healed is a grace, not an achievement. It is a gift of God . . . not something that Lancelot achieves" ("Malory's Diptych *Distinctio*," p. 250). (I am indebted to Kevin Whetter for pointing out Allen's comment.) Andrew Lynch suggests that the Urry episode reflects not "grace"

but Lancelot's "greatness as a knight"—i.e., chiefly his prowess (*Malory's Book of Arms*, pp. 45–46). Elizabeth Edwards briefly discusses the healing of Urry as a "nostalgic text" that reassembles the Round Table knights for the last time, to see "an unwhole knight [bring] the whole court together to witness an act of holiness." She suggests that "the healing itself is a matter of simple contiguity . . . of the right knight with the wound" (i.e., the healing is a matter of coincidence; Lancelot just happens to be "the right knight" to heal Urry) but adds that "divine favor" does mark the healing. "The whole function of the tale," she concludes, "is to mark Lancelot . . . as 'hede of all Crysten knyghtes,' (3:1259.9)" (*Genesis of Narrative*, pp. 167–68). Batt sees the episode as "extending divine grace to earthly values," suggesting that in the event both "the chivalric [code], and Lancelot as its representative" receive God's grace (*Malory's "Morte Darthur,"* p. 153). More recently, Raluca Radulescu has suggested first that "Lancelot's spiritual state is developing, not declining . . . between the Quest and 'Healing' [of Sir Urry]," thus reconciling both secular and sacred chivalry; second, that Malory presents in the healing a public miracle, as opposed to the private "Grail experiences"; and third, that the healing shows Lancelot as indeed the "best knight" ("Malory's Lancelot and the Key to Salvation," pp. 93–94).

26. For a full discussion of the chamber episode, see Hanks, "Malory, the *Mort[e]s*."

27. *La Mort le Roi Artu*, pp. 115–17; *Stanzaic Morte Arthur* (lines 1768–1865 for the episode).

28. *La Mort le Roi Artu*, pp. 115–16; *Stanzaic Morte Arthur*, lines 1804–7; cf. *Works*, 3:1165.10–13.

29. *La Mort le Roi Artu*, p. 116.

30. Batt, *Malory's "Morte Darthur,"* p. 167.

31. C. David Benson, "Ending of the *Morte Darthur*," p. 230.

32. *William of Malmesbury's Chronicle*, p. 315; Wace, *Roman de Brut*, p. 333; Layamon, *Selections from Layamon's "Brut,"* p. 118.

33. Vinaver notes Malory's originality in the passage (*Works*, 3:1654–55, note to 3:1242.3–33).

34. Alan J. Fletcher suggests that Malory takes his phrase from the Latin burial service: "Deus . . . cui non pereunt moriendo corpora nostra, *sub mutantus in melius*" (God . . . For whom our bodies, dying, do not perish, but *are changed for the better* [emphasis mine in both instances] ("King Arthur's Passing," p. 23).

35. Edwards, *Genesis of Narrative*, pp. 175, 177; Batt, *Malory's* Morte Darthur, pp. 177–78.

36. Pochoda, *Arthurian Propaganda*, p. 34; *Works*, 1:xcix.

37. Edward Donald Kennedy, "Malory's Guenevere," pp. 40, 44; Cherewatuk, "Saint's Life," p. 67.

38. Dosanjh, "Rest in Peace," pp. 65–66.

39. *La Mort le Roi Artu*, p. 261; the Middle English *Stanzaic Morte Arthur*, pp. 108.3866–109.3881.

40. Cherewatuk suggests that Malory has built into his characterization of Lancelot, from the Grail story onward, the three-part structure of medieval Christian confession: contrition, confession, and satisfaction (the action of penance). Lancelot's groveling on the tomb represents penance, or satisfaction. The real close of the book, then, is Lancelot's final act of satisfaction (his death), and that close also represents a Christian comedy ("Malory's Launcelot").

41. Cherewatuk makes a similar point, suggesting that Lancelot and Guinevere are "not free to resist" their love, or at least not until, like Guinevere as the story closes, "they reject their bodies and become truly whole or holy" (*Marriage, Adultery*, p. 52).

42. This conclusion has not been universal. It has been debated at length, with many arguing that the human love of Lancelot and Guinevere is essentially unforgivable. Vinaver ignores the debate: since he sees the climax of the story to be Arthur's death, he ends his series of "Commentary" essays with observations about that death, wholly ignoring the deaths of Guinevere and Lancelot (3:1626). F. Whitehead proposed the "human love" view in 1963, suggesting that Lancelot should have renounced such affections. Whitehead adds that Malory's point is no longer that penance opens the gates of heaven but rather that "human affection" endures ("Lancelot's Penance," pp. 112–13). C. David Benson agrees, putting his conclusion even more strongly; noting the Christian references in the closing sections, he concludes that they are superficial: "for all their Christian coloring, these references . . . refer to this world rather than the next." In fact, Benson concludes, "Malory constantly uses the language of Christianity and describes his heroes going to heaven, but he has no real interest in the metaphysical. His focus remains on this world and his religion is sentimental" ("Ending of the *Morte Darthur*," p. 235).

Helen Cooper supports the "holy end" argument. She writes that the great loves of literary romance arise out of the irresistible attraction of each lover to the other, and that this is the defining characteristic of great loves, of which the two greatest in the Middle Ages are Tristan and Isolde and Lancelot and Guinevere. There is "no way out" for Malory's lovers, but this fact does not condemn them. She adds, "Malory does not make the morality easy for himself or his readers. . . . Malory's God is on the side of the lovers." Their godliness appears in the healing of Sir Urry, Guinevere's good end, and Lancelot's similar good end (*English Romance*, pp. 321–23). Michelle Sweeney proposes a middle ground in the holy end–human love debate, suggesting that one finds at the close "yet another one of Malory's deeply awkward happy endings"; though both Guinevere and Lancelot take up religious lives, each remains tied to the other. The tie remains: Guinevere was to have a good ending, as forecast in the May passage, because "whyle she lyved she was a trew lover." Lancelot now has a good ending, too ("Divine Love," pp. 75, 76).

43. A sequence of chapters in Christina Hardyment's recent *Malory* presents a distinctly pro-Malory stance toward the various crimes of which he was accused but never convicted: rape, insurrection, theft, cattle-lifting, etc. See her chapters titled "Nemesis," "Ravisher of Women?," "In No Wise Guilty," "At War with the Law," and "Knight Prisoner" (pp. 273–357).

Adulterated Love: The Tragedy of Malory's Lancelot and Guinevere

Corey Olsen

Sir Thomas Malory's account of Lancelot and Guinevere's love affair in the final sections of the *Morte Darthur*, beginning with Lancelot's reunion with Guinevere after the Grail Quest and ending in their cloistered separation, has had a strongly polarizing effect on his readers. In these final books, Malory consistently focuses the spotlight on the relationship of Lancelot and Guinevere, holding up these two great and tragic lovers as exemplars of noble and virtuous love. At the very end of the narrative, however, Malory turns and has both Lancelot and Guinevere piously repent of their relationship and live the remainder of their brief lives in tearful contrition and harsh penance for their sins. Malory critics in general seem to have found the shift between these two views of Lancelot and Guinevere's love so jarring that they are compelled to question the sincerity of one of them.

The critical responses have therefore fallen into two basic camps. One view is that the appearance of religious zeal at the end of the text is purely formal, or even disingenuous. In this reading, Malory's principles undergo no significant alteration, and his faith in the worldly values of love and chivalry remains firm to the end. The other view is that Malory recognizes the spiritual and moral shortcomings of those worldly values and ultimately turns away from them, pointing his readers in the end to higher, eternal realities. The first view has been the dominant one. Eugène Vinaver insists that, at the end of the narrative, there is "no comfort to be found in religious explanations."[1] C. David Benson asserts that Malory has "no real interest in the metaphysical" world, claiming that Malory's "focus remains on this world and his religion is sentimental."[2] F. Whitehead states flatly that to treat Malory's narrative "as though it were an improving religious work" is to "place the emphasis where Malory has resolutely refused to put it."[3] Karen Cherewatuk, however, strongly argues for the second view, insisting that Malory, in the ending to his work, is trying to "inspire readers to worldly renunciation."[4] Beverly Kennedy also makes a compelling argument that Lancelot rejects worldly values and achieves genuine Christian sanctity in the end.[5]

Other critics attempt to find some common ground, arguing that although Malory's conclusion shows a genuine interest in salvation, Malory maintains a fundamentally worldly perspective throughout. Fiona Tolhurst suggests that it is Lancelot and Guinevere's earthly love that makes them worthy of salvation; thus she maintains that neither Guinevere nor Lancelot actually repents and turns away from their relationship.[6] R. T. Davies does allow that the lovers repent, yet he still sees Malory as postulating a God who is "on the side of the truly chivalrous though they are sinful."[7] Both take the Christian language of Malory's ending more seriously than Vinaver, Benson, or Whitehead, but both understand that language as serving a worldly rather than a spiritual end. Such readings seek simply to remove the tension between Malory's depiction of the lovers' repentance and his earlier praise of their relationship by reading in the ending a mere pseudo-spirituality that firmly endorses Malory's earthly values. In other words, even the critics that seek to reconcile the spiritual and the worldly readings of the ending still end up merely taking sides between them.[8]

In the midst of her argument, Beverly Kennedy makes a comment in passing that, in my estimation, cuts straight to the heart of this scholarly dilemma. Having presented evidence from the text that suggests that Lancelot and Guinevere are not, in fact, "abed" when Aggravaine and Mordred begin pounding on the bedroom door, Kennedy points to Lancelot's protestation of innocence and remarks that "Malory has given us enough evidence to be able to believe Lancelot if we wish."[9] The wishes of the critics are precisely the issue, both in that particular interpretive decision and in the larger understanding of Malory's emphasis in his conclusion. Evidence for both sides is clearly present in the text. Lancelot and Guinevere *do* repent of their relationship and turn to God. Malory also *does* put Lancelot and Guinevere's love forward as the paramount example of good, virtuous love. These are the facts. Scholarly attempts to deal with these facts have found common ground primarily in their insistence that we, as readers, must choose which of these statements we wish to believe.

My contention is that Malory, conscious of the apparent contradiction, insists *both* on the virtue of Lancelot and Guinevere's love *and* on the genuineness of their repentance and religious zeal at the end. In this essay, I will argue that Malory embraces both of these readings, undertaking a deeply thoughtful and highly sensitive depiction of the moral, spiritual, and emotional complexities of Lancelot and Guinevere's relationship. First, I will carefully investigate Malory's definition of "good" and "vertuouse" love by examining his "two emphatic and extended defenses of human love":[10] Elaine of Astolat's defense of her love for Lancelot and Malory's prolonged discourse on the month of May. Then, I will examine how Malory positions Lancelot and Guinevere's affair in relation to this theory.

❖

Elaine's death scene challenges the idea that love is fundamentally sinful. Elaine's unrequited love for Lancelot finally drives her to her deathbed, where she still persists in lamenting Lancelot and complaining of her love for him. Her confessor is distressed and "bade hir leve such thoughtes" (2:1093.1). The priest is plainly concerned that her thoughts at this crucial moment seem to be dwelling on worldly things. Elaine, however, will not be forestalled, and she corrects the priest. Elaine insists that love is not inherently sinful. She is an "erthely woman" (2:1093.3–4), and therefore she claims: "my belyve ys that I do none offence, though I love an erthely man, unto God, for He fourmed me thereto, and all maner of good love comyth of God" (2:1093.5–7). Good love is a natural part of God's created order, Elaine maintains, and therefore it is not in conflict with God's will.[11]

Elaine does not insist that all love comes from God. Only "good love," one human creature loving another "unto God," has divine origin. Elaine goes on to assert that her love for Lancelot falls into this category, and in doing so, she provides some basic characteristics of "good love." First, "good love" is exclusive, faithful, and enduring; Elaine says of Lancelot that "I take God to recorde, I loved never none but hym, nor never shall, of erthely creature" (2:1093.9–10). Second, it is sexually pure; Elaine insists that she is "a clene maydyn . . . for hym and for all othir" (2:1093.10–11).[12] Such love, marked by chastity and abiding faithfulness, Elaine understands as both coming from God and being directed back unto God, and thus her confessor's anxiety is groundless, for good love cannot itself draw her away from God. The beatific smile on Elaine's face after her death (2:1096.16) suggests that her assessment of love in general and her love in particular have received a divine stamp of approval.

Elaine's death triggers a discussion in Arthur's court about constraint in love. Lancelot observes that "love muste only aryse of the harte selff, and nat by none constraynte" (2:1097.23–24). Arthur immediately concurs, remarking that "with many knyghtes love ys fre in hymselffe, and never woll be bonde; for where he ys bonden he lowsith hymselff" (2:1097.25–27). On one level, Arthur is simply agreeing with Lancelot, confirming that love is lost when one attempts to bind or constrain it.[13] In the immediate aftermath of Elaine's death, however, we can easily see another sense in which love may be said to be impossible to constrain. Not only is love necessarily spontaneous, it is also irresistible. Elaine confesses: "I had no myght to withstonde the fervent love, wherefore I have my deth" (2:1094.2–3). Lancelot's love for Guinevere is also unconstrained in this sense, and in this context Arthur's reference to being bound and losing oneself strikes a much more solemn note, especially when uttered in the very presence of Elaine's corpse.

The spontaneity and irresistibility of love receive further explanation in Malory's primary theoretical exposition of love, the long and rather peculiar passage that Vinaver positions at the opening of his Knight of the Cart section. The passage provides a segue between the account of the Great Tournament and the narrative sequence that begins with Guinevere and her knights riding out "onmayynge" in the woods and fields (3:1120.17). Here, Malory chooses to pause and expand the idea of "good love" of which Elaine provided only a preliminary sketch. Later, I will return to the relevance of the May passage to the Knight of the Cart episode itself, but first I want to consider the passage purely as an articulation of Malory's insistence on the interrelationship among love, nature, God, and virtue.

In describing the effects of May on lovers, Malory repeatedly employs imagery from nature. He claims that in May "every lusty harte begynnyth to blossom and to burgyne" (3:1119.2–3). He then emphasizes the connection with a more extended simile: "For lyke as trees and erbys burgenyth and florysshyth in May, in lyke wyse every lusty harte that ys ony maner of lover spryngith, burgenyth, buddyth, and florysshyth in lusty dedis" (3:1119.3–6). Through these images, Malory reinforces Elaine's depiction of herself as an "erthely woman" who was formed by God to love an "erthely man." Malory goes beyond a merely metaphorical connection between humans and vegetation, literalizing the effect of nature on lovers by suggesting that in May "all erbys and treys renewyth a man and woman" (3:1119.10–11). Just as God has formed flowers to grow in spring, so he has designed men and women to love each other.

Malory's nature imagery also sheds light on Elaine's protestations of the irresistibility of her love for Lancelot. Like other natural processes, the burgeoning of love in a lover's heart is an involuntary activity, a process as inevitable and unwilled as growth or puberty. This process seems to be especially inevitable in good people, for Malory claims categorically that "there was never worshypfull man nor worshypfull woman but they loved one bettir than anothir" (3:1119.25–26). Malory further suggests that the same natural process works to recall and renew people whose attitudes and behaviors lead to "fyeblenes of nature and grete disworshyp" (3:1119.20–21). So great is the natural, spontaneous power of love that even people debased in nature and vitiated by their own actions will find themselves in May calling "to their mynde olde jantylnes and olde servyse, and many kynde dedes that was forgotyn by neclygence" (3:1119.11–13). The natural power of love is even, to a degree, redemptive.

Malory places love in a larger context of other human actions and responsibilities that are also, by extension, a part of God's plan for "erthely" people. Malory advises: "lyke as May moneth flowryth and floryshyth in every mannes gardyne, so in lyke wyse lat every man of worship florysh hys herte in thys world" (3:1119.22–24). The connection between nature and love that Malory has been establishing in the May passage is, in Malory's vision, only a portion of a larger mandate for virtuous and worshipful action. From the beginning of the discussion, Malory makes it clear that, in describing the effects of May on "every lusty harte" (3:1119.2–3), he is not speaking exclusively of love. It is not merely love but "lusty dedis" that "spryngith, burgenyth, buddyth, and florysshyth" in a lover's heart (3:1119.5–6). This is why, when remarking on the universality of love among worshipful people, Malory goes on immediately to add: "and worshyp in armys may never be foyled" (3:1119.27–28). In this sense, in love and in the performance of "lusty dedis," both of which spring naturally from the heart according to God's natural order, is one to "florysh hys herte in thys world." The chivalric and the amatory worlds are inextricably linked, and each is a natural, wholesome part of God's design.

Not content with the general claim that good love and worshipful chivalry come from God, Malory also clarifies exactly how the Christian knight's service to God and to his lady should be related. He starts by asserting unequivocally the fundamental primacy of God's claim, explaining that one is to flourish one's heart in the world "first unto God, and next unto the joy of them that he promysed hys feythe unto" (3:1119.24–26). Such a prioritization is intuitive; no one would expect Malory to say that, in principle, one's lady should come before God. Later, in clarifying how one should pursue "worship in armys" (3:1119.27–28), he specifies: "firste reserve the honoure to God, and secundely thy quarell muste com of thy lady" (3:1119.28–29). This construction echoes the same priorities—God first, the lady second—but it goes beyond prioritization to suggest an interesting overlap between these two motivating forces. Both are imperative. A worshipful deed must be done both for one's lady and for God.[14] There is no tension here, no competing claims. God's right to the honor of a deed is preeminent, logically, for he is the source of all that is good and worshipful. But the deed will also flow naturally from the romantic love that springs forth and burgeons in an earthly man's heart, for that is how God formed him. If God is the first cause of worshipful deeds, love is the means by which God makes that goodness flourish in his creatures.

Malory calls such love "vertuouse love" (3:1119.30), and the central virtues with which he associates it are truth, faithfulness, and "stabylité." Elaine has already provided a paradigm for faithfulness: enduring, exclusive devotion. Malory seems to be invoking this same sense when he refers to a knight's beloved as the one "that he promysed hys feythe unto" (3:1119.25–26).[15] "Stabylité" is perhaps the central term that he uses to characterize "vertuouse love." Associating "stabylité" with faithfulness (3:1119.18), Malory first describes unstable lovers as those who "lay aparte trew love." Instability is more than just inconstancy. Unstable lovers also "deface" and undervalue "trew love," setting at "lytyll or nowght, that coste muche thynge" (3:1119.18–19); their love is marked by disrespect for the purity and the preciousness of true love. Along the same lines, Malory also persistently links instability with concupiscence. If one is subject to one's passions, "sone hote sone colde" (3:1120.2), stability is not possible, for "heete sone keelyth"

(3:1120.1). Notice the difference between being compelled, as Elaine is, by the power of nature and being a slave to one's desires.[16] The former brings forth "trew love"; the latter defaces that love.

When Malory describes the remarkable chastity of "olde love" (3:1120.2–3), he states that "then was love trouthe and faythefulnes" (3:1120.5). "Trew" love, love that is stable in this larger sense, encompasses both chastity and faithfulness, just as Elaine claims that her love for Lancelot does.[17] In this context, therefore, "trouthe" and "faythefulnes" are not merely synonyms. "Trew" love, or "good love" as Elaine calls it, is not only constant but "vertuouse," and sexual temperance is centrally located among its virtues. If this is so, then a "trew lover" would be a lover who is not only constant to her beloved but also chaste and respectful of the value and nature of her love, recognizing it as coming from God. Elaine, it appears, was just such a lover, and the connections between the May passage and her deathbed protestation would seem to set her up as the obvious exemplar for this "vertuouse love" that Malory is extolling. But Malory does not point to Elaine for his illustration; he points to Guinevere, inviting us to apply these principles of "trew love" to the relationship of Guinevere and Lancelot.

Such an application is complicated, to say the least. Adulterous lovers (who are also committing treason) might be faithful, but can they be "trew" and "vertuouse" in the senses in which Malory uses those terms? There are also many moments in which Guinevere hardly seems like a "trew" lover in anyone's sense of the term. She turns on Lancelot and banishes him from the court in petty jealousy over his prudent defense of other ladies, disregarding his explanations and calling him a "comon lechourer" (2:1047.2). She refuses even to consider any explanation of his wearing Elaine's sleeve, condemning him as a "false, traytoure knyght" (2:1080.30). While Elaine is nursing Lancelot with such "dyligence and labour" (2:1085.12) that "there was never woman dyd never more kyndlyer for man" (2:1082.31–32), Guinevere is wishing him dead (2:1080.29). How can these outbursts of pettiness and spite[18] be reconciled with her identification as a "trew lover"?

These blemishes might be explained away, to some extent, as the product of the mere excess of love. Even Elaine, who loved only with good love, was guilty of excess; the only sin she accuses herself of is loving Lancelot "oute of mesure" (2:1094.1).[19] The excess involved in Elaine's love even pushes her toward compromising her oft-proclaimed chastity. When Lancelot refuses to be her lawful husband, she offers herself as his paramour as the only alternative to death. Could the moral lapses in Guinevere's relationship with Lancelot be seen in this same light? Might not her occasional overreactions be overlooked and even her treason be mitigated by conceding that, though her love was true, she loved Lancelot out of measure?

It is possible, but Malory's narrative does not allow the moral complications of Lancelot and Guinevere's relationship to be so easily categorized and dismissed. After rescuing Guinevere from the stake, Lancelot insists to Arthur that Guinevere is "as trew a lady unto youre person as ys ony lady lyvynge unto her lorde" (3:1188.14–15) and that Guinevere herself is "both tru and good" (3:1188.36). Later, when Lancelot is returning Guinevere to Arthur at the order of the pope, Lancelot makes before Arthur the formal claim that Guinevere is "trew and clene to you" and a "trew lady unto you" (3:1197.8–10). Ironically, of course, Lancelot's protestations of Guinevere's "truth" seem themselves patently untrue. We *know* that Guinevere has been unfaithful to her husband, in Melleagaunt's castle at the very least. If Lancelot's claims to Guinevere's "truth" ring persistently false at this moment, might not the earlier "lytyll mencion" by the narrator that Guinevere is a "trew lover" be equally open to skepticism? Are we to see the whole May passage, as Terence McCarthy suggests, as an elaborate attempt at spin control, a desperate expedient Malory adopts to try to justify the adulterous pair in the eyes of his readers, despite evidence to the contrary?[20]

As it happens, the May passage has rather the opposite effect. The narrative context that Malory provides for his commendation of Guinevere in the Knight of the Cart demonstrates that he has no desire to avoid the apparent conflicts in his depiction of her love. Rather, Malory uses his praise of Guinevere's truth as a lover, along with the accompanying explanations, as an introduction to the only episode in the last two books in which he openly depicts Guinevere and Lancelot committing adultery. In thus bringing together his highest praise for the virtues of Guinevere and Lancelot's love with the most unquestionable manifestation of their guilt and sin, Malory almost forces his readers to confront the moral ambiguity of Lancelot and Guinevere's relationship.

In the Knight of the Cart, Melleagaunt reinforces the theoretical teachings on love in the May passage with a practical illustration of instability, duly accompanied by "fyeblenes of nature and grete disworshyp" (3:1119.20–21). Melleagaunt's choice to kidnap Guinevere during a Maying outing emphasizes his instability. The queen and her knights are celebrating May, demonstrating their allegiance to that temperate month so intimately associated with natural, virtuous love. The attire of the Queen's knights is indeed an almost comical literalization of Malory's earlier description of May's effect on lovers' hearts. The knights are "bedaysshed wyth erbis, mossis and floures in the freysshyste maner" (3:1122.2–3), as if their entire bodies were springing, burgeoning, budding, and flourishing "lyke as trees and erbys burgenyth and florysshyth in May" (3:1119.3–4). Melleagaunt, meanwhile, is contemplating the treacherous, cowardly ambush of these blooming lovers and the violent ravishing of the queen, the object of his desires. If there has ever been an instance of a foolish and unstable lover appearing like "wynter rasure" to "arace and deface grene summer" (3:1119.14–15), this is it.

Melleagaunt's case is also a caution against judging lovers too swiftly or superficially. On the surface, Melleagaunt's love seems faithful, since he has loved Guinevere "passyngly well" and "so had he done longe and many yerys"

(3:1121.8–9). [21] His love has emphatically not, however, endured without any "lycoures lustis" on his part (3:1120.4). Lancelot recognizes this when he rebukes Melleagaunt for presuming "to touche a quenys bed whyle hit was drawyn and she lyyng therein" (3:1133.11–12). Lancelot emphasizes the prurient intentions underlying this act, noting that even Arthur, her husband, would only have done so if "hit had pleased hym to have layne hym downe by her" (3:1133.14–15). It is easy to overlook Lancelot's rebuke of Melleagaunt's startling impropriety in light of Lancelot's own rampant hypocrisy in making it. [22] But what exactly would Malory have us believe would have happened had Melleagaunt burst in upon a sleeping and unbloodstained Guinevere in her own bed, unclad and accompanied only by her ladies, as he had apparently been contriving to do? It is possible to see, in Guinevere's insistence that her wounded knights be quartered in her own chamber, her prudent desire for some kind of safeguard against just such an assault on her person. Both Lancelot and Guinevere are well aware that Melleagaunt's love for Guinevere is decidedly not "vertuouse love."

The most important function of Melleagaunt's character, however, is the light that it casts on Lancelot, Guinevere, and their love. Melleagaunt openly and formally accuses Guinevere of treason, but his actions also serve as an indirect indictment of Lancelot's character. [23] As I mentioned above, Lancelot's rebuke of Melleagaunt's intrusion into the queen's bed is, under the circumstances, pointedly (though apparently unconsciously) ironic, drawing our attention to Lancelot's own, and far more profound, sexual transgression in lying by the queen as only Arthur should presume to do. Guinevere's outraged scolding of Melleagaunt upon her kidnapping is just as ironic, as the scathing accusations she directs at her craven captor also apply, in a sense, equally well to her noble rescuer. [24] Is Lancelot a "traytoure knyght" (3:1122.8)? In thought, yes, and he soon will be in deed. Is he a "kyngis sonne and a knyght of the Table Rounde" (3:1122.10)? Certainly. Does he "dishonoure the noble kyng that made the knyght" (3:1122.11–12)? Not yet openly, but this matches Arthur's own accusations of Lancelot, later on. Does his adultery with the queen shame "all knyghthode and thyselffe and me" (3:1122.12–13)? Arguably so, though again not yet in the public eye. The primary difference, indeed, is Guinevere's own consent. This may make Lancelot less despicable than Melleagaunt, but at the expense of implicating Guinevere in the crime as well. Other sections of Malory's narrative may allow the criminality of Lancelot and Guinevere's relationship to remain submerged, but Melleagaunt's intervention brings it forcibly to the readers' attention.

The farcical judicial combat between Lancelot and Melleagaunt further showcases the tenuous moral position into which Lancelot and Guinevere's relationship places them. Melleagaunt challenges Lancelot, relying on the justice of his cause in the face of Guinevere's apparently manifest guilt. In the combat, Lancelot is, of course, in the right only on the most slender of technicalities, and as Keith Swanson points out, Malory in this scene departs from his source in order to emphasize Lancelot's active manipulation of this technicality.[25] Despite Lancelot's solemn recognition that "God ys to be drad!" (3:1133.29), the judicial combat draws our attention to exactly how shaky Lancelot's moral ground is and how close his relationship with Guinevere is bringing him to an open defiance of God and right.

It is important, however, not to be rash and one-sided in assessing Lancelot and Guinevere's love during the Melleagaunt incident, for Malory simultaneously presents two distinct views. The similarities of Melleagaunt's position to Lancelot's may insist that we recognize the culpability of Lancelot and Guinevere's affair, but the enormous differences between Melleagaunt and Lancelot as characters simultaneously serve to buttress our understanding of Lancelot's virtue and rectitude.[26]

I have argued above that Melleagaunt's desire for Guinevere is shown to be concupiscent and thus unstable, in the terms of the May passage. Near the end of the Melleagaunt episode, Malory moves decisively to prevent us from tarring Lancelot with the same brush just because he does have a sexual encounter with the queen. When Lancelot is in prison, he is unreliably guarded by a woman who attempts to extort sex from him in exchange for his freedom. Although the attempted seduction may itself be clumsy, the temptation inherent in the situation increases as Guinevere's trial approaches. Lancelot, however, never wavers, proclaiming that "if there were no mo women in all thys londe but ye, yet shall nat I have ado with you" (3:1136.11–12) and adding that "as for my distresse, hit ys welcom, whatsomever hit be that God sendys me" (15–17). Lancelot is resolute in his virtue, submitting himself explicitly to the will of God.[27] Even as he ultimately grants the woman's reduced demand of a kiss, Lancelot emphasizes that his kiss is not a moral compromise, stating flatly that "and I undirstood there were ony disworshyp for to kysse you, I wold nat do hit" (25–26). The incident of the amorous jail keeper seems to serve little function other than helping to restore some degree of confidence in Lancelot's sexual temperance and faithfulness to God. By introducing it, Malory ensures that Lancelot's assignation with Guinevere in Melleagaunt's castle doesn't lead us to the false conclusion that Lancelot is either enslaved by his passions or wholly dismissive of God's moral demands.

Lancelot's interactions with Melleagaunt himself also impress upon the reader the idea that, despite the circumstantial similarities, Lancelot and Melleagaunt are entirely different in moral character. The most persistent difference between the two is Lancelot's courage. Where Melleagaunt is laying dishonorable ambushes for unarmed knights and sending archers to kill Lancelot's horse from a distance, Lancelot is, without hesitation, storming a well-defended castle, single-handedly and even unmounted. While Lancelot is issuing challenges to fight Melleagaunt and all his "felyshyp" at once (3:1127.25–27), Melleagaunt is kneeling in timorous surrender at Guinevere's feet without daring to give battle, even at a tremendous advantage. Melleagaunt's unflagging cowardice and Lancelot's unselfconscious heroism are revealing, considering the persistent link between good love and good chivalry that the May passage establishes. If Melleagaunt's "dysworshyp" is just what we would anticipate in so unstable a lover, Lancelot's "worshyp in armys" is likewise what we would expect to see in a "vertuouse" lover, the paragon of Arthurian chivalry.

When, therefore, Lancelot boldly states to Melleagaunt, almost immediately after his adulterous assignation with Guinevere, that "I fared never wyth no treson" (3:1134.17–18), we must pause before hearing his declaration as mere hypocrisy. Once again, the immediate context elevates our moral understanding of Lancelot, giving us a Lancelot honestly planning a fair fight with an enemy busily plotting an underhanded betrayal. Lancelot may be committing adultery with the queen, but he is not by nature a "traytoure knyght," as Melleagaunt is. Lancelot is, through nature, "a man of worshyp and of proues," even a "trew man" (3:1134.28–31). Lancelot and Guinevere may both be involved in treason, but Malory insists nevertheless that both are, in themselves, "trew."

The Knight of the Cart episode pushes us in contradictory directions, inviting us to look unflinchingly at the gravity of Lancelot and Guinevere's crime while still appreciating their "trouthe," "stabylité," and, therefore, goodness as people. Although it would greatly simplify things to focus only on one or the other, Malory persistently presents both. If the Knight of the Cart were the only sequence that manifested this peculiar division, it would be tempting simply to dismiss the apparent praise of Lancelot's character and to read in the passages that express it merely a bitter irony. But Malory demonstrates the same narrative pattern elsewhere, rarely allowing his readers to relax into either wholehearted approval or unruffled disapprobation of Lancelot and Guinevere's relationship.

Malory's management of the blame for the downfall of the Arthurian court is a good example. The collapse of Arthur's realm has many contributors, but it is Lancelot and Guinevere who provide the occasion. Lancelot's "prevy thoughtes" are "sette inwardly to the quene" (2:1045.13–14). These private, inward desires lead to "prevy" meetings together (2:1045.19). Ironically, the end result of all this priviness is exposure,[28] for they had "such prevy draughtis togydir that many in the courte spake of hit"[29] (2:1045.19–20). On the first page of the Book of Sir Lancelot and Queen Guinevere, the road that leads from the inward desires that Lancelot harbors for Guinevere through scandal to catastrophe is already being laid. In the beginning of Slander and Strife, however, Malory introduces a new factor: the "prevy hate" that Aggravaine and Mordred have "unto the quene, dame Guenyver, and to sir Launcclot" (3:1161.11–13). What was preparing to be a clear-cut condemnation of Lancelot and Guinevere's love as the primary socially destructive agent is qualified by the introduction of a separate and even more openly destructive force. Which are we to see as more responsible for the disaster, Lancelot and Guinevere's "prevy" love or Aggravaine and Mordred's "prevy" hatred? Lancelot and Guinevere are not exonerated by any stretch, but they certainly seem less like villains while Aggravaine and Mordred are around.

One of the most fascinating ways in which Malory renders moral judgments of Lancelot and Guinevere uncertain is the remarkable reluctance that his narrator betrays whenever the narrative catches Lancelot and Guinevere in an unambiguously compromising position. When Lancelot goes to bed with Guinevere in Melleagaunt's castle, for instance, the narrator seems to want to rush quickly past the act itself, saying only: "to passe uppon thys tale, sir Launcelot wente to bedde with the quene" (3:1131.28–29). Although he does not here avoid the bald fact, he shows an inclination to downplay it.

When Lancelot and Guinevere are finally cornered by Aggravaine, Mordred, and their gang, who intend to catch them in the act, the narrator's coyness manifests itself again. First, the narrator prepares the reader with a little description of Lancelot setting forth for Guinevere's chamber: "So sir Launcelot departed and toke hys swerde undir hys arme, and so he walked in hys mantell, that noble knyght, and put hymselff in grete jouparté" (3:1165.5–7). This description savors strongly of the epic, and it makes Lancelot's errand sound positively heroic. There is not the faintest hint of condemnation here for Lancelot's visit to the queen, or even of his imprudence in disregarding Bors's warnings.

Once Lancelot and Guinevere are together in her chamber, Malory pulls back, saying: "And whether they were abed other at other maner of disportis, me lyste nat thereof make no mencion, for love that tyme was nat as love ys nowadayes" (3:1165.11–13). Initially, this remark sounds like mere shyness on the narrator's part, akin to his swift glance past their previous bedchamber encounter.[30] But the addition of the final comment, the contrast between Lancelot and Guinevere's love and love "nowadayes," should make us pause. Remember that in the May passage, "olde love" was associated with chastity and love "nowadayes" with sexual intemperance.[31] By reminding us of the remarkable self-control of antique lovers like Lancelot and Guinevere, Malory invites us to see the whole scene in a completely different light.[32] In doing so, we may recall that Lancelot had told Bors before he left him that his intention that evening had been only to "go and com agayne and make no taryynge" (3:1164.30–31), and it is hard to imagine Malory's temperate lovers leaping instantly into bed upon his arrival, as the brief stay would have required. In fact, Malory's reminder of the difference between Lancelot and Guinevere's situation and a parallel situation in the modern world turns what seemed only a decorous evasion into the foundation of a genuinely plausible argument for Lancelot and Guinevere's innocence on that particular evening.[33]

Once more, the point is not that Malory is trying to exonerate the lovers completely. Whether they are in bed or not on this particular night, they are guilty of adultery—there is no possible uncertainty about that. What is interesting, however, is that Malory goes out of his way to *generate* uncertainty at this pivotal moment.[34] If the narrator had not brought up the issue of whether or not they were "abed," no one would ever have asked the question. At the same time, if Malory had wanted simply to clear Lancelot and Guinevere and turn them into victims, he could have just said conclusively that they were not in bed. Instead, he complicates the situation, choosing the moment of the ostensible proof of their guilt to remind us that Lancelot ("that noble knyght") and Guinevere (a "trew lover") are virtuous beyond the scope of modern-day lovers.

By doing so, Malory prevents his readers from judging Lancelot and Guinevere themselves too harshly. Malory also creates this effect, for instance, by placing in Lancelot's mouth, as he defends his presence in Guinevere's chamber, another phrase that is also linked to previous discussions of virtue and love. As Lancelot prepares to charge into battle against Aggravaine and his band, he swears that he came to Guinevere "for no maner of male engyne" (3:1168.8–9), that is, with no evil design or scheme. Earlier, in a brief aside cataloging the knightly virtues of the noble Sir Gareth, Lancelot observes that "in hym ys no maner of male engynne, but playne, faythfull an trew" (2:1089.2–3). Lancelot understands the virtues opposite to "male engyne" to include truth and faithfulness, the defining virtues of the "olde love" that Malory invokes in the chamber scene. Lancelot did not come to Guinevere's chamber, as Melleagaunt had done previously, for "male engyne." Lancelot insists that he is not that kind of lover, and, like Gareth, not that kind of man.

There is yet another moment in which Malory, using parallel phrasing, opposes "good love" to "male engyne" (2:1054.18–19), and that is in Bors's verbal defense of Guinevere following the Poisoned Apple incident. Both defend character, and both insist that the principals entered into the unfortunate and apparently compromising circumstances with pure intentions. But in both cases, regardless of the intentions and the personal virtues of the principals, irrevocable harm was still done. Guinevere may be innocent, but Sir Patryse is still dead; Lancelot and Guinevere may not have been abed, but the Round Table is still mortally wounded. No matter how temperate their meeting on the fateful evening may have been, no matter how virtuous their love in principle, their relationship has still helped to bring the Arthurian world to destruction.

In the final stages of his narrative, Malory presents us with a remarkably complicated and carefully balanced view of Lancelot and Guinevere. Malory associates Lancelot's sexual liaison with the queen at Melleagaunt's castle with the base treason of Melleagaunt himself, but he also emphasizes the enormous difference between the moral fiber of those two very different knights. He points to the crucial role of Lancelot and Guinevere's relationship in the collapse of the court, but he also raises up some real villains to demonstrate the kind of malice and treachery that are utterly alien to Lancelot and Guinevere's characters. He arranges to have the adultery finally exposed by having Lancelot and Guinevere caught together, yet he reminds us, even in that moment, of the remarkable virtue associated with their love. This delicate poise between praise and blame for Lancelot and Guinevere that Malory maintains does not, I contend, stem from any internal conflict on Malory's part. I do not see Malory torn between an admiration for Lancelot and Guinevere's love on the one hand and some sense of moral duty on the other. Malory is not, as many modern critics are, choosing one side or the other. Rather, he appears to suggest a perspective on Lancelot and Guinevere that embraces both the good and the bad that he insistently places before us. Malory makes no apology for Lancelot and Guinevere's adultery; it is a sin, a crime, and a major contributor to the collapse of the court. However, Malory also never allows his narrative to condemn Lancelot and Guinevere as people. Their actions may be wrong, but they, and even their love, are "trew" and "vertuouse." Malory is attempting to condemn the sin while still asserting the basic goodness and nobility of these particular sinners.

Lancelot and Guinevere's relationship, as Malory depicts it, is fundamentally tragic. If theirs were only a story of two people whose passions overcame their virtue (as is the case in most modern film versions of the story, for instance), everything would be simple. In such a case, the terrible consequences of their relationship would be only the natural results of their sin; at least, we would have something clear and obvious to point to as the cause of the trouble. The story could entail much suffering and the characters could be sympathetic and pitiable, but the moral would still be obvious.

The story of Malory's Lancelot and Guinevere is quite different. Their love is "trouthe and faythefulnes" (3:1120.5); Malory assures us on several occasions that their love is virtuous beyond the capabilities of us lesser, modern people. Their love is of the kind designed and intended by God for his creatures. It is, in a sense, only the circumstances that render their love sinful at all, the tragedy that Guinevere happens to be the wife of Lancelot's king.

The moral of this story is far from obvious. It is easy enough to say that we should affirm Lancelot and Guinevere as good and admirable people and embrace the ideals of their love while condemning the adulterous circumstances in which that love was manifested. Malory invites us to do all three of these things. This sounds fine in theory, but what does such a moral mean in practical terms? From the lovers' perspective, how are they to distinguish between the aspects of their love that are to be celebrated and cherished and those that have led them into moral and social catastrophe? How exactly would they and their love need to change in order to be reconciled with God's moral laws? This is the dilemma that Malory's praise of Lancelot and Guinevere's virtuous love creates.

I speak of a "moral of the story" and the practical application of that moral because I believe that Malory's narrative shows significant interest in the actual emotional and spiritual complexity of this situation.[35] For an illustration, I would like to return to Lancelot's vows and declarations of Guinevere's innocence after they have been officially condemned by Arthur. As I discussed before, Lancelot swears that Guinevere is "as trew a lady unto youre person as ys ony lady lyvynge unto her lorde" (3:1188.14–15) and that Guinevere is herself "both tru and good" (3:1188.36). Malory's treatment of the lovers' moral character might make the second, more general, claim plausible, but what are we to do with the first one? There seem to be only two possibilities: either Lancelot is simply and knowingly lying or he is, in some sense, deluding himself.

One can imagine a third possibility: that Lancelot is trying here, as he has before, to equivocate, to stand on a technicality. If we understand, as I have argued we should, that Lancelot and Guinevere were not in bed when they were trapped in her chamber, Lancelot's protestations here become much easier to understand, and they fit more cleanly into the pattern established by previous events. Lancelot defies Melleagaunt's accusation on a technicality. He knows that Guinevere is guilty of adultery, but, since she isn't guilty of sleeping with one of the knights in the room, as Melleagaunt claims, Lancelot can understand his defense to be technically justified and the queen to be, in a sense, innocent. The same scenario would apply if Lancelot and Guinevere were not in bed when Aggravaine and Mordred started pounding on the chamber door. The technicality involved there is even more slender, but it is comparable. In this case, Lancelot could still know that he and Guinevere have committed adultery in the past and yet say to Arthur "full knyghtly" (3:1197.3) that "they that tolde you tho talys were lyars" (20).

Yet there is more to Lancelot's claims than just equivocation. Lancelot is accused of being a "traytoure knyght" by Aggravaine. Now, Lancelot may be guilty, but that does not in itself make this accusation true. We can understand this concept of the disparity between his guilt and his moral state easily enough by considering the parallel situation that Malory provides: the murder of Sir Gareth, Lancelot's devoted follower. Lancelot did in fact kill Gareth, but that does not mean that Gawain's frenzied accusation that Lancelot is a "false, recreayed knyght" is true (3:1189.1). He may be guilty, but Gawain's accusation is nevertheless unjust. The same is true of his relationship with Guinevere. Aggravaine initially tells Arthur that "Launcelot lyeth dayly and nyghtly by the quene" (3:1161.20), depicting them as abandoned lechers. This accusation is as unjust to their relationship as Gawain's claim that Lancelot slew Gareth and Gaheris deliberately to spite Gawain is unjust to Lancelot's character (3:1189.22–23). Lancelot knows and properly maintains that Guinevere is not a harlot but rather "both tru and good" (3:1188.36).

And yet, they *are* guilty of adultery. The evidence being used against them (Aggravaine's entrapment) may be misleading. The love between Lancelot and Guinevere may be virtuous and good. But this still doesn't make Guinevere "as trew a lady unto youre person as ys ony lady lyvynge unto her lorde" (3:1188.14–15), a claim which it seems that Lancelot, on some level, genuinely believes.[36] Malory has gone to some lengths to create the conflicted and confusing web of guilt and innocence, of sin and virtue, in which Lancelot and Guinevere find themselves tangled. After the death of King Arthur, Malory turns to the task of extricating them.

Prior to the collapse of Arthur's court, Guinevere might be fairly described as shortsighted. She shows a distinct tendency to react to what she observes immediately, giving no regard to extenuating circumstances or possible alternative explanations. As Bors tells her of Lancelot's wearing Elaine's token and of his injury, Bors shows himself willing to give Lancelot the benefit of the doubt as far as his wearing the sleeve is concerned, asserting that he "dare say he dud beare hit to none evyll entent" (2:1081.2). Guinevere is not, considering herself to have been "betrayed" (2:1080.26) and dismissing Lancelot as a "false, traytoure knyght" (30). Earlier, when Lancelot had begun defending other ladies in order, in part,[37] to shield his relationship with Guinevere from growing suspicion, Guinevere sees only that his "love begynnyth to slake" (2:1045.32–33). Even after he offers a long explanation of his reasons for his behavior, she is unmoved, calling him a "false, recrayed knyght and a comon lechourere" and banishing him from her sight now that her eyes have been opened to his "falsehede" (2:1047.1–4). The sudden change that comes upon Guinevere after Arthur's death is so profound that it can only be understood as a genuine conversion experience.[38] Not only does she "lete make herselff a nunne" and take upon herself as "grete penaunce" as "ever ded synfull woman in thys londe" but her whole demeanor alters, and "ever she lyved in fastynge, prayers, and almesdedis" (3:1243.5–9). Guinevere does not merely retreat to a nunnery; she radically redirects her life, such that "all maner of people mervayled how vertuously she was chaunged" (3:1243.9–10).

When Guinevere meets Lancelot for the last time, she demonstrates startling new clarity and penetration of vision. Before, she had been so narrowly focused on their relationship that she could see little else, not even, at times, Lancelot's stratagems for safeguarding that relationship. Now she sees the consequences and ramifications of their relationship with an insight that completely eclipses Lancelot's own understanding.

Two things Guinevere now sees particularly clearly. The first is the role of her relationship with Lancelot in the downfall of the court and, therefore, her own culpability. When Lancelot approaches her in the nunnery, she declares plainly to her companions: "Thorow thys same man and me hath all thys warre be wrought, and the deth of the moste nobelest knyghtes of the worlde" (3:1252.8–10). Guinevere offers this observation as a mere statement of fact; the steadiness of her acceptance of her guilt is remarkable. She does not at any point say anything to shift responsibility away from herself, nor does she make her fault out to be greater than it is by reviling herself extravagantly. Instead, she calmly recognizes her guilt and speaks of her intention to seek God's help to "amende my mysselyvyng" (3:1252.29).[39]

In addition to recognizing her contribution to the national calamity, Guinevere also demonstrates a wholly new insight into her relationship with God. When Lancelot and Guinevere are trapped and Lancelot starts making contingency plans in the likely event of his death in combat at her chamber door, Guinevere declares: "Wyte thou well that I woll neuer lyve longe aftir thy dayes. But and ye be slayne I woll take my dethe as mekely as ever ded marter take hys dethe for Jesu Crystes sake" (3:1166.25–28). Her death at the stake, she claims, would be just like the burning of a martyr; she compares her devotion to Lancelot to a saint's devotion to Christ.[40] The implication that Lancelot is to her what Christ should be to a Christian is a serious and a telling one, particularly since the parallel is rather eerily apt. In all of her troubles, it is to Lancelot that she had ever turned for salvation; in this same scene she states her faith that if Lancelot were to escape her chamber, "I wolde nat doute but that ye wolde rescowe me in what daunger that I ever stood in" (3:1165.35–36). His have been the self-sacrificial wounds suffered to purchase her redemption from the fire; his, the blood shed for her justification. From the nunnery, Guinevere sees the issue of her own salvation in its larger, eternal context. Having recognized her own culpability and her "mysselyvyng," she understands her need for a spiritual rather than a merely physical champion. Her "truste" is now no longer in Lancelot but in "Goddis grace" and "Hys Passion of Hys woundis wyde" (3:1252.13–14).[41]

Earlier, in her pettiness and narrow-mindedness, Guinevere had banished Lancelot from her presence. In the end, now that she sees their situation with wisdom and clarity, she does it again. Guinevere is both firm and unrelenting in this resolve. Her order to Lancelot is unequivocal: "I commaunde the, on Goddis behalff, that thou forsake my company" (3:1252.20–21). To her own wishes, she has added the stamp of divine authority. Guinevere remains absolutely steadfast in her renunciation of her relationship with Lancelot. Even on her deathbed, knowing that Lancelot is being sent to her, her dying request of God is not to "see syr Launcelot wyth my worldly eyen" (3:1255.37).[42]

The phrase "worldly eyen" is a resonant one in the final, penitential segment of Malory's narrative. Literally, Guinevere refers to her physical eyes. She is prepared to meet Lancelot in heaven but does not want to encounter him again in this life. The phrase also serves to invoke the change in her perspective that has so marked her postconversion outlook; she no longer looks at herself or her relationship with worldly eyes. In this sense, then, her final petition to God might also be heard as a last prayer for the strength to avoid stumbling at the end of the race, for the perseverance to prevent a relapse into her old way of thinking about and perceiving Lancelot.

Having examined Guinevere's repentance, we must nevertheless not forget Malory's earlier insistence upon Lancelot and Guinevere's "vertuouse love." If their love is good love and comes from God, why should Guinevere repent of it?

First of all, Guinevere never does actually renounce the love that she and Lancelot have had; she only cuts off any future interaction between them. Guinevere does not condemn their past love itself. She does recognize the role that it has played in the national tragedy, admitting that "thorow oure love that we have loved togydir ys my moste noble lorde slayne" (3:1252.10–11), but she never characterizes their love as vicious in itself. Even the explanation of why she is prohibiting any further relations between them points rather to the circumstances and practical consequences of their affair than to any revulsion at the love itself. She says: "as well as I have loved the heretofore, myne harte woll nat serve now to se the; for thorow the and me ys the floure of kyngis and knyghtes destroyed" (3:1252.23–25). Her thoughts of the terrible results of their relationship are too awful, too painful for her to bear its continuance.

Moreover, even in her renunciation of their relationship, Guinevere refers to their love as a source of good, linking it with God. Guinevere banishes Lancelot from her presence twice in quick succession. The first time, she invokes their love: "I requyre the and beseche the hartily, for all the love that ever was betwyxt us, that thou never se me no more in the visayge" (3:1252.18–20). The second time, she invokes God's authority: "I commaunde the, on Goddis behalff, that thou forsake my company" (3:1252.20–21). Note that she refers to their love not as an object of disapproval but as a source of good and a resource to be appealed to in her attempt at moral reformation, for both herself and Lancelot. In fact, her twofold injunction recalls the harmonious interaction between God and the lady as the dual causes of good chivalric deeds that Malory outlined in the May passage. If their love is good love, it should, with its chastity, temperance, and stability, equip them even for the termination of their worldly relationship.

Indeed, Malory anticipates exactly this reformative role for "trew" love when he defines it in the May passage, remarking that one of the natural effects of May is to help even immoral, unstable lovers call to mind "olde jantylnes and olde servyse, and many kynde dedes that was forgotyn by neclygence" (3:1119.11–13). Love has natural morally recuperative and even redemptive tendencies. Moreover, Guinevere's own redemption is specifically anticipated in Malory's "lytyll mencion" on her behalf, when he remarks not only that she was a "trew lover" but also that "therefor she had a good ende" (3:1120.13). The "good ende" referred to must be her spiritual reformation; there is simply no other sense in which Guinevere had a good end. The important word, however, is "therefor": Guinevere's repentance and her good spiritual end are made possible by the truth and faithfulness of her love.[43]

Lancelot's journey to repentance is longer and more reluctant than Guinevere's. Although he seems able to see farther than Guinevere does prior to her conversion, Lancelot is much more resistant to changing his perspective than she shows herself to be.

Malory explains Lancelot's internal dilemma at the outset of the Book of Sir Lancelot and Queen Guinevere. Lancelot's "semynge outewarde" is to God, while his "prevy thoughtes" and "his myndis" are "sette inwardly to the quene" (2:1045.13–15). Lancelot is not merely a hypocrite, however. As Karen Cherewatuk characterizes him, he is "a fractured Lancelot, caught between two worlds."[44] Malory tells us right away that Lancelot's privy mental occupation with Guinevere is a barrier to his spiritual life, assuring us that, had Lancelot's devotion to God been unadulterated, "there had no knight passed hym in the queste of the Sankgreall" (2:1045.15–16). What is more, Lancelot knows that this is the case. In his explanation to Guinevere concerning his new custom of defending many ladies, Lancelot admits that the Grail Quest "may nat be yet lightly forgotyn" (2:1046.12–13), and he recognizes that he owes his failure in that quest to the lingering of his "prevy thoughtes" on Guinevere (8–11). Nevertheless, despite this recognition, he immediately goes on to explain a second motive for defending other ladies: the desire to better conceal their love and prevent "sclaundir and noyse" (2:1046.28). Lancelot may be aware of the deep division within him, but that awareness does not in itself help him out of his dilemma.

Lancelot is not, however, merely a man with some sort of bad habit or sinful tendency of which he lacks the willpower to rid himself. The heart of Lancelot's problem is that the thing hindering his devotion, his love for Guinevere, is itself an extremely good thing.[45] I have tried to demonstrate how this dynamic is at work in Lancelot's oaths and attestations in the aftermath of his rescue of Guinevere from Arthur. Bolstered by the accusation's poor foundation and malicious motivation and brimming with reverence for the honor and virtue of his love in general and his beloved in particular, Lancelot is able to maintain the case for Guinevere's innocence without conscious duplicity. Lancelot is so wrapped up in the nobility of his love with Guinevere that he becomes almost completely blind to the simple but uncompromising fact of its adultery, the circumstance that taints this otherwise virtuous love and brings Lancelot's devotion to his lady into conflict with his devotion to God.

Lancelot's love for Guinevere so dominates the narrative in the Book of Lancelot and Guinevere, in fact, that it is easy to downplay or even completely lose sight of the spiritual half of Lancelot's dilemma. The episode of the Healing of Sir Urry, which C. S. Lewis called "perhaps the greatest of all passages peculiar to Malory,"[46] serves as a salient reminder; it introduces nothing really new, but it brings our attention back to Lancelot's understanding of his spiritual state.

When confronted with the healing task, Lancelot demonstrates a clear belief in his own unworthiness, attesting: "never was I able in worthynes to do so hyghe a thynge" (3:1152.14–15). He soon proves that this is not just a rhetorical gesture designed for show, for he repeats his statement of humility in his secret prayer, asking for the power to heal Urry "by the grete vertu and grace of The, but, Good Lorde, never of myselff" (3:1152.23–25).[47] Lancelot's prayer for Urry, however, is far from a selfless intercession on the wounded knight's behalf. He petitions that his "symple worshyp and honesté be saved" (3:1152.21–22). While this request is obviously self-interested, it is not necessarily grounded in vanity, in the desire simply to avoid exposure and disgrace before the whole court. One's honesty is certainly not saved in any meaningful way just by having misdeeds hidden from the public. Lancelot's appeal hints at a genuine desire for redemption, even though he does not yet see how to grasp it.

Lancelot's tears upon the granting of his prayer emphasize this desire as well as how far removed he yet is from achieving it. A great deal of critical attention has been devoted to Lancelot's tears;[48] I want to focus more on the clearest cue that Malory provides his readers for their interpretation: the memorable description of Lancelot weeping "as he had bene a chylde that had bene beatyn" (3:1152.36). By comparing Lancelot to a beaten child, Malory describes not only the nature of Lancelot's pain but its larger context. Catherine Batt makes the connection between the image of the beaten child invoked in the context of Lancelot's receiving of mercy and grace from God and the scriptural teaching that "whom the Lord loveth, he chastiseth."[49] Batt argues that the combination of the act of grace and the disciplinary simile mark Lancelot, in Malory's mind, as a specially chosen and beloved child of God.[50] This connection, once made, seems inevitable. Lancelot's tears, undoubtedly accompanied by an overwhelming welter of different emotions, come in response not to punishment but to grace; Lancelot feared a public rebuke, and it did not come. There is an interesting irony in the situation that speaks to Lancelot's confusion of spirit. The New Testament teaches Christians to receive trials and suffering with joy, perceiving in them God's love. Lancelot, by contrast, receives God's mercy, being spared a sore trial and much suffering, and he perceives in that mercy a rebuke. Lancelot's encounter with God's grace in this episode leads him to recognize, on a more visceral and emotional level than his previous declarations, just how little he deserves it.

The healing of Urry is not a turning point, however; only a reminder, a moment in which Lancelot's spiritual crisis, generally submerged since his return from the Grail Quest, breaks through the surface.[51] Lancelot does not emerge from this event with his eyes opened, as Guinevere's will later be opened, for instance. Instead, we see him continue in the throes of the same dilemma for most of the rest of his life.

Even when Lancelot has his final meeting with Guinevere, his perspective is still what it was at the beginning of the Book of Sir Lancelot and Queen Guinevere. When Guinevere ends her long speech renouncing any continuation of their relationship and suggests that he marry another, Lancelot responds: "Nay, madame, wyte you well that shall I never do, for I shall never be so false unto you of that I have promysed. But the same desteny that ye have takyn you to, I woll take me to, for to please Jesu, and ever for you I caste me specially to pray" (3:1253.2–6). Notice that although Lancelot does cite pleasing Jesus as a motivation toward the eremitical life, it is not the primary one. First, in Lancelot's eyes, comes his faithfulness to Guinevere. He rejects marriage and worldly joy not out of a conviction to repent before God but because he refuses to be "false unto you of that I have promysed." Even his pledge always to pray for Guinevere "specially" suggests not a personal reformation but a continuation of their previous relations, merely shifted onto new ground. He was always her defender in the physical realm, and now he seeks to be her spiritual champion. Lancelot is not repenting; he is planning to become a hermit errant.

Guinevere herself is frankly skeptical of Lancelot's intention. She comments: "A, sir Launcelot, if ye woll do so and holde thy promyse! But I may never beleve you . . . but that ye woll turne to the worlde agayne" (3:1253.7–9). With her thorough and honest grasp of their spiritual situation, Guinevere perceives both Lancelot's need for repentance and his current lack of true contrition. Lancelot's reply demonstrates the ambivalence of his spiritual convictions. He admits that he had had no plans for an eremitical existence when he arrived, but that, to the contrary, he had intended to take Guinevere back to his realm so they could continue with the "erthly joye" (3:1253.20) of their love. Lancelot chooses the hermitage only when he finds her intent on renouncing their relationship: "sythen I fynde you thus desposed, I ensure you faythfully, I wyl ever take me to penaunce and praye whyle my lyf lasteth" (3:1253.22–24). In the Grail Quest, it was only their relationship that kept him from forsaking "the vanytees of the worlde" (3:1253.14). If she is truly determined to end their relationship, then he will go through with becoming a hermit, but he makes it clear that in entering a hermitage, he is falling back on his second option.

Lancelot's request for a last kiss is the final evidence of his lack of a truly penitent heart. Having just sworn to "ever take me to penaunce and praye whyle my lyf lasteth" (3:1253.23–24), he adds: "Wherfore, madame, I praye you kysse me, and never no more" (25–26). The "wherefore" in this request is almost comical. A man who can say "Since I have sworn to give up worldly pleasure, kiss me" is probably not wholehearted in his penitential conviction. Throughout this final meeting, Lancelot shows that, despite his decision to become a hermit, he is still seeing Guinevere and their relationship with worldly eyes.

The penance that Lancelot undertakes, however, is not merely some kind of farce. The Healing of Sir Urry episode alone would be enough to show us that Lancelot's desire for spiritual wholeness is quite genuine. But even when he becomes a hermit and later a priest, he has still not resolved the internal conflict that has dogged him since the Grail Quest. Lancelot's reaction to seeing Arthur's tomb draws our attention to the fact that Lancelot still lacks real contrition. His response to the visual evidence of Arthur's destruction is wholly impersonal; he cries out: "Alas! Who may truste thys world?" (3:1254.12). Lancelot does not express any sense of his own role in the downfall of Arthur and the Round Table. Guinevere opens their last conversation with a frank recognition of their culpability in the disaster, and both her new devotion to God and her termination of their relationship are premised upon this basic understanding. Lancelot still lacks this insight. He follows through on his pledge to do penance because he promised to, and, he explains, "yet wyste ye me never false of my promyse" (3:1253.11). But that very motivation is deeply ironic in light of his treason against Arthur, to whom he certainly was false, a treason that he has yet to repent of or to confess, even to himself.

It is not until the burial of Guinevere that Lancelot's long division of heart finally achieves resolution. The message in Lancelot's supernatural vision confirms that he must bury Guinevere "in remyssyon of his synnes" (3:1255.15). Obviously, the penitential actions he has been dutifully performing are not enough. Lancelot's "semynge outewarde" (2:1045.15) is perfectly correct, but, then again, it generally has been. God knows that Lancelot still has yet to put his "prevy thoughtes" fully behind his actions.

When Lancelot swoons at the burial, we are initially invited to understand the event as another image of Lancelot's internal division between God and his love: the priest groveling inconsolably at the tomb of his dead lover. This seems to be the reaction of his companion, the former bishop, who rebukes Lancelot, saying "Ye be to blame, for ye dysplese God with suche maner of sorow-makyng" (3:1256.24–25). Lancelot disagrees, just as Elaine once disputed a similar clerical rebuke, replying that he trusts he does "not dysplese God, for He knoweth myn entente" (3:1256.26–27). Lancelot's reference to his "entente" here is compelling. For Lancelot, his "entente," his "prevy thoughtes," has always been where the problem lay. Lancelot's subsequent statements appear to confirm that he has now undergone a genuine change of heart. Lancelot explains that he was overcome by the memory of the corporate greatness of Arthur and his queen; in this I heartily agree with Karen Cherewatuk's correction of Larry D. Benson's reading, wherein she asserts that "hir" in the following quotation is intended as a plural rather than as a feminine singular pronoun.[52] Seeing Arthur and Guinevere reunited at last after he himself divided them, Lancelot is forcibly reminded of "hir beaulté and of hir noblesse, that was bothe wyth hyr kyng and wyth hyr" (3:1256.29–30). He is struck not by Guinevere's personal beauty but by the beauty and greatness of Arthur and Guinevere as a couple; this is the vision that affects him so deeply. Remember, Lancelot does not swoon when he sees Guinevere's corpse by itself; his reaction is not just shock and love-longing at the sight of his beloved lying dead. Lancelot finally, at her tomb, sees Guinevere not with "worldly eyes" but within the larger framework of his duty to Arthur, his king, and the still larger framework of his moral duty to God. And within these frameworks, Lancelot failed both Arthur and Guinevere profoundly.

The fruit of this revelation is Lancelot's long-delayed conviction of his own sins.[53] He reflects on "how by my defaute and myn orgule and my pryde that they were bothe layed ful lowe" (3:1256.33–34), finally taking responsibility for his actions. Recognizing Guinevere's grand role in Arthur's court, something he had always disregarded in his focus on his own love, Lancelot realizes to the full how glorious was that which he helped destroy. His experience at Guinevere's entombment leaves his heart not only affected but overwhelmed.

Lancelot's final, extreme acts of penance through which he literally mortifies his flesh reflect the completeness with which Lancelot's once-divided mind has been unified. He turns away from "erthely joye" with an almost shocking thoroughness. Lancelot's suffering is not merely an expression of self-loathing, however; it is a cleansing. Earlier in the narrative, just before Elaine dies, she asks for God's mercy and requests that the "unnumerable paynys that I suffir may be alygeaunce of parte of my synnes" (2:1093.14–15). Her petition seems to be granted, for in her death she "lay as she had smyled" (2:1096.16). Lancelot, too, smiles beatifically in death; indeed, the joy at his death is so great it spills over in his companion's laughter. Lancelot's sufferings seem also to have been accepted as purgatorial, and he is taken directly to heaven by an angelic escort.

The fervor of Lancelot's last penance might seem to promote a final abandonment of all earthly love, but it is important to fit the penitential sequences in the last portion of the narrative into the larger theoretical framework Malory has previously developed. Elaine has established early on, with her stalwart resistance to her confessor's admonitions, that not all love needs to be repented. God created earthly women and men to love each other, and the love that he inspires in them by nature is virtuous love, marked by truth, faithfulness, and stability. Many people, especially "nowadayes," pursue only a bastardized version of love, dominated by concupiscent desires. Some people, however, especially back in King Arthur's days, do maintain the old, natural, good love. This virtuous love, originating as it does from God, is not itself sinful, and therefore a knight blessed with such love can serve God and his lady simultaneously, with no conflict or rivalry between them.[54]

That is all just theory, however. In practice, things are always more complicated. Elaine's love, pure though it was, tragically causes her death because of its circumstances. Through no fault of her own, she fell in love with one who could not return her love, and thus she died. Lancelot and Guinevere's love, which was also virtuous and true, also ends tragically because of its circumstances. Their love was good, but their actual, physical relationship was a sin. The fact that one's love is virtuous in quality does not mean that that love is therefore permissible in all situations. Lancelot and Guinevere's relationship was adultery, which remains a mortal sin no matter how true or faithful they were. Their love was noble, beautiful, and even virtuous, but to pursue it under adulterous circumstances is still to rebel openly against God's moral law and, in this instance, also to betray their benevolent and worshipful king.

Thus, Lancelot and Guinevere's love became tainted by their sin. This is why Lancelot experienced the internal conflict that he did. I have shown that Lancelot's division of loyalties between God and his lady was not just a natural consequence of the limitations of human love. Rather, it was an indication that there was something fundamentally *unnatural* about his love, for in natural love God and one's lady are in harmony. This tainting of good love by sin also explains why Lancelot and Guinevere don't just run off and get married after Arthur's death. Their relationship, even though founded on virtuous love, was responsible for the deaths of King Arthur and many others. Their relationship had been prosecuted in defiance of right, and that defiance joined with other causes to bring about an enormous calamity. In the end, Lancelot and Guinevere could not repent sincerely of their sin and yet continue in the relationship that had been the very substance of that sin, even after the circumstances had changed. This is the heart of their tragedy: the purest and most noble of loves between two of the greatest lovers ever had to be voluntarily abandoned. Guinevere's assessment in the nunnery was right. Their love had been adulterated past recall. It could not be cleansed; it could only be severed.

Even though Lancelot and Guinevere's relationship could not be healed, however, *they* still could. As I have previously argued, through even their most morally compromising moments, as in their tryst in Melleagaunt's castle or their fateful meeting in Guinevere's chamber, Malory never encourages the condemnation of the lovers themselves. In the end, he shows them both redeemed, bringing them to a full understanding of their transgression and showing their honest and heartfelt repentance. In doing so, he again affirms the nature and quality of their virtuous love. Because they were true lovers, they had a good end.

NOTES

1. Vinaver, introduction to *The Works of Sir Thomas Malory*, 3rd rev. ed., 1:xcix. In this paper, all quotations from Malory's text come from this edition and will be noted parenthetically by volume, page, and line numbers.

2. C. David Benson, "Ending of the *Morte Darthur*," p. 235.

3. Whitehead, "Lancelot's Penance," p. 112.

4. Cherewatuk, "Saint's Life," p. 73.

5. Beverly Kennedy, *Knighthood*, pp. 296–346.

6. Tolhurst, "Why Every Knight," p. 144.

7. Davies, "Worshipful Way," p. 161.

8. Some critics have seen in Malory's narrative a genuine division of heart between the spiritual claims of Christianity and worldly chivalric values. Robert L. Kelly's claim that

Malory leaves us in the end two irreconcilable Lancelots is one such example ("Wounds, Healing," p. 191). See also the essay by D. Thomas Hanks, Jr., in this collection; he concludes that Lancelot and Guinevere sin knowingly, but that their love is both noble and irresistible, and that they receive forgiveness for it.

9. Beverly Kennedy, *Knighthood*, p. 313.

10. Larry D. Benson, *Malory's "Morte Darthur,"* p. 231.

11. Although Davies links Elaine's defense of her love to the overt casuistry practiced by male interlocutors of the dialogues of Andreas Capellanus, C. David Benson states that Elaine's assertion that "loyal romantic love is not repugnant to God is echoed throughout the end of the *Morte Darthur*" (Davies, "Worshipful Way," pp. 165–66; Benson, "Ending of the *Morte Darthur*," p. 225).

12. Elaine's only lapse in chastity is her offer to take Lancelot as her paramour. This moment certainly does not stain her love with concupiscence, however, as she only makes this offer to Lancelot as a second (and rather desperate) choice to honorable marriage. I will return to this point later.

13. It is possible to read Arthur's elliptical comment to Lancelot as an indication that Arthur has picked up more of the subtext of Lancelot and Guinevere's exchange than they are aware of. "Lowsith" can be understood to mean either "loseth" or "looseth." In either case, we can perhaps hear Arthur warning Lancelot that when a knight is bound by love, he often loosens certain restraints on himself that could result in his losing himself.

14. Davies comments on the simple hierarchy, but does not note the further elucidation of this relationship between God and the lady ("Worshipful Way," p. 163).

15. McCarthy points to the repeated emphasis on faithfulness to a lover as a central principle of good love throughout the *Morte*, quoting as an example Lancelot's outrage at hearing of Tristram's marriage that seemed to mark him as an "untrew knyght to his lady" (*Introduction to Malory*, p. 64).

16. Janet Jesmok, in her treatment of Lancelot and Guinevere's encounter in Melleagaunt's castle, rightly points out Malory's emphasis on their sexual self-restraint in the context of the May passage. However, her insistence that the frankness and intimacy of Guinevere and Lancelot's "loving talk" before they go to bed also directly fulfills the language of the May passage is more problematic, given Malory's insistence on the chastity of "old love" ("Malory's 'Knight of the Cart,'" pp. 113–15).

17. Malory's explanation of the extraordinary virtues of "old" love calls into question Larry D. Benson's assertion that the Arthurian days were "a past so distant that adultery can be at least partially excused." Malory does not suggest a sliding scale of morality here, but if anything, he implies that the moral expectations of these antique figures of heroic virtue should be higher, not lower, than in the corrupted modern times (*Malory's "Morte Darthur,"* p. 233).

18. Many have commented on Guinevere's frequent unpleasantness in this portion of the narrative. Jesmok points out that Malory has systematically deviated from his sources here in order to transform Guinevere into a shrew ("Malory's 'Knight of the Cart,'" p. 109).

19. Lancelot also recognizes this fault in his conversation with Arthur and Guinevere next to Elaine's body, praising her virtues and devotion but observing that she loved him "oute of mesure" (2:1097.12–13). Lancelot therefore attributes her death to this excess rather than to his rejection of her in itself.

20. "In the May passage Malory does his best to enhance the reputation of Lancelot in preparation for events where his virtue will be questioned" (McCarthy, *Introduction to Malory*, p. 66).

21. McCarthy calls Melleagaunt "the typical lover" (*Introduction to Malory*, p. 52).

22. It is also natural to attribute the rebuke at least in large part to Lancelot's desire to draw attention away from the obvious evidence of Guinevere's guilt that has just been displayed.

23. In a recent article, Jesmok emphasizes the connections Malory establishes between Lancelot and Melleagaunt, especially the "blurring of Lancelot's and Melleagaunt's identities" as Lancelot stands in for Melleagaunt in his early duel with Lamorak and fulfills Melleagaunt's fantasies by sleeping with Guinevere in his castle ("Double Life," pp. 87–88).

24. Other critics have also noted the broad applicability of Guinevere's condemnation. See, for instance, Robert L. Kelly, "Wounds, Healing," p. 187, and Elizabeth Edwards, *Genesis of Narrative*, p. 154.

25. Swanson, "God Woll Have a Stroke," p. 167.

26. Swanson also makes this observation, noting that Melleagaunt's vice "accommodates and even invites a generous evaluation of Lancelot" ("God Woll Have a Stroke," p. 168). Although the focus of my own argument will be on Lancelot and the complementary (and indeed complimentary) effect of the parallels between him and Melleagaunt, I concur with Jesmok's compelling argument that Malory also uses the incident "as a tribute to Guinevere as queen and paramour," elevating her in our regard as well ("Malory's 'Knight of the Cart,'" p. 109).

27. Beverly Kennedy sees this refusal in the face of temptation as evidence already of Lancelot's repentance for his very recent sexual indulgence with Guinevere (*Knighthood*, p. 297).

28. McCarthy observes the trend as well, pointing out that at this point in the narrative, many "private sentiments are having distressing public repercussions" (*Introduction to Malory*, p. 68).

29. Beverly Kennedy argues convincingly that "draughtis" here most likely refers to private walks or strolls (*Knighthood*, p. 286). I have never seen contrary evidence presented.

30. Davies argues that Malory here seeks to "screen the conduct of the two lovers" ("Worshipful Way," pp. 160–61). Robert L. Kelly sees Malory's indirection here as reflecting his own reluctance to admit that Lancelot and Guinevere are in bed together ("Wounds, Healing," p. 190). C. David Benson attributes the indirection to a general lack of interest in "erotic passion" ("Ending of the *Morte Darthur*," p. 228).

31. Beverly Kennedy also establishes this connection, observing that "Malory seems to be asking his readers to keep in mind as they decide for themselves . . . whether or not the lovers have been 'abed' on this occasion" (*Knighthood*, pp. 311–12).

32. Hanks gives us a convincing snapshot of this new perspective, arguing that Malory "paradoxically deepens the relationship between Guinevere and Lancelot while he virtually cancels out their adultery," adding that not only does Malory make the bedroom encounter "less fleshly, less adulterous, than in his sources" but "he makes it virtually sacramental" ("*Mort[e]s*," pp. 83–85).

33. The compelling idea that Lancelot and Guinevere were not in bed at all on the night they are ambushed is not crucial to my argument, but it is persuasively urged by Beverly Kennedy (*Knighthood*, pp. 309–13) and Batt (*Malory's "Morte Darthur*," p. 167). Although Malory does, as Kennedy suggests, leave his readers free to decide whether or not the pair are in bed, his reference to the May chapter constitutes an insistence on the peculiar character of Lancelot and Guinevere's relationship, namely its truth and temperance. Any reading of this passage that makes a radically different assumption, judging the couple's behavior on how men and women in modern times might be expected to act, ignores this plain directive.

See, for example, Swanson's statement that "the reader may legitimately deduce from the narrator's reticence that the lovers were 'abed'" ("God Woll Have a Stroke," p. 171).

34. Elizabeth Edwards aptly remarks that "while Malory's version of events *seems* to be predicated on the fact that the lovers have been taken in the act . . . the rest of the book seems intent on unraveling that certainty" (*Genesis of Narrative*, pp. 161–62).

35. Although critics such as Ann Dobyns, D. S. Brewer (in the introduction to his *Morte Darthur, Parts Seven and Eight*), and Andrew Lynch have argued against a "psychological" reading of Malory's characters, Felicia Nimue Ackerman presents a good apology for reading Malory's characters, as I am here doing, as to some extent reflecting human psychology ("'Every Man of Worshyp,'" pp. 32–42).

36. One can, of course, construct a cynical reading of Lancelot's character that sees him as brazening out an untruth because he knows that his unrivaled prowess will necessarily sway the outcome of a judicial combat, should anyone take him up on his repeated challenges. This reading, however, ill suits the understanding that Lancelot displays, especially when trapped in Guinevere's chamber. Hanks tellingly demonstrates that Lancelot actually is prepared to give himself up before he is treacherously attacked ("*Mort[e]s*," p. 82). Beverly Kennedy and Catherine Batt both draw attention to Lancelot's calling to Jesus: "Be Thou my shylde and myne armoure!" (3:1167.5–6). Kennedy observes that Lancelot talks throughout this scene like a wrongly accused and holy man (*Knighthood*, p. 312), and Batt observes that his language bespeaks his "innocence and moral integrity" (*Malory's "Morte Darthur*," p. 167).

37. Beverly Kennedy argues that a desire to stay true, to some degree, to the "perfeccion" he undertook on the Grail Quest makes up a portion of his motivation for defending other ladies besides the queen (*Knighthood*, pp. 286–87).

38. Jesmok argues that a major change in Guinevere's character can be observed after the death and interment of Elaine of Astolat ("Malory's 'Knight of the Cart,'" p. 108). I find this plausible, but although Guinevere's most egregious moments of shortsightedness might be said to be over by the time of the Knight of the Cart episode, this earlier reformation is dwarfed by the change she undergoes when entering Amesbury.

39. Although McCarthy asserts that "Lancelot and Guinevere express no guilt for any sexual sin," it is hard to see what else Guinevere could be referring to by her "mysselyvynge" here (*Introduction to Malory*, p. 69).

40. Several critics point to the significance of Guinevere's martyrdom language here. C. David Benson argues that it emphasizes her "heroic public role," disregarding the spiritual significance of Guinevere's martyr imagery ("Ending of the *Morte Darthur*," p. 230). Edward Donald Kennedy, Batt, and Hanks all find in it evidence of some measure of piety, or at least its precursor, in Guinevere (Kennedy, "Malory's Guenevere," p. 38; Batt, *Malory's "Morte Darthur*," p. 167; Hanks, "*Mort[e]s*," p. 85). I cannot agree; Guinevere is using Christian language here only as a metaphor with which to illustrate her devotion to Lancelot. This speech demonstrates her distance from, not her nearness to, genuine Christian devotion at this point in the narrative.

41. C. David Benson remarks that, in this final conversation between Lancelot and Guinevere, "Jesus is mentioned, but he seems decidedly secondary" ("Ending of the *Morte Darthur*," p. 236. This may be true as regards Lancelot, but it is hard to see how one can say the same of Guinevere. Edward Donald Kennedy disagrees, asserting that Guinevere is "concerned with her own sinfulness and salvation" ("Malory's Guenevere," p. 38).

42. Tolhurst takes Guinevere's prayer not to see Lancelot again before her death as evidence of "her inability to break her earthly attachment through her new lifestyle" ("Why

Every Knight," p. 144). Hanks, in his essay in this volume, concurs with Tolhurst; he suggests that Guinevere would not need to make this prayer were she not still drawn to Lancelot (see p. 22).

43. Tolhurst divorces Guinevere's "good ende" from her repentance in the cloister in claiming that, although she was a model nun, Guinevere had a good end because she was a good lover ("Why Every Knight," p. 144). This rather oversimplifies the situation, separating two things that Malory works to bring together. Davies comes closer in suggesting that "fidelity in love conduced to Gwenyver's final fidelity to God," but even this construction underplays the link that Malory establishes between Guinevere's love and her spiritual reformation, postulating that her love was only a model for, rather than an agent of, her repentance ("Worshipful Way," p. 161).

44. Cherewatuk, "Born-Again Virgins," p. 56. Nathan C. Starr argues that Malory depicts Lancelot as "a complex and very appealing person" ("Moral Problem," p. 471).

45. Vinaver also famously argued that the end of the Round Table comes about through "tragic greatness" and the conflict between "two goods." Vinaver, however, did not see Christian morality as part of that conflict, insisting that "all doctrine shrivels before the conflict of 'two goods' and the desolation it brings" (*Works*, 1:xcix).

46. Lewis, "English Prose *Morte*," p. 20.

47. Raluca L. Radulescu claims that this is Lancelot's first moment of genuine humility ("'Now I take upon me,'" p. 294). I agree that it is a remarkable example of humility for Lancelot, but it is not quite unique: he makes a very similar gesture in his conversation with Guinevere about defending ladies, saying that even what he did accomplish in the Grail Quest was "of Hys grete mercy, and never of my deservynge" (2:1046.5–7).

48. For an excellent summary of various interpretations of Lancelot's tears, see Earl R. Anderson, "'Ein Kind wird geschlagen,'" p. 46.

49. Hebrews 12:6 (Douay-Rheims version).

50. Batt, *Malory's "Morte Darthur,"* p. 157.

51. McCarthy calls the Urry incident a "total vindication of Lancelot," and Radulescu suggests that Urry's healing is "clearly designed to redeem Malory's favorite knight from the stain of adulterous sin and disloyalty" (McCarthy, *Introduction to Malory*, p. 45; Radulescu, "'Now I take upon me,'" p. 285). I agree with Robert L. Kelly in his insistence that the episode "cannot be understood as part of a pattern of cause-and-effect development" ("Wounds, Healing," p. 191).

52. Cherewatuk, "Saint's Life of Sir Launcelot," p. 68.

53. No single point in the conclusion of Malory's narrative demonstrates the choosing of sides among critics that I described at the outset of this essay more clearly than Lancelot's swoon and his subsequent repentance. Readings of this passage are highly polarized, and the description of the nature of Lancelot and Guinevere's love and its association with virtue and redemption tends to be forgotten, even among those critics who emphasize Lancelot's persistence in loving Guinevere until his death. One interesting exception is Edward Donald Kennedy, who argues that Guinevere is pivotal in Lancelot's ultimate conversion, giving her credit for "saving" him ("Malory's Guenevere," p. 42). Kennedy does not, however, explicitly connect Guinevere's work of salvation to the nature of their love or to the May passage; indeed, he says relatively little of the actual process or mechanism by which Guinevere leads Lancelot to salvation.

54. Malory much earlier offered a glimpse of this kind of innocent love in Perceval's slightly naïve description of "synles" love to King Mark (1:679.27).

Endless Virtue and Trinitarian Prayer in Lancelot's Healing of Urry

Sue Ellen Holbrook

In Sir Thomas Malory's *Morte Darthur*, where chivalry is a way of life, moral principles operate with vigor but not necessarily with signs of Christianity. Not all characters displaying chivalric values are identified as Christian or even religious. Moreover, those who are secular Christians frequently indicate their faith just incidentally, such as hearing Mass or expostulating, as Gareth does, "Jesu, wolde that the lady of this Castell Perelus were so fayre as she is."[1] However, in the episode where Sir Lancelot heals the festering, bleeding wounds of Sir Urry, certain chivalric virtues are explicitly adjoined to a Christian belief system. My purpose is to show how in this controversial episode the Christianity of Round Table knights is made to matter and the virtues of the healer are bound to a mystery central to their religious faith, the Trinity.

To fulfill this purpose, I begin with an anecdote from a fifteenth-century collection of edifying literature, for it provides a heuristic for discerning signs of Christianity and is particularly apropos of Lancelot. The next two sections compare the virtues of exemplary Christian holy men and the charism of healing with Lancelot's portrayal in the chivalric atmosphere of the Urry healing event. Then I examine the details and unusual aspects of the Urry healing, including its public atmosphere, absence of medical treatment, ritualistic employment of touch, and use of a prayer to the Trinity unique in the *Morte*. The following two sections explain why the Trinity is the most complex component in the Urry healing and show how fifteenth-century English people expressed an intense, albeit rare, regard for this doctrine similar to Malory's. Finally, suggesting that the story of Lancelot's curing of Urry is only one of various narrative models for attempting to sustain communal relationships in the *Morte*, I conclude that once the components of this healing event are understood, the episode stands out as a distinct instance in which the thriving of chivalric communal morality is linked to Christian sacred belief.

Christian Virtue

A knight who had done "many euylles and moche harme, and wolde conuerte hym to god" asked a holy man if God received sinners in his grace. The holy man answered, "'Ye,' and shewed to hym by many reasons and auctorytees of holy scrypture." But the knight still doubted. Therefore, the holy man showed to him this example: "'Yf thy mantell be rente or broken in ony parte, wylt thou incontinent caste it awaye?' The knyght answered to hym, 'Nay, but I shall make it agayne & amende it, and it shall serue me as it dyde byfore.' Thenne sayde the holy man, 'Ryght so, my frende, is it of god. For how well that thy soule be broken by synne, neuertheless our lord casteth it not awaye, but by very penaunce & pure confessyon shal make it hole agayn by his grace.'"[2] Read in books or heard in sermons, exempla such as this one taught medieval Europeans not just how to conduct themselves honorably, for as J. Ian H. McDonald observes, "every culture has some notion of virtue or moral excellence,"[3] but how to do so within a Christian paradigm.

The virtues inculcated in professional religious, like that holy man in the anecdote, and secular people, like that knight, were not unique to members of the Christian faith community. Christian morality had been "forged," as McDonald puts it, in a "crucible," which contained both "Graeco-Roman" and "Jewish Hellenistic elements."[4] The moral qualities and procedures in the Christianizing crucible included, for instance, the many branches of the cardinal virtues of wisdom, justice, fortitude, and temperance from the Stoic tradition and the cultivation of sorrow from the Judean tradition—the penitence in the exemplum. Although monastic Christians were expected to develop virtues to a greater degree than secular Christians were, both understood that moral excellence was necessary for their concept of salvation. In the paradigm evident in the anecdote, virtuous living for Christians is linked with the belief that their God had created human beings with a soul that, like the knight's mantle, they might damage through evil and harmful acts but also amend by penitence, resumption of virtuous ways, and God's grace.

That knight in the anecdote, who feels "broken by synne" but learns that there is a way for his soul to be made whole again by God's grace, brings to mind Sir Lancelot at several points during the Grail Quest and its aftermath in the *Morte*.[5] It is during the aftermath, following Lancelot's delivery of Queen Guinevere from Melleagaunt's accusation of treason, that Malory sets a story he invented through perusing his "Freynshe boke" (3:1145.1): the episode in which the young knight Urry arrives at King Arthur's court in hope of curing his wounds.[6] In effecting this cure through the grace of God, Lancelot manifests four virtues to be regarded below within chivalric and Christian frameworks: humility, obedience, sorrow, and *caritas*, that is, charity in the sense of love for others.

Virtue and the Charism of Healing

As Maurice Keen explains, traditional chivalric qualities—courage, loyalty, and prowess—formed a "code of honor" developed from the martial function of knights within a "secular ideology," but writers, whether of history, like Jean Froissart, or romance, like the author of the prose *Lancelot*, could hardly imagine a "purely secular ethic, divorced from a religious framework of value."[7] The religious orientation of the virtues Lancelot exhibits in the Urry story—humility, obedience, sorrow, and *caritas*—will become more conspicuous if these virtues and their relationship to each other are looked at first within the Christian framework provided by fifteenth-century English sayings and narratives, like the story of the knight who had torn his cloak, intended to edify laity in accessible, memorable terms.

That humility is the linchpin to salvation is pithily expressed by one wise elder this way: "Right soo as it is Impossyble a shyp to be sure without nayles, also it is Impossyble to be saued without mekenesse."[8] Although humility, closely aligned with patience, is taught as a way to control anger, it is also the antidote to vainglory. One edifying anecdote illustrates the Christian perspective on vainglory in terms relevant to the competitive striving to win worship among Malory's knights. A high-placed man of the world is shown a vision of two men on horses carrying a long piece of wood athwart their shoulders and trying to enter through the gate of a temple. However, they cannot get through, for one will not "meek himself" to the other because each wants to be the first to enter. These men "betokeneth those . . . the which in their offices were proud and will not humble himself the one toward the other in despising the word of god that sayeth 'My children learn of me, for I am humble and sweet in heart and by this mean ye shall find the salvacyon of your souls' [Mt. 11.29]." Such "proud folk," the expositor concludes, "have no part in paradise."[9] As Keen points out, the impetus to earn honor by making a name for oneself, a virtue in chivalry, was regarded in priestly teaching as vainglory and the "archetypal failing of the knighthood and nobility."[10] Although Lancelot was accused of such pride during his quest for the Grail,[11] Malory will make him the last, not the first, in the Urry story (see Mk 10:31, Mt 20:16, and Lk 13:30). Far from trying to be first, he will be a knight who feels painfully reluctant and expects that without divine mercy he will be dishonored in an attempt at "so hyghe a thynge" which he is not "able in worthynes to do" (3:1152.14–15). That is humility.

Related to humility is obedience, that is, giving over one's will to God directly or through a spiritual advisor. For knights, obedience is related to the traditional secular quality of loyalty in service to their lord. The following exemplum, however, illustrates an aspect of obedience particularly relevant to men whose way of life involves them as members of a community, as chivalry does in the *Morte*. A senior brother tells another about his vision of four orders in heaven. The fourth and highest order consisted of those that were "submytted unto" the subjection of "theyr faders spyrytuall as relygyouses" that make vows. That order, he says, had "more noble astate than the other & for this cause they bare atte theyr neckes colers of golde." Why are the cenobites the most noble? Unlike the almoners and the desert hermits, they "gaue them selfe all togyder to god under the subgeccyon of other, whereby theyr meryte is more greter in honour." Obedience, then, "openeth the heuens" and "lyfteth the man vnto heuen."[12] In the story of Urry, it will be as a member of the Round Table community that Lancelot subjects his will to Arthur and as a member of the Christian faith community that he subjects his will to God. For once in Lancelot's life the two communities will merge, and when in due time he, by then a priest and hermit himself, dies, "angellys heue up syr Launcelot unto heven" (3:1258.9).

Also related to humility are two other virtues that will appear in the Urry story, sorrow and the compassion conveyed by *caritas*, charity in the sense of love for others. The cultivation of sorrow may be channeled into repentance, as explained earlier, or into another mode of compunction, such as longing to see the face of God, fear of the final Judgment, or anguish over the condition of humankind.[13] For instance, a holy father explains that to be saved, we should "wepe without ceassyng, for our lorde wyll that our soules be tormented & scorged by contrycyons & waylynges, and atte the last we shall haue that we aske of hym."[14] To this explanation of why God approves of contrition and wailing may be joined a teaching that explains why the humbled heart is the precursor to *caritas*—love of others, which, like repentance, is a virtue from Hellenistic Judaism:[15] "Alle the vertues that a Relygyouse myght perfourme, without humilyte they can not prouffyte hym nothyng. For humylity is the messager of charyte, in hauing the whiche men be with god, whiche is the same charyte."[16] One expression of compassionate love is to care for the ill.[17] Lancelot's compassion for the sick young knight brought to Arthur's court is incontrovertible, and though Lancelot will be the last hope for making Urry whole, Lancelot will not leave him forsaken. Yet, perhaps the most disputed element of the story is Lancelot's weeping.[18] In the penultimate section below on the healing Spirit, I interpret his weeping as an instance of compassionate "charite."

To summarize: once all the elements of the Urry healing are examined, one sees that Lancelot is a man who is "with God" through a humbled, contrite, and loving heart.

Finally, in anticipation of the scenario Malory creates for the healing of Urry and with respect to scholarly controversy over Lancelot's successful intervention, a word about holy healing is in order. First, in edifying literature, physical healing is a charism, a gift from God to those advanced in virtue. Some people graced with this charism heal only through prayer, but most, as Lancelot will do, combine prayer with direct touch—embrace, forehead, lips, finger, or hand. Occasionally, these holy healers are asked to attend an ailing person, but just as in the scenario Malory constructs, more often the sick are brought to them, sometimes having to wait until the holy one appears while witnesses wait as well. These healers are never arrogant about a successful outcome, for that is up to the Lord. After curing a maiden who was "seke of a sykenesse the moost horrible that hath be seen," St. Anthony explains: "Nonc ought to come to me for to recouuer helth. For to giue helthe to seke men apperteyneth to the Sauyoure of the worlde."[19] Lancelot will express the same point. Second, God withholds charisms when no one is virtuous enough to deserve them. This view is heard in an edifying anecdote having the same bitter nostalgic note that Malory is wont to sound about how the present has fallen from the golden days of the past. A brother asks an ancient father "why the Relygyouses at this tyme presente labouryng gete not therby some grace as dyde the aeged Relygyouses." The old father answers that "charyte was thenne so grete that euerychone by vertuouse werkes drewe his neyghbour on hyghe, but now all the worlde applyeth theym to ylle, and eueryone ledyth his neyghbour in to helle, and for thys cause there ys none that geteth any grace."[20] When Lancelot, as a member of a chivalric community that is breaking down, is graced with the charism of healing, he is, at least temporarily, uplifting the whole fellowship.

Healing Urry

Urry suffers from three wounds on the head, three on the body, and one on the left hand, inflicted by an earl's son in a tournament in Spain before Urry slew him "by fortune," that is, by accident. In revenge, the dead knight's mother, a sorceress, had "wrought by her suttyle craufftis that sir Urry shulde never be hole . . . untyll the beste knyght of the worlde had serched hys woundis," which she boasts will never happen (3:1145.10, 16–20). Evidently assuming that such a knight will be a Christian, Urry's mother has taken her son in a horse litter and his sister Fyleloly through "all londis crystened" for seven years, the same magical-mystical number as her son's wounds. They find Arthur at Carlisle when they cross from Scotland "into the bondes" of England (3:1145.28–32). The time is auspicious, near Pentecost, the liturgical festival at which, as a sermon in John Mirk's collection of ca. 1400 explains, "holy church specially calleth" the Holy Ghost to "haue helpe and grace and parte of al the dole that he maketh than to alle . . . that been able to receyue his yeftes," which include filling "hertes wyth pyte & compassyon to alle that ben in disease,"[21] as Urry is. In response to Urry's mother's appeal for relief for her son's affliction, Arthur promises that if "ony Crystyn man may heale" him, then "here shall youre son be healed" and bids all kings, earls, dukes, and knights present to assemble on the "medow," where Urry is laid (3:1146. 23–24. 32). "[W]e muste begynne at kynge Arthur," says Malory, for he was that "tyme the moste man of worshyp crystynde." Calling him "moste noble crystynd kynge," Urry says, "I am at the mercy of God and at youre commaundemente" (3:1147.2–4,

14–15). After the king and all the others have tried unsuccessfully to heal the wounds, they wait, quietly watching, "no man say[ing] nothyng," for Lancelot to come. It is into this suspenseful atmosphere of hope edged with anxiety that Lancelot is finally "aspyed . . . rydynge towarde them" (3:1151.2–4).

When Lancelot has arrived, he evinces meekness, obedience, and his Christian faith. He refers to Jesus twice in response to the king's insistence that he search the wounds, which Lancelot sees as an act of presumption: "Jesu defende me . . . that I should presume upon me to enchyve that all ye, my lordis, myght nat enchyve." When Arthur commands him, saying "Ye shall nat chose," Lancelot responds "Jesu deffende me frome that shame" of taking upon himself "to towche that wounded knyght in that entent that I shulde passe all othir knyghtes." Arthur clarifies the purpose: "ye shall nat do hit for no presumpcion, but for to beare us felyshyp." He then adds why Lancelot is obliged to touch Urry: for if "ye pre-vayle nat . . . there ys no knyght in thys londe that may hele hym" (3:1151.20–32, 1152.1–3). Then Urry appeals to Lancelot: "I requyre the, for Goddis sake, heale my woundis. For methynkis ever sytthyn ye cam here my woundis grevyth me nat so muche as they ded" (3:1152.9–11). For the third time Lancelot invokes Jesus and expresses humility in the face of a task requiring power greater than medical skill: "Jesu wolde that I myght helpe you. For I shame sore with myselff that I shulde be thus requyred, for never was I able in worthynes to do so hyghe a thynge." But kneeling down, he obeys his king: "I muste do your commaunde-mente, whyche ys sore ayenste my harte" (3:1152.12–17). The subjugation of his will to his king's will is clear.

When Lancelot begins, he does so with an act that none of the others per-formed: he makes a formal prayer. The moral qualities of humility and obedience that Lancelot has displayed so far also imbue this prayer: "And than he hylde up hys hondys and loked unto the este, saiynge secretely unto hymselff, 'Now, Blyssed Fadir and Son and Holy Goste, I beseche The of Thy mercy that my symple wor-shyp and honesté be saved, and Thou Blyssed Trynyté, Thou mayste yeff me power to hele thys syke knyght by the grete vertu and grace of The, but, Good Lorde, never of myselff'" (3:1152.18–25). He clearly knows that, as Anthony said, giving health to the sick appertains to the Savior of the World, not to him.

Lancelot's emphasizing three in naming the members of the Trinity is repeated in the method by which Lancelot handles the wounds: first the three on the head, then the three on the body, and finally the seventh on the left hand. As he ransacks the three head wounds, they "bled a lytyll; and forthwithall the woun-dis fayre heled and semed as they had bene hole a seven yere"; after he searches the three body wounds, they "healed in lyke wyse"; after he searches the hand, "anone hit fayre healed." The repetition of the language reinforces the triadic ritual of the process. When Lancelot finishes, Arthur and all the kings and knights "kneled downe and gave thankynges and lovynge unto God and unto Hys Blyssed Modir.

And ever sir Launcelote wepte, as he had bene a chylde that had bene beatyn"
(3:1152.27–32). This copious outpouring of sorrow fits the description of a soul
scourged by contrition and wailing.[22] Arthur then has priests and clerks in the
"most devoutiste" way bring Urry into Carlisle, with "syngyng and lovyng to God"
(3:1153.1–3).[23]

Healing and Prayer

Many scenes of wounded knights being tended have been presented previously in
the *Morte*, but the Urry healing event stands out from the others in several ways.
First, it is the most public of these healings: it is located on a meadow, an area
ample enough for a gathering of 110 men and also the chivalric space on which
these knights hold their tournaments; it is thus a place for wounding yet also
for winning worship together. In addition, the event involves the Round Table
knights as an order identified with their faith; they are exerting solidarity in agreement with their leader's conviction, implied in response to Urry's mother, that as
Christian knights they are obliged to aid the suffering. Noticeably, the Carlisle
clergy are only accessories and appear only at the end.

Second, this healing is among the few accomplished without medical treatment. To be sure, probing a wound, like staunching blood, is a medical procedure.
A physician "sechiþ and serchiþ causes of circumstaunces of sikenesses," according to the medical treatise in Bartholomew the Englishman's *On the Properties
of Things*, and "refusiþ noȝt to grope and handele and to wype and clense priuey
membris and wounds of seke men."[24] Accordingly, in Malory's Sankgreal, when
the truncheon of a spear breaks off in Melias's side, Galahad carries him to an
abbey and removes it; then, in an act more clearly physical than that in the *Queste
del Saint Graal*, an old monk formerly a knight "ransacked" him, concluding that
he can heal him in seven weeks (2:885.25–31).[25] But in Urry's case, handling the
injuries has become a ritual necessitated by the condition of the sorceress's spell. In
a similar ritual earlier in the *Morte*, Lancelot cures Meliot de Logris, at his sister's
request, of his bleeding wounds. These injuries must be "serched with" cloth and a
sword collected from the corpse of the knight, Gilbert, who had injured Meliot.
Whereas his source, the *Perlesvaus*, includes the damsel, Malory limits the act to
Lancelot and expands the ritual by detailing the method of searching with the
two talismans: Lancelot "towched his woundys" with the sword and then "wyped
his woundys" with a piece of the bloody cloth wrapping Gilbert (1:279.23–26,
281.35–36, 282.1–3).[26] Lancelot and Meliot's sister are identified as Christians by
their references to Jesus and God, but these do not pertain to the healing ritual;[27]
rather, the context is magical.

A Christianized instance of wounds healed without medical treatment takes
place in Malory's Tristram story when Ector and Perceval battle in a forest while

independently looking for Lancelot. This healing does involve prayer, although the words are not given. Identities unknown to one another, they fight with swords, leaving both with fifteen wounds that bleed so much they can hardly stand and are "at the poynte of dyyinge." Perceval, described as a knight "in whom the verrey fayth stoode moste in," kneels down and prays "devoutely unto All-mighty Jesu." A maiden brings the "Sankegreall," of which Perceval has a glimmering because he is a "parfyte mayden"; and "furthwithall they were as hole of hyde and lymme as ever they were in their lyff." In this adventure, the holy vessel holds a relic, "parte of the bloode of Oure Lorde Jesu Cryste," as Ector explains to Perceval. Rather than the curative effect of the relic, however, the point displayed is Perceval's holiness, not because his prayer summoned the vessel but because he was able to see it; as Ector comments, the vessel "may nat be sene . . . but yff hit be by a parfyte man" (2:815.28–29, 816.28–36, 817.1–10).

In Malory's Grail section, another healing of a knight occurs without medical treatment, this one viewed by Lancelot half-awake at a cross near a chapel. This knight suffers from an unspecified sickness and prays for himself, but like Urry he is transported in a horse litter and like Perceval's cure, his involves the Grail. Lancelot hears his lament as he asks when the Grail will relieve his suffering: "A, sweete Lorde. Whan shall thys sorow leve me, and whan shall the holy vessell com by me wherethorow I shall be heled? For I have endured thus longe for litill trespasse" (2:894.15–17). Then, self-propelled, come a candlestick and altar table from the chapel, followed by the vessel. In both the *Queste* and the *Morte* the knight is instantly healed after praying in the presence of this holy object, but Malory adjusts the details. Rather than fall off the litter onto the ground and join his outstretched hands as the French knight does, Malory's sick knight "sette hym up, and hylde up both hys hondys," a gesture more like Lancelot's in the Urry event. In addition, whereas the French knight prays "Gracious Lord God, who through this Holy Vessel that I now set eye on hast performed so many miracles," Malory's knight refers to the Lord being within the vessel: "Fayre swete Lorde whych ys here within the holy vessell, take hede unto me, that I may be hole of thys malody." Finally, instead of dragging himself over to kiss and press his eyes to the table as the French knight does, Malory's knight touches the Grail itself: "on hys hondys and kneys he wente so nyghe that he towched the holy vessell and kyst hit" (2:894.25–30).[28] Malory's adjustments harmonize this event with a later vision of Lancelot's (2:1015.30–34) in which the Grail is not a reliquary like the one in the Perceval scene in the Tristram story but a ciborium, which holds the consecrated bread taken in the sacrament of the Eucharist, the Christians' sacred meal of bread that is the body of Christ and wine that is his blood. As Malory says correctly, the Lord is "here within" (2:894.27) by virtue of the consecrated bread in which the real presence of Christ resides; the realness of that presence is depicted in the later vision.

Those two miraculous healings after prayer involving a sanctified container bring up the third extraordinary aspect of healing Urry: the features of Lancelot's prayer. The work of John Cassian, which profoundly influenced the Benedictines among others,[29] helps to discern these features. Cassian defines four kinds of prayer, based on 1 Timothy 2:1: supplication for pardon for misdeeds, vow, intercession, and thanksgiving.[30] The prayer of the infirm knight Lancelot sees while half-awake in the story of the Sankgreal is supplication. The prayer the knights and kings make after Urry's healing is thanksgiving, as are the clergy's processional hymns. Lancelot's prayer on the meadow is clearly intercession. Prayer for intercession, writes Cassian, "proceeds from fervent charity" and "consideration for others' frailty";[31] that is, it proceeds from the previously noted virtue of compassionate love that might bring God's grace.

Other elements in Lancelot's intercession include both brevity and secrecy, the formal subjugation of his will, and the posture of sacrifice. Lancelot says his mere fifty-word prayer "secretely unto hymselff" (3:1152.19–20). Hence, as Cassian observes on the value of secret prayer, it is made to the "searcher not of voices but of hearts."[32] Furthermore, in asking to be given "power to hele thys syke knyght by the grete vertu and grace of The, but, Good Lorde, never of myselff" (3:1152.23–25), Lancelot asks for something that is in "conformity only with the Lord's will, not ours," which is modeled, as Cassian explains, by the Lord himself "praying in the person of the man that he had assumed . . . 'Father, if it be possible, let this cup pass from me, yet not as I will but as you do'" (Mt 26.39).[33] Finally, in looking east in the symbolic direction of the heavenly Jerusalem and holding up his hands, Lancelot takes the *orans* posture found throughout early Christianity and offers up his prayer as spiritual sacrifice.[34]

One more element of Lancelot's prayer demands notice: the Trinity. In the culmination of his quest for the Grail, a scene discussed below, we readers watch Lancelot look at the Trinity, not so named, while a priest consecrates the bread for the Eucharist. Galahad, near the end of his quest, yearns to die so that, in Malory's addition, his soul can see the "Blyssed Trinité" (2:1032.23).[35] But no prayer in the *Morte Darthur* is made to the Trinity except Lancelot's intercession for Urry.[36]

The Trinity

The simple-seeming concatenation of the three addressees in Lancelot's prayer —"Blyssed Fadir and Son and Holy Goste"—reflects a complex doctrine formulated in an atmosphere of contention over the unity in substance (*ouisa*) of the three aspects, their distinction, and the divinity of each.[37] It would take centuries of theological refinement and church politics before the related doctrines of the incarnation and the unity in substance but not number of the three persons of the Godhead received catholic acceptance in the western church in the form expressed in the "Quicunque," or Athanasian, Creed.[38] By Malory's time, the praise of the three members of the Trinity, "Glory to the Father and Son and Holy Ghost" ("Gloria Patri et Filio et Spiritu Sancto"), was routinely recited in church services, chanted by the cloistered in the offices for the canonical hours, and said by the laity using books of hours in private devotion. The doctrine was taught to clergy and transmitted to laity through sermons, tracts, prayers, and other texts. For instance, an exposition of the Trinity fills the first book in the Latin encyclopedia of natural philosophy *On the Properties of Things*, referred to earlier, which Bartholomew composed in the 1220s while teaching at the Franciscan school in Paris. After laying out the doctrinal concept of three persons but one essence and substance in the "sanctus Trinitas," the book reviews the meaning of the names used for each person, starting with God and ending on Christ and the Holy Spirit. This academic account crossed the bounds of clerical education to become available to laypeople in Jean Corbechon's French translation of 1372 and in John Trevisa's English translation of 1398.[39]

Though far less often than the Virgin Mary and other saints, the Trinity was honored in England in dedications of guilds and churches.[40] In the early fourteenth century, devotion to the Trinity was heightened when the first Sunday after Pentecost was instituted in the western church to honor the Trinity, a festival already favored in England.[41] Thus, Mirk, abbot of a house of Augustinian Canons, incorporates a sermon for Festum sancte Trinitatis between those for Pentecost, from which I quoted earlier, and Corpus Christi Day in the collection he made for preachers but which was also read by laity. In the Circumcision section of the *Golden Legend* Caxton printed in 1484, he describes "a grete and a solempne procession" on Trinity Sunday that he saw in the Church of Our Lady in Antwerp, where the piece of Jesus's foreskin kept as a relic there was "born abowtc."[42] In the *Morte Darthur*, it is "uppon Trynyté Sunday at nyght" that Gawain warns Arthur in a dream to ask Mordred for a truce until Lancelot's forces arrive (3:1233.11).[43]

From the Trinitarian schema of divinity, especially associated with baptism, in the earliest documents of the Christian religion to the "holy feste" of Trinity Sunday, on which "al thre persones in trynyte fader and sone and holy ghooste" were revered,[44] it had been, and would remain, hard to grasp the tripartite yet indivisible concept in which the Father, the Son, and the Holy Ghost are three in number but of the same substance. Among the seventy-seven songs the Benedictine Hildegard of Bingen composed, only one, an antiphon of praise written ca.1158, addresses the Trinity. There it is a "wondrous splendor of arcane mysteries, which are unknown to humankind."[45] Peter Abelard, on the other hand, in his work on the Trinity, begun after becoming a Benedictine monk at St. Denis, discusses the Father, the Son, and the Holy Spirit as attributes of power, wisdom, and benignity belonging to the divine substance, a rational approach showing Abelard's willingness, as John Marenbon observes, to "argue that the divinity is comprehensible."[46] However, his *Theologia Summi Boni* was condemned at the Council of Soissons in 1121, the book was burned, and Abelard was made to recite the Athanasian Creed.[47] The limits of human reason in apprehending the Trinity are heard sternly in the *Mirror of the Blessed Life of Jesus Christ*, which the Carthusian Nicholas Love adapted ca. 1410 from the thirteenth-century Franciscan *Meditations on the Life of Christ*. Here religious and lay readers are warned that they cannot understand this matter "by mannes reson" and therefore whenever they hear or think of the Trinity, they must believe what Holy Church teaches and "go no further."[48] In the life of "Saynt Austyn doctour and Bisshop" in his *Golden Legend*, Caxton adds an anecdote conveying the difficulty of understanding the Trinity by even this theologian.[49] During his days in Antwerp, Caxton saw one of Augustine's miracles painted on an altar at the Blackfriars. While writing his book on the Trinity, Augustine went by the seaside in Africa, where he found a child who was spooning water from the large sea into a little pit in the sand. After Augustine expressed the impossibility of ladling all of the sea into that hole with his little spoon, the child answered, "I shalle lyghtlyer / and sonner drawe alle the water of the See / and brynge hit in to this pytte / than thow shalt brynge the mysterye of the Trynyte and his dyuynyte in to thy lytel vnderstandynge / as to the regard therof For the mysterye of the Trynyte is greter and larger to the comparyson of thy witte and brayne / than is this grete see vnto this lytel pytte. And therwyth the childe vanysshed awey." As in Love, we are then warned not to presume to "muse on hyghe thynges of the godhead ferther than we be enfourmed by our faythe."[50]

Nevertheless, as a way to store the three-in-one concept in mind, Trinity iconography informed the visual imagination whether in pictorial media or, as in the *Morte*, verbal imagery. In art, such depictions might be what David Brown calls incarnational, referring to an event in Christ's life; societal, indicating an interaction taking place; or triadic, emphasizing threeness.[51] An incarnational iconographic approach, known as the throne of grace or mercy seat, depicts God the Father enthroned, arms outstretched to hold a Tau cross on which a much smaller Christ hangs, while a dove symbolizing the Holy Ghost hovers near. A woodcut throne of grace, with the addition of saved souls in a cloth floating, above the cross, on God's lap, designates the Trinity Sunday sermon in the 1486 edition of Mirk's *Liber Festivalis* by the Oxford printer Theodoric Rood. Another approach, suggesting dialogic interaction, makes God the Father and the Son mirror images of each other. For instance, an illustrated initial in a psalter made in England ca. 1230–60 portrays two seated look-alike men, each with a book and a cross-nimbus, their dark-bearded faces turned in three-quarters profile toward a spread-winged dove stretching its head upwards.[52] A similar image occurs in the hours made ca. 1480 in Flanders for William Hastings, Edward IV's Lord Chamberlain and one of Caxton's patrons, praised in the 1481 *Mirror of the World*.[53] A variant of this iconography makes the Son look younger. For example, an initial in a psalter decorated in early fifteenth-century England shows a youthful, dark-haired Son seated to the left of the gray-haired Father, who clasps the Son's hand, again the dove between them.[54] Yet another iconographic approach, triadic faces, represents all three members as men. Images that combine triadic faces with the interactional mode illustrate Caxton's *Golden Legend* and his 1486 edition of Nicholas Love's *Mirror*, called *Speculum vitae Christi*, in two different woodcuts from northern France. For the *Golden Legend*, the full-page frontispiece shows the Trinity centered in a cloud ruffle at the top surrounded by angels with a throng of saints below. On the left of the bench they sit on is the Son, with cross-nimbus, wounds on hands and side, face turned slightly to the right; in the middle is the Father, with tiara, right hand in blessing, left holding an orb; and on the right is the Spirit, crowned, gesticulating, face turned towards the Father.[55] In the smaller *Speculum* drawing, the sisters Peace, Mercy, Sothfastness, and Righteousness stand before the three persons sitting on a canopied throne. On the left is the beardless Son with cross-nimbus and bony ribs exposed but not showing wounds since the incarnation has not happened; in the middle is the hairier Father also with cross-nimbus; and on the right, huddling close, is the young Spirit, with double-nimbus. Each raises his right hand and with the other touches a large bound book lying closed on the Father's lap; the folds of their cloaks mingle beneath.[56] Thus, the image gives the three persons orthodox unity, as the shared gestures and mingled cloaks indicate, but without sameness, as the distinguishing details indicate.

An interactional image of God the Father, the Son, and the Holy Ghost as three men appears in the revelation granted Lancelot as he fulfills his quest for the Grail in a scene that Malory keeps close to its source in the *Queste del Saint Graal*. At the doorway of a chamber in the fortress of Corbenic, having prayed to "Fayre swete Fadir, Jesu Cryste" to see something of what he seeks, Lancelot sees an altar on which sits the "holy vessell" covered with red samite, functioning as a ciborium, and "before the holy vessell" a priest who seemed to be at the "sakerynge" (consecration) of the Mass: "above the prystis hondys were three men, whereof the two put the yongyste by lyknes betwene the prystes hondis: and so he lyffte hym up ryght hyghe, and hit semed to shew so to the peple" (2:1015.11, 25–34).[57] In seeing not bread but the youngest man of the Trinity, here the Son, Lancelot perceives directly Christ's real presence in this oblation.[58] Earlier, Lancelot saw only the ciborium, but now freed from torpor, he sees the divine conversion of an ordinary foodstuff into the body of Christ as the Father and the Spirit put the Son in the hands of the priest blessing and lifting the bread.[59] Galahad, Perceval, and Bors also experience a vision of this mystery when they see Joseph, first bishop of Christendom, elevate a consecrated wafer he has taken out of the holy vessel. However, they see not the Trinity but a child with a face "as rede and as bryght os ony fyre," i.e., the Spirit, who "smote hymselff into the brede, that all they saw hit that the brede was fourmed of a fleyshely man" (2:1029.25–27). Thus, the bread becomes the Son through the operation of the Spirit. After Joseph puts the wafer back into the holy vessel, a man with the "sygnes of the Passion of Jesu Cryste bledynge all opynly" comes out of it and carries it to Galahad to take from it his "Saveoure" (2:1030.4–5.13).[60]

Unlike Lancelot, held to watching at a threshold, the three holier knights participate in their mystical experience of the real presence of Christ in the Eucharistic bread; nonetheless, the Trinity Lancelot sees has doctrinal significance and an iconographic tradition. In Love's *Mirror*, for instance, when Mercy and Reason fail to find anyone who will die to redeem Adam's sin, Peace suggests it be the one who wrote the judgment; Reason decides which one of the Trinity's persons is the best choice; and the Father, the Son, and the Holy Ghost each agrees. As the story of Mary's life and her soon-to-be son's is then taken up, the idea of the full Trinity's involvement in the Son's sacrifice through incarnation, dramatized in the allegory, is conveyed by saying it was ordained by the High Trinity: "When þe plente of tyme of grace was come þe which þe hie Trinite ordeyned to saue mankynd þat was dampnet þorh þe synne of Adam, for þe grete charite þat he hade to mankynd, stiryng him his grete mercy."[61] In Caxton's *Speculum* woodcut, the collaboration of the three members is shown by the three men all touching the book, closed until the "plenty of time of grace was come." In other images, the Father and the Spirit support the Son as he holds a cross, signifying his commitment to incarnation.[62] In the Malory manuscript, Scribe A draws attention to Lancelot's scene, with the marginal note, "[t]he significacion of the Sankgreal that ys called the holy vessel the whiche appeared to sir Launcelot," but not to the one with the other main questers.[63] This *nota bene* probably occurs because of Lancelot, not because of the triad of men he sees. Still, we may note that by attentively following the French *Queste*'s imagery in the two visions of the mystery of the real presence of Christ in the Eucharistic bread, Malory produces a view of this sacrament as continuing the work of the incarnation, work in which the whole Trinity engages dynamically with humankind, as it does in the miracle of Urry's cure.

The Trinity in the *Morte* makes Malory's book one of several editions Caxton printed between 1483 and 1486 in which the Trinity appears in picture or prayer.[64] Besides the previously discussed woodcuts, these include the 1483 *Lyf of Our Lady* to the epilogue of which Caxton contributes a prayer "Vnto the holy and undevyded trynyte / Thre persones in one veray godhead."[65] At the end of the *Golden Legend* story of the fruitlessness of Augustine's attempt to explain the Trinity, a story told also in Mirk's *Festivalis* of an anonymous "grete clerke" instead of Augustine,[66] Caxton adds a prayer to Augustine to be a "medyatour and aduocate vnto thc Blessyd Trynyte / that we maye amende oure synful lyfe in this transytorye world / that whan we shalle departe / we may come to euerlastyng blysse in heuen / Amen /."[67] Caxton's prayer in the preface to Malory's *Morte* in 1485 echoes that one. Caxton reminds readers that all is "wryton for our doctrine" so that we "folowe vertue, by which we may come and atteyn to good fame and renomme in thys lyf, and after thys shorte and transitory lyf to come vnto euerlastyng blysse in heuen, the whiche He graunte vs that reygneth in heuen, the Blessyd Trynyte. Amen."[68] Caxton often concludes prologues with a prayer about this life and the one to come, normally made to "all-mighty God"; only his Malory prologue has the Trinity. If not inspired by the *Morte Darthur* itself, Caxton's prayer here may suggest Trinitarian interest among his patrons.

Lancelot: Trinitarian Prayer, Endless Virtue, and the Healing Spirit

In a certain room in a fifteenth-century hospital in Worcester, the dying could look up from their beds to find the Trinity painted on the ceiling.[69] Although the alliterative *Morte Arthure* opens with a prayer to "God" and "his pris Moder," Robert Thornton, a Yorkshireman of the gentry class with which Malory identified, invoked the Trinity in Latin at the head of this work when he copied it ca. 1440 into his book.[70] One of the few fifteenth-century English hymns to the Trinity reminds readers in its refrain that "in one is all" in the Trinity.[71] For some, whether dying, writing, or praying, to regard the Trinity was to sense triple-fold potency in the interrelatedness of the three persons. Thus, in the closing stanza of a prayer to "crist lord Ihu," we hear "God þe fadir & þe Sone infere / and þe haligaste also, / þat lord ert called lefe & dere / and onefald god withoutene mo, / endeles vertew ay be nere / and wirschippe þat shal neuer say ho. Amen."[72] Lancelot's prayer encompasses this sense of the Trinity's endless virtue and worship, that Malorian word for honor.

The three persons of the Trinity could be characterized by each one's special effect as long as (unlike Abelard's attempt) the properties ascribed belong clearly to all three. Thus, a poem by William Nassington names the might of the Father, the wit of the Son, and the good will of the Holy Ghost and then ravels the three back together as "a God and ane Lord yn threhed, / And thre persons yn anehed."[73] The distinctions in a lyric prayer offer an enriching perspective on Lancelot's prayer. After two verses invoking the "Celestiall father, potencial god of myght" and then two invoking "O benygne Ihu," we hear the final two, beginning "O fyre ververns, enflammed with all grace, / Enkyndlyng hertes with brondes most charitable," which is the "holy gost by name; / the thrid person . . . Of parfite loue thow art the gostly flame / . . . My coumford, my counsell, my parfite charite." The speaker asks the Father to "assist me" to see "thy glorious face" after this life; Jesus to "defend me, withe thy petious woundes fyve" against bodily and ghostly tribulations; and the Holy Ghost to "rescow me . . . by thy preseruacion." Although "coniunctable" to Father and Son, the ghostly flame, which is also the "water of life" and "well of consolacion," preserves and consoles through love.[74] As Hildegard of Bingen writes in two songs, the "life-giving life" that is the "fiery" Spirit pours "ointment on broken and fetid wounds."[75]

We see the Spirit's rejuvenating work in Malory's Sankgreal when, in a passage kept close to the French, ancient Mordrains asks Galahad to let him rest between his arms. Calling him a rose, the flower of "all good vertu, and in colour of fyre," Mordrains remarks that "the fyre of the Holy Goste ys takyn so in the that my fleyssh, whych was all dede of oldenes, ys becom agayne yonge" (2:1025.14–17).[76] In the Urry healing scene, the immediate reaction of Fyleloly and Urry to Lancelot when he arrives combines with the Pentecostal setting to convey the restorative work of the Spirit through the compassion stirred in him. As Mirk explains, Pentecost is a time when the Holy Ghost "flyeth from the soule that is combred wyth deadly synne" to "hem that ben in good lyf to god and to man and haue mercy in herte and compassion of hem in al her need."[77] As soon as Lancelot comes near them, Fyleloly whispers, "Brothir, here ys com a knyght that my harte gyveth gretly unto." Sharing her recognition that this knight may be the one who will make him whole, her brother replies, "Fayre syster . . . so doth my harte lyghte gretly ayenste hym, and my herte gyvith me more unto hym than to all thes that hath serched me" (3:1151.12–16).[78] In the fervor of compassion, a Christian and chivalric virtue, this best knight of the world has enough purity of heart to become the conduit of "parfite charite." Regarding the flow of tears in relation to prayer, Cassian contrasts those "squeezed by a hardened heart from dry eyes" with the "abundance of spontaneous tears" stirred by various virtues, such as distress over hardships weighing down the "righteous."[79] Lancelot, crying as abundantly as a beaten child, shows the contrite and humbled heart pleasing to God, and Lancelot's true love for God and fellow Christians.

For some ascetics, knowledge of the Trinity, to be reached through prayer, consists of a mystical union achieved when virtues, especially love, have purified the soul.[80] Lancelot's prayer is not a step toward mystical union but an intercession made in loving response to a young knight's unceasing, undeserved tribulation of seven piteous wounds. In Wolfram von Eschenbach's thirteenth-century Grail story, in which Anfortas suffers unceasingly from the poisoned wound in his testicles, Parzival prays to the Trinity through the "Gral" on his second visit to Munsalvæsche: "Thrice did he genuflect in its direction to the glory of the Trinity, praying that the affliction of this man of sorrows be taken from him."[81] But he does not then search Anfortas's wound; instead he asks openly the compassionate question, whereupon Anfortas is restored to health at once. Like everyone assembled there and back at Arthur's court, Parzival knows he will ask this question and what the result will be. In Lancelot's case, however, no outcome is predicted, and no symbolic object comes between the prayer-giver and the divine source of healing or the beneficiary: present are only the invisible "in one is all" mystery of the Trinity, one knight's secret prayer out of compassion, humility, and obedience, and his gentle, searching hands.

To conclude, the foregoing examination of how Lancelot makes Urry's wounds whole demonstrates the ways this healing is a Christian event, stark in manifestation yet replete with sacred mystery. We can be moved by this event without knowing much about the Trinity, for the power of three, the tribulations of wounds, and the art of empathetic healing are not unique to Christianity. Yet, through acquaintance with the history, expression in worship, representation in visual media, and moral dimension of this doctrine, we see why in the *Morte* and its cultural context the Trinitarian prayer Malory composes for Lancelot is distinctively Christian and orthodox. Moreover, the episode of Lancelot's healing of Urry reflects Malory's concern with the need to sustain moral life within forms of community. Some of his narrative models for doing so have historic realism, like the public religious funerary custom of the dole that Lancelot, dressed in a "mournyng gown," makes in Dover for Gawain "of fleyssh and fysshe and wyne and ale, and every man and woman he dalt to twelve pence" with "hys owne honde," in sorrow, compassion, and humility (3:1250.24–29).[82] Some are humanist, like the Candlemas tournament, in the telling of which religion is never mentioned, yet virtuous works and choices are on display, as we hear in Arthur's praise of Gareth for holding with Lancelot, "For ever hit ys . . . a worshypfull knyghtes dede to help and succoure another worshypfull knyght whan he seeth hym in daungere," and in Malory's conclusion that "he that was curteyse, trew, and faythefull to hys frynde was that tyme cherysshed" (3:1114.20–22, 31–32). In the model provided by the Urry healing event, Lancelot, at once a member of the Round Table and Christian faith communities, is graced by the charism of healing through the Trinity and draws up his fellows through love.

NOTES

1. Malory, *Works*, 3rd ed. rev., 1:307.34–308.1, 331.19–20. Here and elsewhere I substitute neutral punctuation for Vinaver's exclamation point. Additional references will be given in parentheses in the text.

2. "Seuen chapytres, the whiche the abbot Moyses sente to the abbot Permenius [Poemen]" (*Vitas Patrum*, trans. Caxton, fol. CCCxvi, col. 1–2). The "Seuen chapytres" is one of the *Exhortations of the Holy Fathers*, which, in turn, is one of the texts in the anthology Caxton translated from a French version of the Latin original. Manuscript and incunable copies of the Latin texts were widely available in England. In the passages to be quoted in this study, transcribed from Oxford, Bodleian Library, Arch. G. d. 30, I add quotation marks, expand abbreviations, substitute commas, periods, and question marks for virgules, and occasionally capitalize. The standard source for the Latin anthology is *Vitae Patrum*, ed. Heribert Rosweyde (1617; 2nd ed. 1625 and 1628), which consists of ten books. Although I am using here the 1617 Rosweyde, the text is reprinted in Migne's Patrologia Latinae 73–74. References to Rosweyde will be by item numbers. Thus, the saying about the knight, or soldier (*militante*), is book 6.4.30.

3. McDonald, *Crucible of Christian Morality*, p. 180.

4. McDonald, *Crucible of Christian Morality*, pp. 1, 193.

5. For the Sankgreal, see *Works*, 2:896–99 (Lancelot and the male hermit), 926–35 (Lancelot and the good man, then another male hermit, then a female recluse), and 1014–18 (Lancelot and the old man and other folk in Pelles's castle).

6. P. E. Tucker suggests that Malory was influenced by a version of a noncontinuous adventure in the prose *Lancelot* ("Source for 'The Healing of Sir Urry,'" p. 490). Robert L. Kelly prefers another part of the prose *Lancelot* for the model, Lancelot's initiation into knighthood on St. John's Day ("Wounds, Healing," p. 175).

7. Keen, *Chivalry*, p. 81.

8. Laudable exhortacyons, *Vitas Patrum*, fol. CC, col. 1; Rosweyde, book 3.116.

9. Laudable exhortacyons, *Vitas Patrum*, fol. Clxxxix, col 2; Rosweyde, book 3.38.

10. Keen, *Chivalry*, p. 81.

11. See, for example, *Works*, 2:928.34–36: "thou hast ruled the ayenste me as a warryoure and used wronge warris with vayneglory for the pleasure of the worlde."

12. Laudable exhortacyons, *Vitas Patrum*, fol. CCii, col. 2–CCiiv; Rosweyde, book 3.141.

13. On repentance in the thought of Philo of Alexandria (ca. 20 BCE–50 CE), which fuses Hellenistic and Jewish elements, see McDonald, *Crucible of Christian Morality*, p. 198. On other types of compunction, see John Cassian, "Ninth Conference: On Prayer," *Conferences*, §§XXVI–XXIX, pp. 346–48; and Cassian, "VIIII Conlatio Abbatis Issac Prima," *Collationes XXIIII*, pp. 273–76 (the Latin text; section numbers are the same as Ramsey's).

14. "How men ought to styre them to compunccyon," *Vitas Patrum*, fol. CCxxviv; Rosweyde, book 5.3.27. The gospel is probably Luke 6:21, "Blessed are you that weep now, for you shall laugh," and Psalm 24:4–5, "He who has clean hands and a pure heart . . . will receive blessing from the Lord," or 73:1, "Truly God is good to the upright, to those who are pure in heart."

15. See McDonald, *Crucible of Christian Morality*, on *caritas* with justice in Cicero (p. 191), Philo's "philanthropia" (pp. 197–98), and the command to love one's neighbor (Lev. 19:17) (pp. 69–73).

16. Laudable exhortacyons, *Vitas Patrum*, fol. CCv, col. 1; Rosweyde, book 3.126.

17. Laudable exhortacyons, *Vitas Patrum*, fol. CCv, col. 1; Rosweyde, book 3.156.

18. See, for example, the divergent treatments by Earl R. Anderson, "'Ein Kind wird geschlagen,'" esp. pp. 58–63; and Stephen C. B. Atkinson, "Malory's 'Healing of Sir Urry,'" esp. p. 349.

19. "The Lyfe of Saynt Anthonye Abbot," *Vitas Patrum*, fol. xxxix, cols. 1–2; the English text abbreviates the Latin passage: "Non enim Antonii aut cujusquam hominum omnino hanc esse medicinam, sed Dei solius, qui et quibus vellet, et quo vellet tempore daret sanitatem" (*Vitas Patrum* book 1 *Vita Beati Antonii Abbatis*, chap. 28). For modern English, see Athanasius, *Life of Anthony*, p. 44, chap. 56.

20. Laudable exhortacyons, *Vitas Patrum*, fol. CCx, col. 1; Rosweyde, book 3.181.

21. John Mirk, "Vigilia pentecostes," *Liber festivalis and Quattuor sermones*, sig. [d 7v, d 8], Oxford, Bodleian Library, Bod S. Selden d. 8. The name of the collection is also given as *Festialis* and *Festial*.

22. In the Tale of Sir Gareth, when Arthur's reunion with his nephew fills him with joy, "ever he wepte as he had bene a chylde" (1:358.19–20). The simile conveys copiousness, whether joyful as in Arthur's case or sorrowful as in Lancelot's.

23. The clergy would have been those in the Augustinian priory, founded by Henry I in 1122 and made a cathedral in 1133. Although it was then dedicated to St. Mary (appropriately thanked by Arthur's knights when the healing succeeds), it is now dedicated to the Holy and Undivided Trinity. In her 1899 study of church dedications in England, Frances

Arnold-Forster assigns Carlisle Cathedral's Trinity dedication to the medieval period, around the time of Becket (1:26, 3:78). However, in the current history of Carlisle Cathedral, David W. V. Weston documents the datum that in accordance with Henry VIII's second act of suppression, the priory was dissolved in 1540, and in 1541 the cathedral was refounded and dedicated to the Holy and Undivided Trinity (*Carlisle Cathedral History*, pp. 6 and 18). Medieval paintings of the lives of Anthony and of Augustine are among the decorations, but I have found no image of the Trinity known to have existed there.

24. John Trevisa, trans., "Liber Septimus. De Infirmitatibus et Venenis" (*On the Properties of Things*, 1:437).

25. In *La Queste del Saint Graal*, p. 44, Galahad extracts the steel, i.e., the spearhead, and all the wood: "Et il met la main au fer et le trait hors a tout le fust"; when shown the wound ("li mostrent la plaie"), the monk looked at it and said he would bring the knight back to health in a month: "Et il regarde et dit qui il le rendra tout sain dedens un mois"; in Matarasso's rendering, "He examined it" (*Quest of the Holy Grail*, p. 69).

26. "Lancelot e la damoisele i atochierent l'espee e le suaire, e eles li sont tantost asoagiees, e dist que il se sent bien or a primes que il n'avra garde de mort" (*Le Haut Livre du Graal: Perlesvaus*, 1:348, lines 8477–82).

27. Meliot's sister tells Lancelot she will "abyde tyll God sende you agayne" (1:279.35); Lancelot says "that God me forbede" when Hallewes bids him kiss her, and "Jesu preserve me frome your subtyle crauftys" when she reveals her thwarted plan to embalm his body so she can kiss and embrace it (1:281.6, 21–22).

28. "Et si tost come li chevaliers maladies le voit venir, si se lesse chaoir a terre de si haut come il estoit et joint les mains encontre et dit: 'Bian sire Diex, qui de cest Saint Vessel que je voie ci venir avez fet tant bel miracle en cest païs et en autre. . . . Et lors s'en vet trainant a la force de ses braz jusqu'au perron ou la table seoit. . . . Et il se prent a dues mains et se tire contremont et fet tant qu'il bese la table d'argent et la toche a ses euz" (*Queste*, p. 59; *Quest*, pp. 82–83).

29. On Cassian's influence, see Fry, *Rule of St. Benedict*, pp. 58–59.

30. Cassian, "Ninth Conference," *Conferences*, §IX p. 336; *Collationes XXIIII*, p. 260.

31. Cassian, "Ninth Conference," *Conferences*, §XV.1, p. 338; *Collationes XXIIII*, pp. 262–63.

32. Cassian, "Ninth Conference," *Conferences*, §XXXV.2, p. 353; *Collationes XXIIII*, p. 238.

33. Cassian, "Ninth Conference," *Conferences*, §XXXIV.6, p. 352; *Collationes*, p. 281.

34. See Cassian, "Ninth Conference," *Conferences*, §XXXVI.1, pp. 353–54; *Collationes XXIIII*, p. 283. Cassian's reference is to Psalm 141:2, "the raising of my hands like an evening sacrifice."

35. See *Queste*, p. 274; *Quest*, p. 280.

36. This observation extends to the prayers in various colophons in the Winchester Manuscript, which are addressed to "blyssed lorde" on fol. 346v, "Blessed Ihu" on fol. 409, and "Ihu" on fol. 449. There is also a request that readers pray that "god" send the author good deliverance on fol. 148. The rhymed prayer printed by Caxton, in the end part missing from the manuscript, refers to "Iheu" (Malory, *Caxton's Malory*, 1:600).

37. See Chadwick, *Early Church*, p. 130; J. N. D. Kelly, *Early Christian Doctrines*, pp. 232, 243–49, 255–58.

38. For instance, among the forty-five verses of this creed, critical lines for the Trinity include "The Father is from none: not made nor created nor begotten. The Son is from the Father alone, not made nor created but begotten. The Holy Spirit is from the Father and

the Son: not made nor created nor begotten but proceeding" (J. N. D. Kelly, *Athanasian Creed*, p. 19, verses 21–33). The corresponding Latin is "Pater a nullo est factus nec creatus nec genitus. Filius a Patre solo est, non factus nec creatus sed genitus. Spiritus sanctus a Patre et Filio, non factus nec creatus nec genitus sed procedens." The Quicunque, another title for the Athanasian Creed (from "Quicunque vult," "whoever wishes," the first words of the Athanasian Creed), is likely to have originated in southern Gaul ca. 500; see pp. 35, 109–13. For its use in instruction of those to be baptized and as a test of orthodoxy and its eventual incorporation into psalters and the divine office in the west, see pp. 41–44. For Augustine's influence, see p. 90.

39. Bartholomaeus Anglicus, *De Proprietatibus rerum*, pp. 4–45. For Trevisa, whose translation was published by Wynkyn de Worde ca. 1495, see *On the Properties of Things*. For Corbechon, see Bartholomaeus, *Le Livre des propriétés des choses*.

40. In London, for instance, including wards outside the city limits, only three of the forty-seven pre-sixteenth-century religious ("parish") guilds were dedicated to the Holy Trinity; see Unwin, *Gilds*, Appendix A, pp. 367–70. In her 1899 census of church dedications in England, Arnold-Forster traces 636 to the Trinity (*Studies in Church Dedications*, 1:17) and 2,161 to St. Mary "the Blessed Virgin" (1:41); 238 of the Trinity dedications are pre-Reformation (3:2).

41. See Arnold-Forster, *Studies in Church Dedications*, 1:25–26, and also Trinity Sunday in *Catholic Encyclopedia*; it was instituted under Pope John XXII (1316–34).

42. Caxton, *Golden Legend*, fol. viii, col. 2 (London, British Library C. 11. 1. 8), EEBO (Early English Books Online).

43. Malory finds Trinity Sunday in the fourteenth-century stanzaic *Morte Arthur*, lines 3160–69, 3196–221 (*King Arthur's Death*, pp. 88–89). No festival is named in the early thirteenth-century French *La Mort le Roi Artu*, chap. 176.

44. Mirk, "Festum sancta Trinitatis," *Liber festivalis* (1483), sig. e ii^v. On Trinitarian schema, see J. N. D. Kelly, *Early Christian Creeds*, pp. 22–23; with baptism pp. 30–49.

45. #26 Laus Trinitati (Hildegard, *Symphonia*, p. 142), lines 5–6: mirus splendor archanorum, / que hominibus ignota sunt.

46. Marenbon, *Philosophy of Peter Abelard*, p. 55.

47. Abelard, "Historia Calamitatum," pp. 20–25. For a later version, *Theologia Scholarium*, Abelard was tried for heresy at Sens in 1140 but despite Bernard of Clairvaux's prosecution was not ultimately condemned; see Clanchy, *Abelard*, pp. 306–25.

48. Love, *Mirror of the Blessed Life of Jesus Christ*, p. 23.

49. The story is also told in Mirk's *Liber festivalis* of an anonymous "grete clerke." See Caxton's 1483 "Festum sancta Trinitatis," *Liber festivalis*, sig. e iiii–verso. The version in this edition exists also in the other recension of Mirk's collection published by Rood in 1486 (sig f [6–verso], col. 1) and de Worde in 1493, and also edited by Erbe from Oxford, Bodleian Library MS Gough Eccl. Top.4 (Mirk, *Mirk's Festial: Collection of Homilies*, pp. 167–68).

50. Caxton, *Golden Legend*, fol. CClxvi verso, col. 2–CClxvii, col. 1. For Augustine's *On the Trinity*, see Chadwick, *Early Church*, pp. 235–36, and J. N. D. Kelly, *Early Christian Doctrines*, pp. 271–79.

51. David Brown, "Trinity in Art," p. 330.

52. Reproduced in Rickert, *Painting in Britain*, fig. 103c.

53. Reproduced in *The Hastings Hours*, fol. 20v. On Hastings as Caxton's patron, see prologue and epilogue in the *Mirror* (*Prologues and Epilogues of William Caxton*, ed. Crotch, pp. 52, 57).

54. Rickert, *Painting in Britain*, fig. 175.

55. Caxton, *Golden Legend* frontispiece; Hodnett, *English Woodcuts*, #237.

56. Love, *Speculum vitae Christi*, sig. a [8v]–b ii, Cambridge University Library, Inc 4018 [3.J 1.1] (EEBO); drawing on sig. b ii (Hodnett, *English Woodcuts*, #313). See Love, *Mirror of the Blessed Life of Jesus Christ*, pp. 16–19, for the comparable segment, and p. 243 note to 16.14–18.26 on the source in Bernard of Clairvaux's sermon on the Annunciation.

57. See *Queste*, p. 255; *Quest*, p. 262.

58. In interactional and triadic imagery, the Son may look the same age as the Father or look younger; similarly, the Spirit, if represented in male form, may be mature or young. Here, the two men holding the younger man have to be the Father and the Spirit, for these are the two persons of the Trinity that work in conjunction to produce the mysterious presence of the Son in the bread.

59. On the development of the doctrine of the Eucharist and theories of likeness or conversion as to how the bread was really Christ's body yet also bread and thus "eucharist, being composed of two elements, a terrestrial one and a celestial," see J. N. D. Kelly, *Early Christian Doctrines*, pp. 196–98, 211–16, and 440–55. The treatise on the "sacrament of cristes blessede body" adjoined to Love's *Mirror* uses both likeness and conversion explanations in defense of this sacrament; see Love, *Mirror of the Blessed Life of Jesus Christ*, pp. 223–26.

60. See *Queste*, pp. 269–70, and *Quest*, pp. 275–76.

61. Love, *Mirror of the Blessed Life of Jesus Christ*, p. 22.

62. For instance, in the Hastings hours the Son and his mirror-image Father together hold a scepter behind the fluttering dove while with his other hand the Son supports a plain cross, its vertical staff extending down to the firmament of the world, thus symbolizing his descent. See Turner's commentary in *Hastings Hours*, p. 119.

63. Malory, Winchester Manuscript, fol. 401v for Lancelot; fols. 405v–406 for the others.

64. Caxton had been planning to publish the *Morte* since 1481, the year he announced it in *Godfrey of Boloyne*; see Painter, *William Caxton*, p. 146.

65. *Prologues and Epilogues*, p. 85. Painter assumes the verses are Caxton's (*William Caxton*, p. 132).

66. Quoted from Caxton's 1483 "Festum sancta Trinitatis" (Mirk, *Liber festivalis and Quattuor sermones*, sig. e iiii–verso). The version in this edition exists also in the other recension of Mirk's collection published by Theodoric Rood in 1486 (Mirk, *Liber festiaales*, sig f [6v] col. 1) and de Worde in 1493, and also edited by Erbe from Oxford, Bodleian Library MS Gough Eccl. Top.4 (Mirk, *Mirk's Festial: Collection of Homilies*, pp. 167–68).

67. Caxton, *Golden Legend*, fol. CClxvii, col. 1.

68. Malory, *Caxton's Malory*, 1:3.

69. Described by Colin Richmond in "The Visual Culture of Fifteenth-Century England," p. 194.

70. In Lincoln Cathedral Library MS 91, Thornton's incipit is "[h]ere beginnes Morte Arthure. In Nomine Patris et Filii et Spiritus Sancti. Amen pur Charite. Amen." See *Alliterative Morte Arthure* in *King Arthur's Death*, p. 115 and lines 1–2. On Thornton, see summary in Thompson, *Robert Thornton*, pp. 2–5.

71. #52 "In One is All" (*Religious Lyrics of the XVth Century*, pp. 82–83).

72. #60 "Christ, Defend Me from My Enemies" (*Religious Lyrics of the XVth Century*, pp. 93–95, lines 67–72). This is a translation of a Latin hymn by Berenger of Tours (d. 1088), which precedes it in Corpus Christi College Oxford MS 274 (note p. 312).

73. "Religious Poem" (*Religious Pieces in Prose and Verse*, p. 59), lines 1–8.

74. #51 "A Prayer to the Three Persons in the Trinity" (*Religious Lyrics of the XVth Century*,

pp. 80–81), lines 2, 17, 33–34, 41–44, 46; 14–16, 23–24, 40; 36, 38. "Vervens" in line 33 is a spelling of "fervens" (fervent); see editor's note p. 81.

75. #24 Spiritus sanctus vivificans vita (Hildegard, *Symphonia*, p. 140), line 1: vivificans vita; line 6: ungit vulnera; #27 O ignee Spiritus (p. 141), line 1; (p. 146), lines 47–48: quia tu preciosissimum ungentum es / fractis et fetidis vulneribus. In translating the Latin, I have consulted Barbara Newman's literal prose translations of #24 (p. 141) and #27 (p. 147).

76. See *Queste*, p. 263; *Quest*, p. 269.

77. Mirk, "Vigilia Pentecostes," *Liber festivalis* (1483), sig. [7v].

78. Arthur uses the phrase "myne herte gyvyth me" in responding to the tall, well-built young man (Gareth, as it turns out), who arrives on horseback, enters the hall leaning on two well-dressed men, and asks the king for the gift of food and drink for a year. Arthur responds, "[A]ske bettyr . . . for this is but a symple askyng; for myne herte gyvyth me to the gretly, that thou arte com of men of worshyp" (2:294.17–20). Here "that" means "because" (see 3:1435 note to lines 18–20); i.e., although Arthur does not yet know his blood relationship to this "fayre son," the king feels certain that this "goodlyest yonge man . . . that ever they all sawe" will "preve a man of right grete worshyp" (2:293.28–29; 294.17, 20–21). In this case, the unidentified visitor bears signs of his social status in his build, companions, etc., yet not knowing this petitioner is his nephew, Arthur also recognizes something special about his lineage. Similarly, Urry and Fyleloly, without knowing who Lancelot is when he arrives, sense something special about him. While literal contextual cues, such as the sudden silence Arthur commands of the waiting knights, would stimulate that sense, Mirk's explanation of the Spirit in the context of Pentecost seems applicable to what Fyleloly and her brother feel: the "beste knight of the worlde" has arrived.

79. Cassian, "Ninth Conference," *Conferences*, §XXX.1, p. 348; *Collationes XXIIII*, p. 277.

80. Notably, Evagrius Ponticus, whose work influenced Cassian and also the Cistercians. See Evagrius, *Praktikos and Chapters on Prayer*, pp. vii–xviii, and *Praktikos #3*, Prayer #3 and 52; also *Ad Monachos*, #67, 110, and 136.

81. Wolfram, *Parzival*, pp. 394–95.

82. See also Karen Cherewatuk's essay in this collection.

Christian Rituals in Malory: The Evidence of Funerals

Karen Cherewatuk

In his classic study, *The Making of the Middle Ages*, R. W. Southern analyzes the place of religion in Chrétien de Troyes's romances:

> Chrétien, as an author, was neither religious nor, in intention at least, anti-religious. Religion was part of the furniture of his stories—indeed an essential part, for religious observance was one of the elements of good breeding. But the Christianity of Chrétien is an affair of externals, providing plenty of bishops and clerks to add to the dazzling throng, and a rich pageantry of miters and crosiers at weddings. The real internal religion of the heart was untouched by Christianity. There is in Chrétien none of the melancholy, none of the sense of the sinfulness of the heart, which we sometimes find in Malory. Chrétien probes the heart, but it is ... not yet made tender by the penetration of strong religious feeling. There is nothing in Chrétien like the passage of the *Morte d'Arthur* when Guinevere takes leave of Lancelot.[1]

According to Southern, Christianity for Chrétien involves exterior trappings, which he metaphorically describes as "furniture" in the room of romance. In contrast, Southern finds interior religious life in Malory. For Malory's Christianity Southern employs a second metaphor, the "prob[ing of] the heart."

A good many Malorians would argue, *contra* Southern, that Malory shows even less interest in Christianity than Chrétien. First, Malory's narration typically focuses on action and events rather than providing description. Outside of the Grail Quest, there is no full depiction of religious panoply. Hence, the rambling house of the *Morte Darthur* is even more lightly furnished than Chrétien's. Second, Malory's turn toward the heart, what Southern calls his "penetration of strong religious feeling," these critics explain as a conflict of romantic love and chivalric duty[2] or as a shift in genre.[3] For these critics, the "melancholy" of the *Morte's* ending derives not from "the sense of the sinfulness of the heart" but from loss of romantic love or male fellowship.[4] In general, these critics hold that the religious

77

elements at the close of the *Morte* are plot devices providing resolution to the oft-cited problem of divided or conflicting loyalties, as when Fiona Tolhurst argues that Lancelot and Guinevere "achieve salvation as much through their earthly love of each other as though their repentance."[5] With Southern, others have argued that Lancelot and Guinevere's turn to God provides consolation for the destruction of the Round Table.[6] Analyzing specific textual details, some have found strains of fifteenth-century spirituality in the *Morte*, noting Malory's familiarity with Eucharistic practice,[7] his use of embedded prayers,[8] his careful articulation of confessional language,[9] his increased use of hagiographic motifs,[10] and his reliance on motifs derived from Christian exempla.[11] Whatever the scholars' predispositions on the question of Christianity and Malory, all can agree that in turning to the lovers' separation at the end of the *Morte Darthur*, Southern turns to *the* pivotal scene: the lovers' parting, after Gawain's and Arthur's deaths and before Guinevere's and Lancelot's. Recognizing the significance of these scenes of death, this essay approaches them in a fresh way, applying the evidence of death and funeral rites to the question of Malory's engagement with late medieval Christianity. My method involves, first, reporting the details of late medieval funeral practices in order to fill out for modern readers elliptical formulations that would have been intuitively grasped by fifteenth-century audiences; and second, suggesting ways in which the "dolorous deaths and departings" of Gawain, Guinevere, Lancelot, and even King Arthur can provide evidence of the characters' experiencing Southern's Christian "feeling." In short, my question is this: As the principal characters move into the house of death, do they find an eternal home? My answer relies on the reader's willingness to resist dividing the furnishings of romance into separate rooms called "the sacred" and "the secular." My argument will controvert other scholars' reluctance to see "the sacred" and "the secular" as overlapping domains.

To begin at the most basic level of Christian belief, passages throughout the *Morte Darthur* presume the existence of the soul. Thus when the sinless Galahad dies, "so suddeynly departed hys soule to Jesu Cryste, and a grete multitude of angels bare hit up to hevyn" (2:1035.15–16).[12] When the virtuous heathen Palomides smites off the head of the pagan Corsabryn, however, "therewithall cam a stynke of his body, whan the soule departed, that there myght nobody abyde the savoure. So was the corpus had away and buryed in a wood." Corsabryne's corpse is hauled off to the woods not only because of the stink of his soul but because consecrated ground is reserved for Christian burial, and "he was a paynym" (2:666.13–16). In contrast, even though he received his death wound attempting regicide, the deceased Accolon is "brought unto the chirche" (1:149.33). Throughout the *Morte Darthur*, knights and ladies die and are buried, their corpses interred in consecrated space: a hermitage (1:119.6), a priory (2:812.18), a chapel (3:1232.17), a church (1:77.23–24, 2:1059.26). In Malory's England, commoners were buried in the churchyard while members of the gentry or nobility came to their final rest, like Accolon, within a church or monastery. In his shorthand, Malory glosses the funerals of his noble characters with the phrases "bury this knyght rychely" for Harleus le Berbeus or, for Perceval's sister, "buryed her as rychely as them oughte a kynges doughter" (1:80.21 and 2:1033.17–18).[13] These formulae, I think, refer not simply to the sumptuousness of the tomb but to the care taken for all due ceremony, from burial of the body to recitation of masses for the deceased's soul. Thus King Pellinore offers as payment the harness of a deceased man "and charged the heremyte with the coorse, that servyse sholde be done for the soule" (1:119.9–10). The noun "soule" can appear in simply formulaic references to death—as in the phrase "anone departed the soule frome the body" (2:945.14–15)—or to Christian doctrine as in this reference to "the Sonne of the Hyghe Fadir that lyght within a maydyn and bought all the soules oute of thralle" (2:892.12–13). Concern for the soul is most evident, however, when a character utters prayer in the face of violent death, as does Sir Collgrevaunce at Sir Lyonell's hands: "Fayre swete Jesu Cryste, that I have myssedo, have mercy uppon my soule!" (2:973.8–9). The same pattern occurs in requests for prayers for the deceased, as when Malory memorably suggests that his audience pray for Tristram's soul: "all maner jantylmen hath cause to the worldes ende to prayse sir Trystram and to pray for his soule. Amen, sayde sir Thomas Malleorré" (2:683.2–4). The author also seeks prayers for his own soul as well as for deliverance from his current trial: "I praye you all jentylmen and jentylwymmen that redeth this book of Arthur and his knyghtes from the begynnyng to the endynge, praye for me whyle I am on lyve that God sende me good delyveraunce. And whan I am deed, I praye you all praye for my soule" (3:1260.20–24). I accept Catherine Batt's warning that "one cannot make a priori assumptions about Malory's religion on the basis of social placing,"[14] that is, the author's status as a gentleman does not determine his religious orientation, especially given the current debate about gentry participation in parish life versus more private practices of devotion.[15] Yet the last two passages I cite show Malory breaking the narrative frame to speak in his own voice about a practice he assumes as a norm: prayer for the deceased. At the very least, we can assume that the author held to the doctrine of the immortality of the soul and the efficacy of prayer for speeding that soul through the pains of purgatory to heaven.

Given this belief, Malory consistently treats characters who do not die suddenly to deathbed ministration, to which practice I now turn.[16] In fifteenth-century England, Catholics received Holy Communion once a year, at Easter, after confession or "shrift" and penance. The preliminary shrift ensured that the penitent had reconciled with all in the community—family, neighbors, associates—so that the parish's taking of the Easter sacrament truly embodied the Eucharistic body. The single exception to the annual communion came at the point of death. The late medieval rites that preceded death ensured that the soul passed out of the body in a state of grace; these sacraments strengthened the Christian's resolve to resist the demons who would attempt to provoke heresy as the body suffered death. That resolve was needed by both Christians strong in the faith and the less confident. In relating her near-death experience in the long text of the *Showings*, for example, Julian of Norwich narrates how after "I tooke all my rites of Holy Church" and even had trained her eyes on the crucifix as a reminder of Jesus's salvific death, the room seemed "as if it had be mekil occupied with the fends."[17] In an apparently early predeath experience, Margery Kempe, who was unable to make her final confession, was tormented by devils who bade "hir sche schuld forsake hir Crystendam hir feyth, and denyin hir God."[18] While Julian's experience follows step by step the journey toward death outlined in the popular fifteenth-century manuals on the *ars moriendi*,[19] Margery's hesitation over an unnamed sin keeps her from the all-important final shrift. In the normal course of death, as opposed to Margery's truncated rite, the dying Christian made his/her shrift, experienced penance, and was "houseled," that is, given the Eucharist. The Middle English and early modern English verb "housel" derives from the Old English *huslian*, to sacrifice, referring to "Sacrifice of the Mass" or "sakering" at which the bread and wine were consecrated.[20] Before administering housel, the confessor at the deathbed could be quite severe, as was Margery Kempe's "when he gan scharply to vndyrnemyn hir."[21] After all, the confessor's goal for the "final examination" was to ensure that the sufferer was free from sin, had reconciled with all other Christians, and was ready to receive the final housel, also known as the *viaticum*.[22] After shrift and housel, the Christian received the final anointing with chrism or unction *in extremis* on the eyes, ears, nose, mouth, and hands. According to St. Thomas Aquinas, the goal of the sacrament of final anointing was the purification of sins, especially those committed through the senses, so that the Christian was prepared "for glory immediately."[23] Many Christians put off final anointing because of the widespread belief that they would be deprived of the full use of their senses should they return to health. Thus, only those certain of death sought this final sacrament. On the deathbed, then, the sacramental pattern of Easter is invoked—shrift, penitence, and Eucharist—as the body (sometimes anointed) releases the soul and it rises, from earthly fellowship to the communion of saints. By demand, however, the English laity made housel or the *viaticum* the centerpiece of their final rights or "rights due," the latter of which is also the phrase commonly used in the fifteenth century for the Easter Communion.

In all the particulars Malory followed fifteenth-century deathbed rite,[24] albeit in his shorthand style. For example, during the Grail Quest, a noblewoman who has been dumb her whole life recognizes Perceval as "Goddes knyght" and leads him to the sege perilous: "Ryght soo she departed and asked a preste, and as she was confessid and houseld thenne she dyed" (2:611.24–25, 30–31). Balin and his brother Balan reconcile with each other before they ask a lady to "sende for a preest, that we may receyve our sacrament and receyve the blessid body of Our

Lord Jesu Cryst."The lady does and the priest "gaf hem her ryghtes" (1:90.33–37). In these scenes Malory thus appropriately sequences the verbs that indicate that the dying have been confessed and houseled. The words of Perceval's sister affirm the laity's insistence on final Eucharist, for "asked she her Saveoure, and as sone as she had reseyved Hym the soule departed frome the body" (2:1004.4–5). It is the dying Lancelot who, aware of his imminent death, explicitly undergoes the full process: he "was howselyd and enelyd [anointed] and had al that *a Crysten man ought to have*" (3:1257.24, italics mine).

Like the deathbed ministration that the fifteenth-century Christian "ought to have," funeral practice was rooted in the firm belief in the efficacy of prayers and sacraments celebrated in memory of the deceased. The Office of the Dead itself consisted of three parts. First, a service of vespers was sung on the night preceding the burial. This service was also called the Placebo, based on the singing of the opening antiphon from Psalm 114:9, "I will please the Lord in the land of the living" ("Placebo domino in regione vivorum"). Second, matins was chanted the next morning; this service also was known as the Dirige or Dirge, based on the recitation of Psalm 5:9, "make straight my path, O Lord, in your sight" (Domine . . . dirige in conspectu tuo viam meam"; numbering follows the Vulgate Bible). Finally, matins was followed, often immediately, by the requiem Mass and burial. The tripartite service of vespers, matins, and Mass was repeated thirty days after the funeral at a celebration called "the month-mind" and then again a year later, at the "year-mind," or "obit," and thereafter annually. The celebration of the month-mind could explain why Lancelot's followers remain together for "a monthe" after his burial (3:1259.25–26).

Among classes who could afford it, care was taken that a large number of mourners attend the funeral to pray for the departed. Rewards for the clerics and the poor who offered prayers at the services could range from a meal to a robe to a monetary donation, and payment was fixed, ranging from "four pence given to priests and clerics who could recite the dirge to a penny or halfpenny for the illiterate poor who could only do a *pater* or *ave* by rote."[25] When John Paston died and his body was brought from London to Norwich, it was accompanied for six days by a priest and twelve poor men with torches. This contemporary of Malory and fellow member of the gentry was mourned at his funeral by twenty-three nuns, thirty-eight priests, thirty-nine choir boys, twenty-six clerics, four torchbearers, a prioress, an anchoress, and an unknown number of friars and the poor.[26] Costs were recorded for the hearse, because the body needed to be transported with appropriate solemnity; for mourning clothes, because the paid mourners needed to match; for food and drink, because they also needed to be fed for the two days of services; for candles and torches around the corpse, because they would visually remind all present to call upon Christ, the living light, for the sake of the deceased; for the "glaser for takyn owte of ii. panys of the windows of the chyrche for to late owte the reke of the torches at the deryge" and re-solder them after;[27] and for the poor-dole, for the funeral was the *last* chance for John Paston to distribute charity, now by proxy, to the poor. If a public demonstration of family status, Sir John Paston's funeral was also a genuine display of faith, a mixture of Christologic symbols and practicality, and the kind of service at which Malory's gentry and noble audiences regularly offered up their prayers for the deceased.

Many deaths in the *Morte Darthur* are described by details familiar from John Paston's elaborate funeral. These funerals pale in comparison to the arrangements that Lancelot makes for the sake of Gawain's soul. Lancelot offers a poor "dole" to "all that wolde com of towne or of the contrey" that consists of a meal of "fleyssh and fysshe and wyne and ale ... and twelve pence" (3:1250.24-27)—and *that* went just to the mourners at the vespers service. "And on the morn all the prystes and clarkes that myght be gotyn in the contrey and in the town were there, and sange massis of Requiem. And there offird first sir Launcelot, and he offird an hondred pounde, and than the seven kynges offirde, and every of them offirde fourty pounde. Also there was a thousand knyghtes, and every of them offirde a pounde; and the offeryng dured fro the morne to nyght" (3:1250.31–1251.5). In putting Gawain to rest, Malory refers to both the vespers service and requiem Mass, yet he emphasizes the monetary offerings of the chivalric mourners. These gifts are so generous that a chantry could be dedicated in Gawain's memory. This type of endowment employed one or more chaplains in reciting masses for the deceased, usually at a side altar or chapel within a church but sometimes at a separate foundation established for that purpose. To Gawain Lancelot had already offered the founding of perpetual chantries, for the souls of Gareth and Gaheris, as repentance for his hand in slaying them. In fact, Lancelot had extravagantly proposed to found "at every ten myles ende ... an hole covente, to synge and rede day and nyght in especiall for sir Gareth sake and sir Gaherys. . . . and there ys none of all thes religious placis but they shall be perfourmed, furnysshed and garnysshed with all thyngis as an holy place ought to be" (3:1199.32–1200.6). Such "proffirs" are indeed "grete," as Gawain asserts (3:1200.14) and as an audience of Malory's contemporaries would have recognized. The founding of even one college of seven monks or priests in memory of Sir John Fastolf, one of the wealthiest men in fifteenth-century England, proved prohibitively expensive for his heirs.[28] With rage, perhaps at the improbity of an offer to found chantries every ten miles from Sandwich to Carlisle, Gawain rejects Lancelot's plan and moves Arthur to war against him. Yet, after Gawain's death, Lancelot honors him with a lavish funeral. Why?

While a modern audience is inclined to explanations of guilt or grief, a medieval audience might interpret both Gawain's and Lancelot's actions as evidence of what Southern calls the "penetration of strong religious feeling." The sacrament of penance or confession requires three steps by the sinner: contrition of the heart, confession of the mouth or shrift, and satisfaction by deeds.[29] Although Gawain had time to make his shrift before his death (3:1231.5–6), it is the letter he writes to Lancelot that attests to the other two phases through which the penitent must pass: contrition and satisfaction. The letter confirms the contrition of heart that Gawain experiences while suggesting his desire to make satisfaction. In particular, Gawain seems to fear dying without having reconciled with his former friend and present enemy, that is, dying "oute of charite" with a member of the Christian community. The wording is John Mirk's, taken from his *Festial*, a collection of homilies that was originally intended to aid parish priests but that ranked among the most popular devotional texts of the fifteenth century. In his funeral sermon, Mirk explains that "þei þat dyeth oute of charite schal haue no parte of þe prayeress of holy chyrch."[30] In his letter to Lancelot, Gawain attempts to heal their fractured relationship. First, Gawain releases him from responsibility for death—"And I woll that all the worlde wyte that I, sir Gawayne, knyght of the Table Rounde, soughte my dethe, and nat thorow thy deservynge, but myne owne sekynge"—and then twice requests that Lancelot visit "my toumbe and pray som prayer more other les for my soul" (3:1231.15–16, 19–20, and 1232.8–10). Lancelot's prayers would indicate reconciliation with Gawain, and hence that Gawain's soul now benefits from "þe prayeress of holy chyrch." Gawain closes by signing "with parte of my harte blood" (3:1232.8). While the phrase bespeaks Gawain's emotion, it also suggests his contrition which, in confessional manuals, is always associated with language of the heart. This deathbed letter thus serves the same function as a medieval will, which was usually as much concerned with spiritual directives and requests as with distribution of property. Having repented his vengeance against Lancelot (3:1232.13 and 16–17), Gawain receives his housel and yields his spirit.

The "doleffull wordes" of Gawain's letter in turn pierce Lancelot's "harte" (3:1249.22), indicating that he, too, experiences contrition of the heart. Lancelot responds to Gawain's death with the panoply of acts of remembrance, cited above: alms-giving, recitation of masses, penance, and prayer. In addition to giving alms and having masses recited for the soul of the deceased, the church directed mourners to pray for and to perform penance for the sake of the deceased. The prayers of survivors were deemed efficacious for reducing the time of suffering in purgatory, while penance undertaken by the living was viewed as a means to resolve the deceased's incomplete satisfaction. In an action that anticipates his behavior on Guinevere and Arthur's funeral monument, Lancelot "lay two nyghtes uppon hys [Gawain's] tumbe, in prayers and in dolefull wepynge" (3:1251.6–7). In fact, the purpose behind erecting a tomb or funeral monument was to elicit prayers, as Balan explains to his brother Balin, "whan we are buryed in one tombe and the mensyon made over us how two bretheren slewe eche other, there wille never good knyght nor good man see our tombe but they wille pray for our soules" (1:90.38–91.2). It is indeed a "good knight," the best in the world, who offers prayers on Gawain's tomb, but where a modern audience sees one religious act, a medieval audience might understand two meanings: Lancelot offers prayers for the sake of the deceased and he weeps for himself, thereby expressing his own sense of contrition.[31] Gawain's funeral services, while not as extravagant as the chantries that Lancelot had proposed earlier for Gareth and Gaheris, reflect the healing of the breach of Malory's metaphoric "two bretheren": Lancelot pays for the entire funeral, dons a mourning gown, distributes the poor-dole with his own hand, and at the requiem Mass offers one hundred pounds *in memoriam*. All these funerary details—from Gawain's shrift to Lancelot's prayers at the grave—are original to Malory, appearing in neither of the major sources for this tale, *La Mort le Roi Artu* and the stanzaic *Morte Arthur*. In Malory's *Morte Darthur*, Lancelot's generosity at Gawain's funeral services sharply contrasts with his offering a mass penny for the Fair Maid of Astolat, that being the smallest possible amount for enrolling a name in a church's bede-roll, a church's annually read list of the names of deceased benefactors (2:1097.35).[32] The Fair Maid's death does not lead Lancelot to moral action or repentance; Gawain's does.

Clearly, Gawain's practice of the *ars moriendi* directs Lancelot to his own repentance. The church intended death and funeral rites to function in just this way. In his sample sermon, Mirk describes funerals as "a myrroure to vs alle" in which the Christian still living is given a reminder to repent before death.[33] Christians were advised not simply to die good deaths but to practice almsgiving, prayer, and bodily mortification, especially as atonement for deadly sin. This is the cornucopia of repentant acts that Queen Guinevere embraces in response to King Arthur's death: "And whan quene Gwenyver undirstood that kynge Arthure was dede and all the noble knyghtes . . . she lete make herselff a nunne, and wered whyght clothys and blak, and grete penaunce she toke uppon her, as ever ded synfull woman in thys londe . . . but ever she lyved in fastynge, prayers, and almes-dedis, that all maner of people mervayled how vertuously she was chaunged" (3:1243.1–10). It is in the last meeting between Guinevere and Lancelot that Southern finds "the melancholy, the sense of the sinfulness of the heart" that he takes as the mark of "the penetration of strong religious feeling." That sense of sin is evident in the speech Guinevere addresses first to her ladies and then to Lancelot:

> Thorow thys same man and me hath all thys warre be wrought, and the deth of the moste nobelest knyghtes of the worlde; for thorow oure love that we have loved togydir ys my moste noble lorde slayne. Therefore, sir Launcelot, wyte thou well I am sette in

suche a plyght to gete my soule hele. And yet I truste, thorow Goddis grace and thorow Hys Passion of Hys woundis wyde, that aftir
my deth I may have a syght of the blyssed face of Cryste Jesu, and
on Doomesday to sytte on Hys ryght syde; for as synfull as ever I
was, now ar seyntes in hevyn.   (3:1252.8–17)

The queen thus articulates the theology of atonement behind her conversion. She
sunders her relationship with Lancelot with firm resolve, explaining her conscious
choice to earn salvation through physical penitence. Thus she specifically refers
to Christ through the traditional imagery of the "Man of Sorrows," that is, to
the bleeding, crucified Savior who earned salvation through his body.[34] Guinevere's credo of freedom from sin through "Goddis grace" and "Hys Passion of hys
woundis wyde" is the Easter message. As we have seen, this doctrine also lies at
the center of the Christian's deathbed ministration. In the *Crafte and Knowledge
For to Dye Well*, the most popular of the English *ars moriendi*, the confessor asks
the dying Christian:

> Ffurst aske hem thys . . . art thow gladde that thow shalt dye in
> the feyth of Cryste? . . . The seconde interrogacion shalbe thys,
> knowelegest thow that oftyntymes and many maner off wyses and
> greuoulsy thow hast offendyd thy Lord God that made the off
> nougt. . . . The iiird interrogacion shal be thys, art thow sory in thy
> herte of all maner off synnes. . . . The fourth interrogacion shall
> be thys, purposyst thow verrayly and arte in full wyll to amende
> the. . . . The ffyfte interrogacion shall be thus, foryeuest thow fully
> all maner off men in thyn herte that euer haue doo the any harme
> or greuaunce. . . . The VIth interrogacion schal be thys, welt thow
> that all maner off thynges that thow hast in any maner off wyse
> mysgoten be fully restoryd ayene as moche as thow mayst and art
> ibounde, . . . and rather loue & forsake all thy goodes of the worlde,
> yeff thow mygth make dewe satisfaccion and noon other wyse?
> The seuenthe interrogacion schalbe thys, beleuest thou fully
> that Cryste dyed for the and that thow mayst neuer be saued, but
> be the meryte of Crystes passion.[35]

As the queen places her faith in Christ's passion and death, she ministers to her
own soul. Because she chose never to see Lancelot again with her "worldy eyen"
(3:1255.37), Guinevere can reasonably hope to see the "blyssed face of Cryste
Jesu" after death. Such a choice is not easy; after all, Malory's sympathy has long
been with the lovers, and his Guinevere swoons three times upon seeing Lancelot.
Yet Guinevere here chooses heavenly over earthly love. After her struggle and
death, the queen receives full Christian burial. Her body is transferred from the
convent at Amesbury to Glastonbury in a solemn procession recalling that of

John Paston: "And there was ordeyned an hors-bere, and so wyth an hondred torches ever brennyng aboute the cors of the quene and ever syr Launcelot with his eyght felowes wente aboute the hors-bere, syngyng and redyng many an holy oryson, and frankensens upon the corps encased" (3:1256.6–10). Her funeral services are marked by appropriate ritual, first performed by her former lover who by this point has repented and taken Holy Orders. Thus, instead of the sought-after final kiss, Lancelot earns the honor of first singing the queen's "dyryge" and "masse" (3:1256.5–6). Like Gawain's death, Guinevere's death and subsequent funeral rite provide moral instruction for Lancelot, as had her earlier repentance. As Edward Donald Kennedy comments about Lancelot, "in rejecting him, Guenevere becomes his guide."[36]

Both Gawain and Guinevere clearly articulate their sense of sin—he in his deathbed letter, she in the scene of her parting from Lancelot—and die having repented. In contrast, the sincerity of Lancelot's penitence is open to question. He takes his religious vows in imitation of the queen's, asserting "the same desteny that ye have takyn you to, I woll take me to" (3:1253.4–5). When she questions his motivation, Lancelot responds with a magnificent profession of faith—not to God but to Guinevere: "And therfore, lady, sythen ye have taken you to perfeccion, I must nedys take me to perfection, of ryght. For I take recorde of God, in you I have had myn erthly joye, and yf I had founden you now so dysposed, I had caste me to have had you into myn owne royame. But sythen I fynde you thus desposed, I ensure you faythfully, I wyl ever take me to penaunce and praye whyle my lyf lasteth" (3:1253.17–24). This is conversion by thwarted desire, as if life at the hermitage is the only choice Guinevere has left Lancelot. His request for a final kiss, his swooning at their departure, and later, his continual groveling on the king and queen's tomb, all depict a man still tied to his former passion.

There is a difference, however, between Lancelot's motives in imitation of Guinevere and his later expression of grief for Arthur and the queen. Upon rising from lamenting upon their tomb, Lancelot explains: "for my sorow was not, nor is not, for ony rejoysyng of synne, but my sorow may never have ende. For whan I remembre *of hir beaulté and of hir noblesse*, that was bothe with hyr kyng and with hyr, . . . truly myn herte wold not serve to susteyne my careful body. Also whan I remembre me how by my defaute and myn orgule and my pryde that they were bothe layed ful lowe . . . sanke so to myn herte that I myght not susteyne myself" (3:1256.27–38, italics mine). In the phrase "hir beaulté and of hir noblesse," Malory's use of "hir" is beautifully ambiguous. The ambiguity of the possessive pronoun derives from the frequent confusion of Middle English "her"—deriving form Old English *hir(e)* and meaning "her"—and Middle English *her(e)*, deriving from Old English *heora* and meaning "their." This plural possessive frequently is spelled as "hir."[37] Malory typically uses "their" or "theyr" for the plural possessive, but according to Kato's *Concordance* there are numerous exceptions,[38] one such case being when "sir Mellyagaunt charged the queen and all her knyghtes that none of hir felyshyp shulde departe frome her" (3:1123.29–30). In this case the possessive "her" refers to the queen's knights but "hir" refers to "their"—that is, the knights'—fellowship. In the scene of Lancelot's grief, Malory either uses "hir" to refer to both the queen and king's beauty and nobility, a point he clarifies in the next clause when he separately refers to Guinevere and Arthur ("that was bothe with hyr kyng and with hyr"); or uses "hir" in the first clause as the singular possessive referring to Guinevere and in the second clause as clarifying the point that his grief extends to both the king and queen. In either case of grammatical construal, at first reading/hearing, the audience might assume Lancelot grieves for Guinevere, but Lancelot's adjective "bothe" shows that he in fact laments for king and queen. Whereas at their parting Lancelot had considered only Guinevere, seven years later his focus has shifted to include both the queen and king and, more important, to highlight the sin of pride—"myn orgule and my pryde"—that he committed. At his final meeting with the queen, Lancelot had not acknowledged any sin on his part. After Guinevere's death, however, the language in which Lancelot expresses his memories insistently bespeaks his atonement, as the queen's had earlier. Lancelot expresses not simply grief for his queen (and king) but the profound pain of contrition, with its emphasis on the language of the heart.

Lancelot lives on longer than all other principal characters of the *Morte Darthur* and hence has longer to repent. After his departure from Guinevere, Lancelot "endured in grete penaunce syx yere," putting on "th'abyte of preesthode" in the seventh (3:1255.3–4). As I have argued in detail elsewhere, Malory articulates Lancelot's acts of atonement more clearly than do his sources and emphasizes hagiographic details indicating that Lancelot earns his final reward.[39] As we have seen in the cases of Gawain and Guinevere, the third stage of atonement is satisfaction for sin. Chaucer's Parson explains that the sinner works satisfaction (appropriate expiation of his/her sins) through "almesse and bodily peyne."[40] Both in confessional manuals like *The Parson's Tale* and in saints' lives, "bodily peyne" or ascetic practices are linked with repentance of the sins of the flesh; in particular, food deprivation is associated with the healing of lechery, of which adultery is a subspecies.[41] This is the "bodily peine" that Lancelot embraces unrelentingly after Guinevere's burial beside Arthur: "Thenne syr Launcelot never after ete but lytel mete, nor dranke, tyl he was dede, for than he seekened more and more and dryed and dwyned awaye" (3:1257.1–3). Critics who interpret Lancelot's acts outside of the late medieval religious context find only undying, if morbid, commitment to the queen. Against the backdrop of penitence, however, the same acts testify to the necessary pain of atonement and to the body as the locus of salvation.[42] It is as hard for Lancelot to repent sin as to leave the queen, for the acts are one and the same, and his attraction to her is so strong that he must continue to repent, even after her death. Malory thus increases the pathos of Lancelot's penitence by layering grief, guilt, and asceticism. After death, Lancelot's corpse is transported "in the same hors-bere that quene Guenevere was layed in tofore that she was buryed" (3:1258.22–23). This association echoes in two registers, the secular-romantic and the sacred-religious, recalling Lancelot's thwarted earthly love and the inevitability of his death in the face of eternity. Lancelot prepares for death as the Christian ought and as both Gawain and Guinevere had before him, with repentance on earth.

Death comes to Lancelot in the seventh year of his penitence. His death scene recalls Galahad's, with a vision of angels "heaving" Lancelot's soul "unto heven, and the yates of heven opened ayenst hym" (3:1258.9–10; cf. 2:1035.14–16). Although at every point Malory increases the hagiographic details that suggest Lancelot's heavenly reward, he does not leave us long at this mystical height. He soon reports the material details of Lancelot's funeral. Malory's hero is conveyed to burial at the castle of Joyous Garde with the kind of rich spectacle beloved by fifteenth-century gentlemen and nobles: Lancelot's face is bared (and therefore, his body must have been embalmed), and a hundred torches burn around his corpse until it is put to rest in the choir of the castle's chapel, as were the bodies of his fictive counterpart, Gawain, and his historic counterpart, the Earl of Warwick, in their respective castles.[43] Lancelot is given a secular rather than a monastic send off, but the mixing of Christian panoply and Ector's chivalric eulogy does not negate religious meaning, as some have claimed. If modern readers attend to the other details of the death and funeral practices accompanying Lancelot's end, they are led to the truth at the center of Ector's final evaluation of the hero: "and thou were the trewest lover, of a synful man, that ever loved woman" (3:1259.14–15). Between the matching terms "trewest lover" and "loved woman" lies "a synful man," now redeemed. In a persuasive analysis of Malory's use of Christian exempla in the Poisoned Apple and the Healing of Sir Urry, Kenneth Hodges argues that "the richness of Malory's religious engagement is not in the simple statement of abstract theological principles but in the application of such abstract principles to the complications of romantic and political life."[44]

Malory's shifting of "the responsibility of moral interpretation" to the reader, whether a member of a fifteenth-century audience or a twenty-first-century Malory scholar,[45] simply will not allow a separation of ideals into sacred and secular categories. After all, the death for which the book is named is patterned on a biblical model: Bedivere's actions with Arthur's sword clearly recall Peter's denial of Christ,[46] and Arthur's status as "rex quondam rexque futurus" hints at Christological resurrection (3:1242.29). And yet, in terms of funeral practice, King Arthur dies unconfessed, unhouseled, and unanointed. In terms of the question of Christianity, Malory's world has never been an either-or, secular or sacred, but both heroic and religious, and in the case of Arthur's death, pagan and Christian. Nonetheless, it is Arthur who, in details original to Malory, helps the weakened Gawain sit up to offer shrift and write his letter; who insists on Gawain receiving "hys sacrament"; and who, retreating to the Celtic mists of Avalon, begs Bors "and if thou here nevermore of me, pray for my soule!" (3:1231.4–6, 1232.13, 1240.34–35). Demonstrating belief in the efficacy of Christian death ritual, Gawain repents on his deathbed; Guinevere as she dies prays never again to see the source of her temptation, Sir Lancelot, for the remainder of her life. At the very least, these and myriad other details in *Morte Darthur* refer to authentic fifteenth-century deathbed and funeral practice. More than that, these funerary details point to Malory's naturally embracing a series of Christian beliefs: the immortality of the soul, the efficacy of prayer, the practice of deathbed ministration and of acts of penitence preceding death, and, most important, heavenly reward for those who have atoned. The shaping of these characters' ends hints at lived practice, to which Malory testifies when, in the final explicit, he seeks prayer for his own soul (3:1260.24). In sequence, Gawain, Arthur, Guinevere, and Lancelot receive such prayers from their survivors. More than mere furnishings, their deaths—narrated in Malory's beautiful, understated style—lay bare the medieval Christian's final struggle for atonement. This critic reads in the very furnishings of the *Morte Darthur*'s great death scenes an interior home for the repentant heart.

NOTES

1. Southern, *Making of the Middle Ages*, pp. 245–46.

2. See, for example, Grimm, "Knightly Love," pp. 76–95.

3. Tolhurst, "Why Every Knight." For the same idea, see Cooper, *English Romance in Time*, p. 322. K. S. Whetter argued that Malory's Arthuriad is a hybrid romance, a "tragic romance," in his *Understanding Genre*, pp. 99–149.

4. On romantic love, see Janet Jesmok's essay in this volume; on male fellowship see the essay by Whetter, also in this volume.

5. Tolhurst, "Why Every Knight," p. 145. For the term "divided loyalties" as employed by earlier critics, see Brewer's introduction to *"Morte Darthur," Parts Seven and Eight*, pp. 26–29; Lambert, *Malory: Style and Vision*, pp. 176–78; Lundie, "Divided Allegiance," pp. 93–111; and McCarthy, *Introduction to Malory*, pp. 88–90.

6. See Brewer's introduction to *"Morte Darthur," Parts Seven and Eight*, pp. 31–33, and Guerin, "'Tale of the Death of Arthur,'" pp. 269–74.

7. Riddy, *Sir Thomas Malory*, pp. 113–38.

8. Noted in the essay by Hanks in this volume.

9. Cherewatuk, "Malory's Launcelot."

10. Cherewatuk, "Saint's Life of Sir Launcelot," pp. 70–73.

11. Hodges, "Haunting Pieties."

12. Here and throughout, I refer parenthetically to the 1990 Vinaver-Field edition (Malory, *Works*, 3rd rev. ed). All quotations from Malory's text come from this edition and will be noted parenthetically by volume, page, and line numbers.

13. See also 1:67.5–6, 1:77.33, 1:90.30–32, 2:1097.34–35, etc.

14. Batt, *Malory's "Morte Darthur,"* p. 134.

15. Using the evidence of wills, Colin Richmond argued in the 1970s and 1980s for

the elites' individualist practice of faith in the fifteenth century. In contrast, Eamon Duffy used parish records to argue in the 1990s for the communal nature of fifteenth-century piety. A representative work by Richmond is "Religion and the Fifteenth-Century English Gentleman" (1984); Duffy's work led to his well-known *Stripping of the Altars* (1992). For Christine Carpenter's mediation of this debate, see her "Religion."

16. In this and the subsequent paragraphs, my summary of deathbed practice and funeral rituals derives from H. S. Bennett, *Pastons and Their England*, pp. 196–207, and Duffy, *Stripping of the Altars*, pp. 302–78.

17. Julian of Norwich, *Shewings*, 3.73–74 and 98–99.

18. Kempe, *Book of Margery Kempe*, 7.29–30.

19. Duffy, *Stripping of the Altars*, pp. 314-18. Rebecca Reynolds has applied the *ars moriendi* to Malory in her article, "Elaine of Ascolat's Death."

20. Malory refers to the moment of transubstantiation or "sakeryng(e)" four times in the Grail Quest, at 2:926.19, 2:1015.30, 2:1029.22, 2:1034.17.

21. Kempe, *Book of Margery Kempe*, 7.16–17.

22. The coinage *viaticum* metaphorically embraces the notion of provision for the journey to the next life.

23. Aquinas, *Summa Theologiae* Suppl.29.1. See also Suppl.32.2 on the sacrament's preparing the Christian for immediate glory and Suppl.32.6 on the purpose of anointing various sense organs of the body.

24. As noted by Brewer in his "Death in Malory's *Le Morte Darthur*," p. 50.

25. Duffy, *Stripping of the Altars*, p. 359.

26. *Paston Letters, 1422–1509*, ed. Gairdner, vol. 4, no. 673. In n. 3 on p. 226, Gairdner cites the "very long but narrow roll" containing this list from Francis Blomefield's eleven-volume *History of Norfolk*, which was published by Blomefield 1736 and 1752 and continued after his death by Charles Parkin. Given that the roll had been lost prior to Gairdner's 1904 publication, Norman Davis does not print it in his definitive two-volume edition of the *Paston Letters and Papers of the Fifteenth Century*. However, the details of John Paston's funeral, as transcribed by Blomefield, are entirely in keeping with practices for members of his estate.

27. *Paston Letters, 1422–1509*, ed. Gairdner, vol. 4, no. 637, p. 228. After the funeral, the candles were typically donated to the church to be used to light the altar during the consecration, a practical gift as well as a visual reminder of the deceased's continued presence at the Eucharistic table (Duffy, *Stripping of the Altars*, pp. 332–33 and 361–62).

28. Sir John Fastolf had no direct heir and left the bulk of his land to his friend and legal advisor, John Paston, on condition that he found a single college at Caister Castle whose residents would provide prayer for his soul in perpetuity. This college never came to fruition both because of the legal imbroglio over Fastolf's will and because of the sheer expense of founding even a single independent institution, as opposed to establishing a chantry in an already existing church or monastery.

In 1456 Fastolf's nephew, Henry Fillongley, reported to him that, in addition to the landed endowment and the cost of the license from the king, "they would ask you for every 100 marks [value of land], that you amortize 500 marks." See Virgoe, *Private Life in the Fifteenth Century*, p. 104. For the version of the will on which John Paston based his claim to Fastolf's estates, with Fastolf's insistence on a college of seven monks or priests, see *Paston Letters*, ed. Davis, 1:88.6–26. Fastolf's endowment was eventually transferred to Magdalen College, Oxford.

29. For a brief summary of the stages of confession and the language associated therewith as applied to Malory's Lancelot, see Cherewatuk, "Malory's Launcelot."

30. Mirk, *Mirk's Festial*, 295.5–6.

31. In the Christian tradition, tears have long been associated with contrition or compunction of the heart. See McEntire, *Doctrine of Compunction*.

32. The bede-roll was the list (roll) of donors to the fabric of a church. On All Soul's Day the entire bede-roll was read aloud, and it was referred to at a parish's guild meetings and each Sunday at the "bidding of bedes" (Duffy, *Stripping of the Altars*, pp. 153–44 and 334–37).

33. Mirk, *Mirk's Festial*, 294.1–6.

34. Twomey, "*Sir Gawain*, Death, and the Devil," pp. 76 and 86–88.

35. David William Atkinson, *English "Ars Moriendi,"* pp. 9–11. The version of the *Crafte and Knowledge for to Dye Well* that I cite was printed by Malory's editor, William Caxton, in 1490. See Atkinson, p. xiii.

36. Edward Donald Kennedy, "Malory's Guenevere," p. 128.

37. See the *Middle English Dictionary*, hir(e) 1 and her(e) 2.

38. The following examples of Malory using Middle English "hir" as Modern English "their" are found in Kato's *Concordance to the Works of Sir Thomas Malory*: 21.13, 23.13, 23.16, 25.22, 25.23, 26.15, 26.20, 26.33, 27.3, 27.6, 27.8, 27.16, 31.30, 32.27, 34.23, 35.36, 36.16, 36.19, 39.9, 39.21, 40.13, 50.23, 50.29, 51.33, 55.35, 76.29, 108.34, 111.33, 120.22, 128.2, 128.19, 128.28, 128.29, 131.35, 131.36, 137.7, 139.6, 161.2, 161.3, 164.12, 200.11, 203.18, 205.20, 211.22, 211.27, 216.16, 216.29, 220.34, 221.22, 223.2, 229.17, 229.24, 230.2, 231.11, 233.20, 234.8, 234.9, 235.6, 238.4, 238.11, 238.21, 239.9, 240.17, 241.16, 243.25, 244.1, 263.13, 265.34, 267.12, 271.1, 276.16, 296.37, 302.8, 347.23, 354.35, 475.28, 489.29, 603.13, 618.29, 619.1, 733.2, 853.3, 868.12, 871.12, 871.13, 906.22, 906.23, 941.18, 1123.29; and as "hyr" at 70.5.

39. Cherewatuk, "Saint's Life of Sir Launcelot," pp. 68–73.

40. See Chaucer, *Parson's Tale*, in *Riverside Chaucer*, p. 325, line 1028.

41. Cherewatuk, "Malory's Launcelot," p. 69.

42. Bynum, "Why All the Fuss about the Body?," p. 15.

43. Brewer, "Death in Malory's *Le Morte Darthur*," p. 255.

44. See also Hodges, "Haunting Pieties," p. 45: "This final recognition that Launcelot cannot save himself by his own greatness diminishes his knightly stature (literally: he loses a cubit in height due to his asceticism [3.1257; XX.12]), but it is the necessary step toward salvation."

45. Hodges, "Haunting Pieties," p. 30.

46. Matt. 26:69–76, Mark 14:66–73, Luke 22:55–62, John 18:25–27.

Rhetoric, Ritual, and Religious Impulse in Malory's Book 8

Janet Jesmok

Religious impulse dominates "The Most Piteous Tale of the Morte Arthur Saunz Guerdon," book 8 of Sir Thomas Malory's *Le Morte Darthur*. Guinevere becomes a nun and an abbess, Lancelot becomes a priest, and his faithful followers take on religious habits. Malory uses religious rhetoric, ritual, and imagery to describe these conversions, suggesting, perhaps, that his epic romance has become hagiography or a religious tract. But have these characters found salvation within a conventional Christian context? C. David Benson comments that "Malory constantly uses the language of Christianity and describes his heroes going to heaven, but he has no real interest in the metaphysical."[1] His comment, I think, must be tempered. Malory does have an abiding interest in the metaphysics of salvation, as D. Thomas Hanks, Jr., discusses in this volume.[2] Further, although Malory's knights' pursuit of religious life reinforces secular homosocial bonds, as Benson argues, Queen Guinevere reveals a clear understanding of sin and salvation. Finally, her movement toward God moves Lancelot and his followers to at least the ritual of religious life, and she leads Lancelot, Malory's abiding interest, to sanctity; Guinevere succeeds where even the saintly Galahad failed. But Malory's religion is usually grounded in *this* life, not the next. His major characters find salvation because they love the things of this world, even as they leave them behind: Lancelot is battered into holiness by his intense love for Arthur, the fellowship, and Guinevere, who, as Malory says, "was a trew lover, and therefor she had a good ende."[3] Malory's conventional Christianity is not always persuasive, but his web of religion, myth, courtly service, and secular chivalry provides an artistically satisfying conclusion that is true to his characters and to this long, complex work.

To understand Malory's religious impulse in book 8, we must first explore his more general view of religion and spirituality and his use of Lancelot du Lake as the crucible of religious and secular conflict. Malory first grapples with religious issues in "The Tale of the Sankgreal" (2:847–1037). Although he attempts to simulate the French *Queste*'s spiritual world when following Sir Galahad and the

Grail knights, his deletions and emphases indicate a secular, chivalric preference. Elizabeth Edwards sees "an entrenched tension between the apparently clerical (possibly Cistercian) aims of redemption and didacticism and the 'knightly' aims of romance. . . . Malory, writing as a knight as he so obtrusively does, occupies a position more like that of the knights he writes about than that of hermits who explain the knights."[4] And so, as is often the case in the *Morte*, Lancelot dominates dramatic interest, embodying the conflicts between religious and secular chivalry. In his treatment of Lancelot's Grail Quest, Malory demonstrates his affinity for the fighting man. Lancelot strives to become part of the holy brotherhood primarily because it represents another quest, a way of proving his worship. His love of this world's beauties and values pulls him back from the spiritual, as readers have often observed.[5] As Lancelot himself says, "whan I sought worldly adventures for worldely desyres I ever encheved them. . . . And now I take uppon me the adventures to seke of holy thynges, now I se and undirstonde that myne olde synne hyndryth me and shamyth me, that I had no power to stirre nother speke whan the holy bloode appered before me" (2:896.2–9). But even in this insightful moment, worldly things mitigate his sorrow: daylight comes and he "harde the fowlys synge; than somwhat he was comforted" (2:896.10–11).[6] Later, at perhaps the height of his Grail experience, Lancelot spends a month on the Grail ship with the corpse of Perceval's sister, "susteyned with the grace of the Holy Goste" (2:1011.30). But instead of being rapt in a timeless spiritual experience, Lancelot becomes bored: "And so on a nyght he wente to play hym by the watirs syde, for he was somwhat wery of the shippe" (2:1011.31–1012.1). Lancelot tries to give himself completely to the quest for spiritual enlightenment, but his very essence undermines the transformation. This wavering in religious pursuits has caused many to see Lancelot as unstable, a trait that may be a tragic flaw but may also be his salvation.

Lancelot's stability (or lack of it) is central to his character development, to his education through suffering, and, ultimately, to his salvation, but critics have failed to agree about this slippery term, which Malory uses in various ways. Mary Hynes-Berry sees Lancelot's instability as "basically a chivalric failing. Capable of great deeds of arms, Lancelot has been motivated time and again not by the true Christian's [*sic*] knight's concern for advancing the greater honour and glory of God but by a selfish interest in aggrandisement."[7] In other words, Lancelot sometimes fails to remember that chivalric excellence is God's gift to be used for God's purposes. Even though the "quarell muste com of thy lady" (3:1119.29), the cause must be just. In contrast, Edward Donald Kennedy defines Lancelot's instability as "his inability to renounce the unstable world that he must abandon if he is to be saved."[8] Because Lancelot's unstable world revolves around Guinevere, he again becomes enmeshed in worldly things after the Grail Quest. If instability means *not* renouncing the world, then stability suggests turning toward the spiritual, as

Dhira Mahoney argues. For her, Malory uses the term "stability" in a religious context, denoting piety, honesty, or goodness: "Malory is not simply confusing stability with holiness. . . . In the context of his Sankgreal, stability means persever-ance in the pursuit of holiness, and connotes withdrawal from the world"; in this, Mahoney agrees with Kennedy.[9] Lancelot's instability, then, signals his failure to devote himself to God, to use his gifts for God's purposes, and to remain true to his Grail promises by ending his illicit relationship with Guinevere.

Yet a few years later, Dhira Mahoney says of Lancelot in book 8 that the "instability that the Grail hermits accused him of is in fact a magnificent integ-rity," suggesting that his inability to renounce Guinevere is admirable.[10] If not virtuous, his fault is nonetheless fortunate because it produces his transforming torment. He is torn between his beloved chivalry, which centers in the queen, and the spiritual excellence he strives for in the Grail Quest, embodied in Galahad. His profound sensitivity to both worlds is, finally, what saves him, not only in the narrative but also as a character. For what would he be without this excruciating conflict? Tristram? Galahad? Neither character captures the reader's imagination the way Lancelot does. His pain reflects our own as he tries to balance reli-gious ideals with earthly passions. The idea that stability—his tenacious loyalty to Guinevere and knighthood—finally saves Lancelot is early suggested by C. S. Lewis, who sees Malory substituting knightly virtue for religious devotion.[11] Lancelot, stable in his devotion to the queen, therefore remains the greatest of earthly knights, notwithstanding his Grail failures. Although readers such as Alfred Kraemer view Lancelot's return to religion in book 8 as a continuation of his Grail experiences and a second chance to reject Guinevere for higher aspira-tions, I will argue that he is saved not by rejecting the queen but by his unwaver-ing devotion to her.[12]

Malory's best-known usage of "stability" supports this view. In the famous May passage on virtuous love that opens "The Knight of the Cart" episode in Vinaver's book 7, Malory describes its importance: "For, lyke as wynter rasure dothe allway arace and deface grene summer, so faryth hit by unstable love in man and woman, for in many persones there ys no stabylité: for [w]e may se all day, for a lytyll blaste of wyntres rasure, anone we shall deface and lay aparte trew love, for lytyll or nowght, that coste muche thynge. Thys ys no wysedome nother no stabyl-ité, but hit ys fyeblenes of nature and grete disworshyp, whosomever usyth thys" (3:1119.14–21).

Reading "stability" in a secular context, Dorsey Armstrong persuasively argues that Lancelot is extremely stable, his allegiance grounded in *this* world, with the "stabylité" of virtuous love.[13] He lapses only when he attempts to achieve the Grail. Although he fails, the Grail Quest begins the necessary suffering that will refine his character in book 8. This stability becomes Lancelot's triumph and salvation as he follows Guinevere to a spiritual level of courteous devotion, ascending the ladder of love, achieving the ideal of courtly worship. Lancelot never refutes his fidelity to Guinevere and secular chivalry, although she, I think, misinterprets his motives when she responds to his commitment to follow her in holy penitence: "A, sir Launcelot, if ye woll do so and holde thy promyse! But I may never beleve you . . . but that ye woll turne to the worlde agayne" (3:1253.7–9). She doesn't see that he loves *her*, not the world itself. Once she withdraws, he no longer cares for worldly things. Although he says that "in the queste of the Sankgreall I had that tyme forsakyn the vanytees of the worlde, had nat youre love bene" (3:1253.13–14), still his choices content him; he would not trade his life for Galahad's. Similarly, Malory, like his hero, remains faithful to chivalric values, even when depicting the pinnacle of spiritual experience in the Grail Quest.[14] His religious vision rises above the mundane, but it never seems to penetrate the next world.

In book 8 Malory remains ambivalent about conventional religion in his portrayal first of Arthur's passing and then of Guinevere's and Lancelot's deaths and the fellowship's dissolution. For most readers, the passing of Arthur represents the *Morte*'s climactic moment. This quintessential mythic scene in which the wounded king disappears in the mist to be healed on the Isle of Avalon completes Arthur's narrative and fulfills the promise of Caxton's title. Although in Malory's *Morte*, Arthur's demise intertwines religious, literary, and mythic motifs, the literary and mythic dominate, with religion largely in the rhetoric.[15] For example, in "The Vengeance of Sir Gawain," Arthur twice calls himself a Christian king (3:1183.9, 1184.6), and various characters invoke God or Jesus at key moments. In his postmortem appearance, Gawain credits God with the opportunity to speak to Arthur: "Thus much hath gyvyn me leve God for to warne you of youre dethe" (3:1234.6–7). Arthur, not realizing that Gawain is a ghost, thanks God for his nephew's return: "now I se the on lyve, much am I beholdyn unto Allmyghty Jesu" (3:1233.32–33). After the battle, Lucan sees Arthur's survival as God's will, warns him of Gawain's prophecy of the king's death, and pleads with him to abandon his vengeance: "and yet God of Hys grete goodnes hath preserved you hyddirto. And for Goddes sake, my lorde, leve of thys, for, blyssed be God, ye have won the fylde" (3:1236.32–1237.1). For Lucan, Arthur's survival is his best revenge. But when Arthur sees "an hondred thousand leyde dede upon the downe," he responds with anger: "Than was kynge Arthure wode wroth oute of mesure, whan he saw hys people so slayne frome hym." He calls on God rhetorically, as most of us do when facing pain or tragedy—"Jesu mercy! . . . where ar all my noble knyghtes becom?"—but his aim is vengeance: "But wolde to God . . . that I wyste now where were that traytoure sir Mordred that hath caused all thys myschyff" (3:1236.9–11, 16–21). In seeking revenge, he goes against the Christian message of forgiveness and the Old Testament warning that vengeance belongs only to God.

Notwithstanding religious rhetoric, in his final actions Arthur embodies the epic warlord. Preparing to attack Mordred with his spear, he speaks like a pagan warrior: "Now tyde me dethe, tyde me lyff . . . now I se hym yondir alone, he shall never ascape myne hondes!" (3:1237.5–6). In the midst of a sea of slain warriors, Arthur chooses vengeance, killing Mordred and receiving a death wound rather than preserving his own life by taking Lucan's advice. Now with one lone companion, Arthur returns Excalibur to the Lady of the Lake, ending his tenure wielding the sword of kingship. The tragically isolated hero who descends the Wheel of Fortune recalls Beowulf rather than a Christian leader or saint. His lone companion Bedivere, after years of devotion to his worldly king, is left, like Wiglaf and the Wanderer, with nothing. He cries out to Arthur: "A, my lorde Arthur, what shall becom of me, now ye go frome me and leve me here alone amonge myne enemyes?" Arthur replies: "Comforte thyselff . . . and do as well as thou mayste, for in me ys no truste for to truste in" (3:1240.29–32). Arthur says nothing of the next world, of God, Christ, penitence, or salvation, expressions that Guinevere's later conversion proves Malory fully capable of. Arthur acknowledges another life only in asking Bedivere to pray for his soul (3:1240.34–35). Vinaver notes the sense of "unrelieved loneliness" in this scene: "There is no remedy for Arthur's wounds, and no truth in the belief in his eventual return. 'I wyl not say that it shal be so.' And when night falls on the plain of Salisbury there is no 'trust left to trust in', no comfort to be found in religious explanations; all doctrine shrivels before the conflict of 'two goods' and the desolation it brings" (1:xcix). With Christianity largely in the rhetoric, Malory presents the desolation of Gethsemane without the redemption.

Malory, unlike King Arthur, offers some religious solace here, as he will after Lancelot's death. Bedivere comes upon a hermitage, meets the former bishop of Canterbury, and decides to turn to a life of prayer and fasting, like one of those knight-hermits who populate the Grail world. Malory here unites the hermitage and the court through ritual. Bedivere takes on holy garb and assumes the bishop's actions, extending the chivalric brotherhood into religious life. But, seemingly impatient, Malory quickly shifts the narrative back to worldly and mythic concerns, especially to Arthur's fame and legacy. He speaks again of the magic ship; of Morgan le Fay, Nyneve, and other magical ladies; of his favored Sir Pelleas, whom Nyneve protected; and finally of uncertainty regarding Arthur. No one sees the corpse, only a fresh grave, and Malory gives us hope: "yet som men say in many partys of Inglonde that kynge Arthure ys nat dede, but had by the wyll of Oure Lorde Jesu into another place; and men say that he shall com agayne, and he shall wynne the Holy Crosse" (3:1242.22–25). The narrator expresses hope for Arthur's return, not for his eternal rest or joy in heaven. Although the rhetoric is tinged with religion—if Arthur survives it is the Lord's will; his next quest will be finding the True Cross—the spirit is heroic and chivalric. Later, with Lancelot's death,

Malory creates a similar pattern: the remaining knights move toward a brother-hood on a higher plane, yet one united by earthly companionship, not theological belief. But first we must look at the only character who belies this generalization, Queen Guinevere.

Only Guinevere fully appreciates the world-change after Arthur's death; she assesses the situation, decides on her future, and, consequently, points the remaining few in a new direction. She accepts full responsibility for Camelot's tragedy—"Thorow thys same man and me hath all thys warre be wrought, and the deth of the moste nobelest knyghtes of the worlde; for thorow oure love that we have loved togydir ys my moste noble lorde slayne" (3:1252.8–11)—and then, armed with Christian belief, she faces her future: "And yet I truste, thorow God-dis grace and thorow Hys Passion of Hys woundis wyde, that aftir my deth I may have a syght of the blyssed face of Cryste Jesu, and on Doomesday to sytte on Hys ryght syde" (3:1252.13–16). In contrast with her earlier crises, where she sees her fate joined with Lancelot's,[16] here she meets her destiny alone. Unlike Arthur's passing, where hope lies only in his bodily return to the world, here faith perme-ates the queen's mortal solitude and imbues her language with religious thought.[17] Her vision transcends this world; as she imagines the next, although her imagery is tactile—"Hys woundis wyde . . . the blyssed face of Cryste Jesu . . . Hys ryght syde"—her sight perceives the supernatural.

In a touching speech, Guinevere's rhetoric, which invokes the major tenets of Christian belief regarding death and the afterlife, strongly counters C. David Benson's assessment that the queen changes only her clothing, never leaving the Round Table's values behind.[18] Her serious sins have brought trag-edy on those she loves, but she makes no excuses. Her salvation lies in contrition and absolution; God's grace and Christ's blood will heal her soul. She refuses to despair that her sin is too grave to be forgiven: "for as synfull as ever I was, now ar seyntes in hevyn" (3:1252.16–17). She prepares herself for the Beatific Vision and a place on God's right hand, humbly trusting in God's grace and the miracle of the Incarnation to effect her healing.[19] Knowing that she must abandon the fruits of her sin, she banishes Lancelot for the last time, for once with complete sincerity. As she prepares for God's kingdom, she advises her former lover to turn toward his earthly one: "And to thy kyngedom loke thou turne agayne, and kepe well thy realme frome warre and wrake" (3:1252.21–23). Notably, in spite of Lancelot's Grail aspirations, she sees him as more earth-bound than she. She asks only for his prayers, again affirming her need for grace in order to be saved. No one in the *Morte* demonstrates a deeper understanding of Christian belief than Guinevere. Malory uses the queen as a model for the other characters and as a catalyst for Lancelot's conversion.[20] As she led Arthur in courtly refinement and Lancelot in courteous love, now she instructs the few survivors in eschatology.

Like all Malory's major characters, however, Guinevere is tethered to this world. As Arthur laments his lost knights, as Lancelot despairs over his beloved king and queen's demise, so Guinevere grieves over Arthur's death and his kingdom's dissolution. Her grief leads to penitence, which centers in her turning away from Lancelot's physical being, always, in the last book, a source of palpable distress. Her renunciation, one of the *Morte*'s most moving moments, signals Malory's preoccupation with the body and its troubling relationship with spirituality. In her study of the Grail Quest, Jill Mann argues that "[i]t is because the intact, inviolate, virgin body is an image of spiritual wholeness that sexual temptations loom so large in the adventures of the Grail knights."[21] If the virginal body signifies integrity in the Grail Quest, at the end of Malory's work, the fragmented body, which has fallen to sexual temptation, emerges as the enemy to be resisted, not to protect virginity but to extirpate the sensual, even the sensuous. Malory reveals the crushing cost for Guinevere in rejecting Lancelot and turning toward God: "And therefore, sir Launcelot, I requyre the and beseche the hartily, for all the love that ever was betwyxt us, that thou never se me no more in the visayge. . . . for as well as I have loved the heretofore, myne harte woll nat serve now to se the" (3:1252.17–24). Her torment focuses on his visage, his bodily presence, the physical lineaments that identify her beloved. As the courtly lover loves first through the eyes, that love now must be dispatched through absence of vision, the symbolic arrow of love torn away. So Guinevere tries to obscure her earthly vision, to put Lancelot out of eyesight so that her illicit love can no longer tempt her. In her last recorded words, she beseeches "Almyghty God that I may never have power to see syr Launcelot wyth my worldly eyen!" (3:1255.36–37). She must close her eyes to *this* world so that she can open them to the next. But the price is heavy: "for there was lamentacyon as they had be stungyn wyth sperys, and many tymes they swouned. And the ladyes bare the quene to hir chambre" (3:1253.31–33). The arrows of love have become the spears of death. In rejecting Lancelot's physical being, Guinevere fails to control her own body and must be carried away. Fittingly, the lovers' deep devotion culminates in this powerful and poignant physical severance. And as we shall see, Lancelot will literally leave his body behind to follow Guinevere.

As always, except when pursuing the Grail, Lancelot allows his queen to lead—"But the same desteny that ye have takyn you to, I woll take me to, for to please Jesu, and ever for you I caste me specially to pray" (3:1253.4–6)—but his movement away from chivalry and toward the Christian life of the spirit is, like his character throughout the *Morte*, problematic. C. David Benson, following Vinaver, observes of Lancelot's vocation: "Jesus is mentioned, but he seems decidedly secondary. The language is religious, but the motive is Lancelot's devotion to the queen."[22] Lancelot's own words underscore his conflicted quest for spirituality: "And therfore, lady, sythen ye have taken you to perfeccion, I must nedys take me to perfection, of ryght. For I take recorde of God, in you I have had myn erthly joye, and yf I had founden you now so dysposed, I had caste me to have had you into myn owne royame" (3:1253.17–22). Clearly, his first desire is to continue his loving relationship with Guinevere now that she is free. Even after her rebuff, he still asks for a parting kiss.[23] The devastating events of Arthur's death and the kingdom's destruction have not affected Lancelot as they have Guinevere. While she assumes responsibility for the tragedy and moves toward penitence, he wants to get on with his (or their) life, to begin again. When finally convinced of her renunciation, however, he follows like a good soldier. Yet his embrace of religious life hides a reality grounded more in "erthly joye" than in the pursuit of perfection.[24]

Malory wants to make a saint of Lancelot, but he doesn't seem to know how.[25] In the last book, Lancelot's religious impulses are at first conventional. Religious rhetoric laces his dialogue, especially in times of stress. When the plotters, led by Mordred and Aggravaine, discover him in Guinevere's chamber, Lancelot often invokes God or Jesus: he cries out that with armor "I shall sone stynte their malice, by the grace of God!" (3:1165.26–27); when his attackers create a noisy scene, he calls on "Jesu mercy" for quiet (3:1166.8–11). Later, he calls Guinevere "[m]oste nobelest Crysten quene" (3:1166.13), and when she speaks of her death, he exclaims: "That shall never be. . . . God deffende me frome such a shame! But, Jesu Cryste, be Thou my shylde and myne armoure!" (3:1167.4–6). This language is surprising for a man supposedly caught in adultery, but as Helen Cooper recently observed, "Malory's God is on the side of the lovers."[26] Confirming his many attempts to exonerate the lovers, Malory uses religious rhetoric to create the feeling that Lancelot and Guinevere are indeed innocents caught in a treacherous web.

Back in Arthur's realm after the Siege of Benwick, Lancelot, in his exhibition of grief, follows Christian orthodoxy. He visits Gawain's tomb and prays for his soul, offers one hundred pounds for masses for Gawain's salvation, and gives alms with his own hands (3:1250.24–1251.5). After Gawain's requiem Mass, Lancelot "lay two nyghtes upon hys tumbe, in prayers and in dolefull wepynge" (3:1251.6–7). These demonstrations of religious fervor, however, soon turn to asceticism, and finally to something more extreme. After meeting Guinevere for the last time, Lancelot first becomes a recluse, leaving all his worldly possessions and accomplishments behind. He prays, fasts, confesses, and asks the bishop of Canterbury to take him as a brother (3:1254.13–18), following Bedivere's path after Arthur's death. But he soon abandons the good works of a lay Christian and assumes a religious habit, later becoming a priest. Lancelot successfully performs the rituals of penitence and the priesthood—"I wyl ever take me to penaunce and praye whyle my lyf lasteth. . . . and there [the bishop of Canterbury] put an habyte upon syr Launcelot. And there he servyd God day and nyght with prayers and

fastynges" (3:1253.23–24, 1254.16–18)—but Malory never reveals what motivates Lancelot's religious conversion, as he does with Guinevere. What he shows
instead, after Guinevere's death, is Lancelot's unremitting pain, to the point of
despair. Instead of finding joy in faith and anticipation of the next world, both
for him and the queen, Lancelot is overcome by grief, focusing only on worldly
loss. As Vinaver writes, "[h]e repents not of the sins he has committed against
God, but of the griefs he has caused his lady and King Arthur. And so there is no
relief to his pain" (1:xcix). Groveling on the tomb of Arthur and Guinevere, he is
inconsolable. F. Whitehead rightly observes that the "lament, and the inordinate
emotion that he displays from this time onwards: the broken slumbers, the refusal
to be comforted, the grovelling on the queen's tomb, are not in keeping with the
monastic way of life he has adopted, and represent the introduction into the calm
of the cloister of those worldly affections he is supposed to have renounced."[27]
Lancelot's grief and penitence reflect a worldliness that Guinevere lacks. While
he yet lives, she is able to transcend the world and to envision her spiritual destiny;
while she lives, however, Lancelot can maintain only the rituals of religious life.
And once she is dead, he loses all will to do anything but die.

In describing Lancelot's grief, Malory again emphasizes the body: "so whan
I sawe his corps and hir corps so lye togyders, truly myn herte wold not serve to
susteyne my careful body" (3:1256.30–32). The world has not become superfluous;
rather, as he looks back at what once was and at what he, through his "defaute"
and "orgule" and "pryde," has helped to destroy, he loses the desire to live. Malory
describes his rapid decline in terms of physical loss as the once great and powerful Lancelot moves from asceticism to suicide by self-denial. Once the queen dies
and truly disappears from his life, *he* begins to disappear, disfiguring the visage
that, in her repentance, she could no longer bear to see. Her deathbed words—"I
beseche Almyghty God that I may never have power to see syr Launcelot wyth
my worldly eyen!" (3:1255.36–37)—prophesy Lancelot's end. After he buries her
next to Arthur, "syr Launcelot never after ete but lytel mete, nor dranke, tyl he
was dede, for than he seekened more and more and dryed and dwyned awaye. . . .
he was waxen by a kybbet shorter than he was, that the peple coude not knowe
hym" (3:1257.1–6).[28] Lancelot's death more closely resembles Elaine of Astolat's
than Galahad's. Malory's emphasis on the body here reinforces Elaine's argument
about the naturalness of loving with one's body and confirms the physicality of
Lancelot's longing.[29] Rather than yearning for God and the spiritual, he is encum-
bered with the world's loss. He shrinks like the Sibyl,[30] but unlike her, he also loses
his voice. His last significant speech occurs when the hermit warns him that "ye
dysplese God with suche maner of sorow-makyng" (3:1256.24–25). Lancelot tries
to defend himself, and if ever he were to express his Christian views, this would
be the time. But he clearly has no sense of how religious belief might console
him. His last words concern the body and this world—"'My fayr lordes,' sayd syr

Launcelot, 'wyt you wel my careful body wyll into th' erthe'" (3:1257.21–22). He asks for the last rites, and, significantly, to be buried at Joyous Gard, a place associated with Guinevere and with Tristram and Isolde's adulterous love.[31] Lancelot twice describes his body as "careful," full of care, bearing the world's pain. Only securing his body in a grave and covering it with earth will quiet his longing, stifle his grief, and salve his pain.

What is surprising, from a theological perspective, is that Lancelot achieves salvation and, judging from the rhetoric of hagiography, a version of sainthood. The bishop has a wonderful dream in which he sees Lancelot at heaven's gate, surrounded by angels. When he goes to Lancelot's bed, he finds him "starke dede; and he laye as he had smyled, and the swettest savour about hym that ever they felte" (3:1258.16–17), the smiling and sweet smell signaling that he is with God. Lancelot has in fact become a martyr to love, his body as battered and subjugated as any Christian saint's. Although he expressed no thought of joining the queen in the next life, he clearly yearned for death as martyrs long for the sight of God. Moreover, rather than rejoicing in the hero's greatest victory, the bishop and his fellow knights, like Lancelot when faced with Guinevere's death, weep and wring their hands, making "the grettest dole . . . that ever made men" (3:1258.18–19).[32] Malory here turns his back on heavenly joy to portray worldly loss. Continuing through Ector's threnody, grief and pain, "wepyng and dolour out of mesure" (3:1259.22), dominate these scenes. Malory displays his hero proudly in death, giving his audience one last glimpse. And perhaps he gently admonishes Guinevere, who could no longer bear to see her lover's face, for here, Lancelot's "vysage was layed open and naked, that al folkes myght beholde hym" (3:1258.30–31). As Whitehead rightly comments: "To treat Malory's *Tale of the Death of King Arthur* as though it were an improving religious work, as though it discussed courtly morality in the light of the doctrine of the Grail, or even as though it showed the world and its vain joys dissolving into nothingness is . . . to place the emphasis where Malory has resolutely refused to put it."[33] Clearly, Malory grieves with his remaining knights, in much the same way that Arthur grieved when his band rode off in the Grail Quest: "Now . . . I am sure . . . shall all ye of the Rownde Table departe, and nevyr shall I se you agayne holé togydirs" (2:864.5–8).

Malory canonizes Lancelot because of his stability—as the queen's lover, a leader of his beloved fellows, Arthur's devoted retainer, the greatest of all earthly knights. With Arthur gone, Lancelot leads the remaining knights in a brotherhood full of Christian ritual, but lacking in clear theology. They adopt Lancelot's road to salvation, following him as he followed the queen. After a long search, Bors finds Lancelot and "whan syr Bors sawe sir Launcelot in that maner clothyng, than he preyed the Bysshop that he myght be in the same sewte. And so there was an habyte put upon hym" (3:1254.32–34). When Lancelot's fellow knights—Blamour, Bleoberis, Galyhud, Galyhodyn, Wyllyars, Clarrus, and

Gahallantyne—discover their leader, they all "toke such an habyte as he had" (3:1254.36–1255.2). Malory's emphasis on clothing rather than belief reveals their religious ritual's physical nature.[34] As a community, they wear the same clothes and then begin to perform the same activities—reading holy books, singing Mass, ringing bells, and doing lowly service—and their motive is clear: "for whan they sawe syr Launcelot endure suche penaunce in prayers and fastynges they toke no force what payne they endured, for to see the nobleste knyght of the world take such abstynaunce that he waxed ful lene" (3:1255.10–13). Again, Malory makes no mention of religious conversion, service to God, penitence, or hope for heaven. Instead the knights do it for Lancelot. When they bring Guinevere's body to the tomb she will share with Arthur, "ever syr Launcelot with his eyght felowes wente aboute the hors-bere, syngying and redyng many an holy oryson, and frankensens upon the corps encensed" (3:1256.8–10). The ritual, which Malory's paratactic sentence structure underscores, unifies the brotherhood. Malory remains true to his chivalric ideal by bringing his last knights together in a community that, though more spiritual, resembles the old times. Together again, they follow their leader. As Fiona Tolhurst comments, "Malory's Arthuriad makes possible, and appears to have as its primary goal, the rebirth of Lancelot within a fictional world that blurs *La Queste*'s clear line between earthly and spiritual chivalry so completely that Lancelot becomes a salvific figure–one who heals Sir Urry and later transforms the surviving Round Table fellowship into a spiritual community."[35] In a sense, the *Morte*'s conclusion turns on its head what Mary Hynes-Berry so rightly says of the French *Queste*: "The stress of the *Queste del Saint Graal* is on [Lancelot's] failure to cut himself away from earthly values and ties and thus his failure to achieve a profound level of Christian experience."[36] Malory's Lancelot achieves the ultimate Christian experience, sainthood, by clinging to his earthly values.

Following Catherine Batt's thesis regarding the remaking of Arthurian literature that "[i]mplicit in our positioning is not simply the burden of interpretation but a responsibility for the constitution of the text itself,"[37] I would suggest that *we as readers* are complicit in Lancelot's canonization, as Malory wants us to be, overlooking his adultery and betrayals, forgiving his sins, and rejoicing with the bishop of Canterbury in seeing our hero at heaven's gate, not delving too deeply into how he got there. Death alone assuages his grief and despair. Judson Allen comments about the healing of Sir Urry that "Lancelot is never more of a sinner than when he is most holy,"[38] and perhaps his final actions bear this out. In the Grail Quest, a hermit admonishes Lancelot to "loke that your harte and youre mowthe accorde" (2:897.29). John Plummer argues that the "eventual lack of accord between heart and mouth, fact and speech, makes Lancelot false to his God and to himself."[39] From a Christian theological perspective, Lancelot is indeed false to his God. But in Malory's estimation, in *his* Christian world,

Lancelot is true to himself, saved because finally his heart and mouth *do* accord when he follows his queen to a life of prayer and denial, even if his reasons are more worldly than Christian. Lancelot's final transformation pleases Malory's God and wins him salvation. Ignoring Christian teaching, Malory uses religious rhetoric and ritual to elevate both courtly devotion and secular chivalry to ways of life worthy of salvation. Derek Brewer long ago observed that "[f]or Malory—and we shall never understand him if we do not understand this—there is no essential incompatibility between the values of Christianity and those of the High Order of Knighthood, of ideal Arthurian chivalry."[40]

NOTES

1. C. David Benson, "Ending of the *Morte Darthur*," p. 235.

2. See Hanks, "'All maner of good love comyth of God,'" in this volume.

3. Malory, *Works*, 3rd rev. ed., 3:1120.12–13. In this essay, all quotations from Malory's text come from this edition and will be noted parenthetically by volume, page, and line numbers. Although I am using Vinaver's edition of Malory's work, I prefer to retain the traditional title, *Le Morte Darthur*.

4. Edwards, *Genesis of Narrative*, p. 98.

5. See, for example, Vinaver's introduction (Malory, *Works*, 1:xc–xcii); Moorman, "'Tale of the Sankgreall,'" p. 195; and Stephen Atkinson, who thoroughly explores Lancelot's experiences in the Grail Quest ("Malory's Lancelot and the Quest," pp. 129–52). See also Fiona Tolhurst's essay in this volume.

6. In his introduction, Vinaver notes that "in the French the singing of the birds is but a means of bringing home to Lancelot his sense of wretchedness" (Malory, *Works*, 1:xci).

7. Hynes-Berry, "Tale 'Breffly Drawyne,'" p. 99. Hynes-Berry notes that "[t]he emphasis on instability rather than adultery as Lancelot's sin is one of the fundamental changes Malory makes [to his source]."

8. Edward Donald Kennedy, "Malory's Guenevere," p. 39.

9. Mahoney, "Truest and Holiest Tale," pp. 121–22. She also provides a helpful critical overview of this topic (pp. 121–25).

10. Mahoney, "Hermits in Malory's *Morte*," p. 15.

11. Lewis, "English Prose *Morte*," pp. 16–17. Lewis argues that "where the originals used specifically religious, Malory uses ethical, concepts: *virtuous* for *celestial*, *knightly* and *virtuous* for the offering of the heart to Christ, *stable* for *religious*. . . . the choice before Malory's knights is not that between 'religion' in the technical sense and active life in the world. They are to go on being knights."

12. In *Malory's Grail Seekers*, Kraemer says that "Lancelot seems troubled by his near miss on the Grail quest and appears to recognize from his son's farewell to him that he could literally taste the cup to the full if only he could be done with Guenivere [*sic*]; during the Grail quest that severance is apparently not possible, but it does occur at the end of the work" (p. 104). But compare Larry D. Benson, who argues in *Malory's "Morte Darthur"* that "Lancelot . . . remains true to Guenevere, and his faithful love for the queen, which prevented his achieving the Grail, becomes the means of his salvation" (p. 244).

13. In *Gender and the Chivalric Community*, p. 150, Armstrong notes that in the Grail Quest, Lancelot tries to function chivalrously in a foreign world: he "persistently misreads, misinterprets, and misbehaves due to his inability to comprehend the spiritual landscape

that suddenly confronts him." She challenges the assessment that Lancelot is unstable, arguing that, in fact, it is his great stability, his complete devotion to Guinevere and secular chivalry, that ensures his failure in the Grail world and, in my reading, his salvation. But Dhira Mahoney disagrees, seeing Lancelot's instability as inevitable once he returns to the courtly world: "Lancelot's fault is less a weakness of character than a failure of his whole being, his self-integrity. He cannot remain in the world and not love." Mahoney, however, reads "stability" in a religious context as "perseverance in the pursuit of holiness, and connotes withdrawal from the world" ("Truest and Holiest Tale," pp. 121, 122). In contrast, Armstrong sees Lancelot's only instability in thinking he can become another Galahad. If Malory's "vertuous love" narrative comments are definitive, he appears to side with Armstrong.

14. Mahoney says of the Grail Quest that "secular and spiritual pursuits could be considered complementary rather than competitive elements of a knightly life" ("Truest and Holiest Tale," p. 110).

15. I use "rhetoric" here in a narrow sense to mean the language of a particular subject, in this case, religion.

16. Dobyns notes, for example, that Malory's repetition of plural pronouns in the discovery scene underscores the lovers' closeness and oneness ("Rhetoric of Character," pp. 344–45): "'Alas!' seyde quene Gwenyver, 'now ar *we* myscheved *bothe*! . . . . I dred me sore *oure* longe love ys com to a myschyvus ende'" (3:1165.22–23, 29–30, my emphasis).

17. Mahoney argues that "Malory has departed from his sources to intensify the queen's penitence" ("Hermits in Malory's *Morte*," pp. 13–14). In the French source, fear for her safety motivates her to enter the convent. Guinevere in the *Stanzaic Morte Arthur* is more worldly and pragmatic than Malory's queen; she does not become so pious and holy that people marvel at the change in her. Further, she is not an abbess.

18. C. David Benson, "Ending of the *Morte Darthur*," p. 236.

19. Larry D. Benson argues that Guinevere's soul-healing "is shown by two passages that Malory invented—Guenevere's gift of prophecy, whereby she foretells her own death . . . and the miraculous vision that announces her death to Lancelot with the divine command that she be buried next to Arthur. . . . our last view of Guenevere is of the good wife, at last reunited with her husband" (*Malory's "Morte Darthur,"* p. 242). See also pp. 242–48 for an insightful reading of the *Morte*'s ending.

20. Her role here reflects Malory's general characterization of Guinevere throughout the *Morte*. He increases her importance in establishing Arthur's kingdom and the Oath of Knighthood, in judging chivalric behavior, and in enhancing Lancelot's greatness. If, for a time, she breaks down in book 7, accusing Lancelot of treachery and recreance, this understandable lapse does not diminish her nobility or importance. See, for example, Edward Donald Kennedy's "Malory's Guenevere" and my discussion of Malory's alterations in "The Knight of the Cart" that transform her from a haughty, courtly lady to a sensitive and responsive lover (Jesmok, "Malory's 'Knight of the Cart'").

21. Mann, "Malory and the Grail Legend," p. 214.

22. C. David Benson, "Ending of the *Morte Darthur*," p. 236. Also see Vinaver's comment that "[w]hen Lancelot comes to avenge the King and the Queen he finds that the Queen has retired from the world. To share her fate he becomes a hermit; not for the love of God, but for the love of the Queen: 'And therefore, lady, sithen you have taken you to perfection I must needs take me to perfection of right'" (Malory, *Works*, 1:xcviii; Vinaver has here normalized the spelling he retains in his edition).

23. F. Whitehead observes that "the two French versions of the *Mort Artu* carefully avoid

any suggestion that Arthur's death has left Lancelot a clear field; indeed, no courtly work in French allows the lovers to build on the prospect of the husband's death. . . . Given the ambiguous relationship between Arthur and Lancelot . . . the proposal seems more than a little indecent. That it is very cynical in this context, where it follows immediately Lancelot's declaration that he 'must needs take him to perfection', is obvious enough. His request for a kiss . . . contributes further to the strangely profane impression that the passage makes" ("Lancelot's Penance," p. 112).

24. As Larry D. Benson observes, Lancelot "remains true to Guenevere, and his faithful love for the queen, which prevented his achieving the Grail, becomes the means of his salvation. . . . Lancelot enters the religious life not because he forsakes his earthly love but because he remains true to it" (*Malory's "Morte Darthur,"* p. 244).

25. See Cherewatuk, "Saint's Life of Sir Launcelot." Although I disagree with her conclusion that Lancelot attains sainthood within a Christian context, she offers insightful readings of Malory's book 8.

26. Cooper, *English Romance in Time*, p. 322.

27. Whitehead, "Lancelot's Penance," p. 113.

28. A cubit is an ancient unit of linear measure equal to the length of the forearm from the tip of the middle finger to the elbow, or about 17 to 22 inches.

29. When asked to forget her love for Lancelot, Elaine retorts: "Why sholde I leve such thoughtes? Am I nat an erthely woman? And all the whyle the brethe ys in my body I may complayne me, for my belyve ys that I do none offence, though I love an erthely man, unto God, for He fourmed me thereto, and all maner of good love comyth of God. . . . And of myselff, Good Lorde, I had no myght to withstonde the fervent love, wherefore I have my deth!" (2:1093.3–7, 1094.1–3).

30. The reference is to the Latin epigraph of T. S. Eliot's "The Waste Land," which, in the translated textual note, reads: "For I once saw with my own eyes the Cumaean Sibyl hanging in a jar, and when the boys asked her, 'Sibyl, what do you want?' she answered, 'I want to die.'" Petronius Arbiter, Satyricon 48.8 (Eliot, *Waste Land*, p. 3). The sibyl, in her old age and despair, has shrunk to only a voice.

31. Mahoney reads this scene differently ("Hermits in Malory's *Morte*," p. 17). Although she agrees that Malory's Lancelot, unlike his source analogues, dies of grief, she argues that his "grief is not aroused specifically by Guinevere's death: at Amesbury, when Lancelot sees her visage, we are told 'he wepte not gretelye, but syghed' (1256.3–4); it is when he sees the queen and the king lie together in their tomb that he swoons and laments. At the archbishop-hermit's reproach he reveals the source of his grief: not the 'rejoysyng of synne' but the memory and the loss of the Arthurian world, of the whole tissue of reciprocated love and mutual obligations that made the fellowship so glorious and so renowned." I would counter that Lancelot's decline, his own inconsolable death wish, begins with Guinevere's death.

32. This dole-making in Malory, both here and at the death of Galahad, needs further exploration. From my limited knowledge, the grief seems out of line with the reader's expectations of rejoicing that Lancelot, after so many struggles, is finally at peace with the Lord. In contemporary hagiography such as *The Golden Legend*, I have found no evidence of such lamenting at the saint's death. This collection, however, cites an interesting analogue to Lancelot's smile and sweet savor in its tale of St. Dominic (August 4) (Jacobus de Voragine, *Golden Legend*, 2:427). A friar, at the moment of Dominic's death, sees Dominic, "the man of God, crowned with laurel and shining with a wondrous brightness, setting out from Bologna." Later, when the sepulcher was opened to transfer the saint's remains, "an odour

of such sweetness came forth that it might have come from a storeroom of perfumes rather than from a tomb." Another nearly contemporary source from Italy, Sister Bartolomea Riccoboni, *Life and Death in a Venetian Convent*, chronicles the deaths of forty-nine holy women but offers only praise for the deceased and belief in their salvation, with no sadness or lamenting.

33. Whitehead, "Lancelot's Penance," p. 112

34. Mahoney comments on clothing in the *Morte*: "In Malory's public world, clothing is frequently an important signifier of a change of inner state, as is the adoption or abandonment of the trappings of knighthood such as armor and horses." She sees the knights' assumption of hermits' habits as a sign of "grief and remorse," of their internal change, rather than as a signal of their brotherhood, their union in a new venture, as I argue above. She stresses that "[t]hough Lancelot and his kinsmen live in a group with the archbishop, their life is not described as a cenobitical one [that is, a life in a religious community, like a convent or monastery]. They are a group of like-minded solitaries living together, not a structured community" ("Hermits in Malory's *Morte*," pp. 16, 19).

35. Tolhurst, "Slouching towards Bethlehem," in this volume, p. 131.

36. Hynes-Berry, "Tale 'Breffly Drawyne,'" p. 95.

37. Batt, *Malory's "Morte Darthur,"* p. xvi.

38. Allen, "Malory's Diptych *Distinctio*," p. 245.

39. Plummer, "*Tunc se Coeperunt*," p. 157.

40. Brewer, "'[H]oole book,'" p. 58.

Christianity and Social Instability: Malory's Galahad, Palomides, and Lancelot

Dorsey Armstrong

As every essay in this volume suggests, Christianity is an important and complicated aspect of the chivalric world of Sir Thomas Malory's *Morte Darthur*. The text enacts a complex and often vexed overlap, interaction, and, on occasion, *opposition* of religious and chivalric identities. Derek Brewer once famously said of the *Morte Darthur* that "[f]or Malory—and we shall never understand him if we do not understand this—there is no essential incompatibility between the values of Christianity and those of the High Order of Knighthood, of ideal Arthurian chivalry."[1] Yet a close analysis of the *Morte* suggests that there *is* a tension between these values, even if Malory seems to be initially suggesting that there is not.[2] The *Morte* wants to represent these ideals as theoretically compatible, but when deployed in the text they often jostle against and conflict with one another. Trouble arises because the relationship between religious and chivalric ideals is so fluid—at times the two overlap almost exactly, while at others they stand in direct conflict with one another, a situation that makes it difficult to talk about them with any consistency or clarity.

Comparing Malory's best-known non-Christian knight, the Saracen Palomides, with his most Christian knight, Galahad, reveals that a consistent inconsistency pervades the chivalric project of the *Morte Darthur*. The values of Malory's text simultaneously pull in two opposing directions—counterposing the ideal of a (limited) meritocracy of knightly skill and chivalric conduct[3] with that of a state of spiritual perfection. While these two models of behavior are not mutually exclusive in theory, in practice they often clash. The struggle to resolve and reconcile these two conflicted and often conflicting idealized identities—honorable knight and devout Christian—contributes significantly to the ultimate collapse of the Arthurian community.[4] Palomides and Galahad are both Christians—the former only in spirit for much of the text, the latter perfect in his faith from the moment he appears. An analysis of their very different religious experiences shows how faith may function simultaneously as support and threat to Arthur's chivalric community. And more than any other knight, it is Sir Lancelot who finally best

107

demonstrates this struggle between chivalric and religious ideals to which Galahad and Palomides have called attention.

The Present Absence

Religion seems to be both everywhere and nowhere in Malory's *Morte*. Kings and knights repeatedly swear oaths "By God!" or "By Jesu Christ!"; before heading out for a busy day of questing, knights routinely hear Mass; the most important challenge presented to the Round Table *en masse* is the quest for the Holy Grail; important events—feasting, tournaments, and indeed, the annual reaffirmation of the founding of the Round Table—are all connected to important days in the church calendar such as Easter or Pentecost. But at the same time, most of the ideals of Malory's Arthurian community are the principles of a secular chivalry; romantic love, not Christian charity, is the driving force of identity construction for the greatest knights. As Jacqueline Stuhmiller has recently argued in her analysis of trial by combat in the *Morte Darthur*, "On the face of it, it would seem that God is not an active participant in the lives of his Malorian constituents and that . . . his only role is to provide the name by which knights swear their most solemn oaths."[5] And while the Order of the Round Table is inextricably bound to the "hyghe feste of Pentecoste," its members are not all required to be themselves Christians.

This fact is, surprisingly, revealed by a religious recluse (Sir Perceval's aunt) in the midst of that most sacred and Christian of knightly forays, the quest for the Holy Grail. The former queen of the Wastelands tells her nephew that "all the worlde, crystenyd and hethyn, repayryth unto the Rounde Table, and whan they ar chosyn to be of the felyshyp of the Rounde Table they thynke hemselff more blessed and more in worship than they had gotyn halff the worlde" (2:906.17–21).[6] This claim strikingly suggests that non-Christian knights may become full-fledged members of the Round Table brotherhood, but her *idea* of inclusiveness conflicts with the *practice* of knightly experience in Malory's text: non-Christians must convert before they are granted full admittance to the brotherhood of the Round Table, and the killing of unbaptized knights (no matter how valiant or skilled) is frequently characterized as both honorable and necessary.[7]

For example, although non-Christian knights such as Sir Palomides are accounted good knights before they convert to Christianity, other knights often make a point of lamenting their non-Christian status even as they praise their knightly prowess, a move that suggests non-Christian knights are not regarded as "full" Round Table knights.[8] Sir Tristram is much concerned with the state of Sir Palomides's soul, and when he learns that Palomides has vowed not to be baptized until he has fought "seven trewe bataylis for Jesus sake" and lacks only one instance of armed combat, he declares: "Be my hede . . . as for one batayle, thou shalt nat seke hyt longe. For God deffende . . . that thorow my defaute thou sholdyste lengar lyve thus a Sarazyn" (2:842.9–12). The text takes care to identify knights as Saracen or Christian, and makes a point of identifying knights who have converted from paganism to Christianity: "sir Palamydes the Saresyn was another, and sir Safere and sir Segwarydes, his brethren—but they bothe were crystynde" (1:343.24–26). Another Saracen who famously converts is Sir Priamus in the account of the Roman War. As Gawain says of his one-time rival: "'this is a good man of armys: he macched me sore this day in the mournyng . . . whan he is crystynde and in the fayth belevys, there lyvyth nat a bettir knight nor a noblere of his hondis.' Than the kynge in haste crystynde hym fayre and lette conferme hym Priamus, as he was afore, and lyghtly lete dubbe hym a deuke with his hondys, and made hym knyght of the Table Round" (1:241.1–11). Significantly, Priamus is not invited into the Round Table fellowship until *after* his baptism.

Although Malory's text never explicitly defines the beliefs and practices of Saracens, it takes care to demonstrate that their unconverted souls are foul and deserving of death: when Sir Palomides kills the Saracen Sir Corsabryne in single combat, Malory tells us that "therewithall cam a stynke of his body, whan the soule departed, that there myght nobody abyde the savoure. So was the corpus had away and buryed in a wood, bycause he was a paynym" (2:666.13–16). In the quest for the Holy Grail, on one of the rare occasions when he kills his opponents, Galahad expresses remorse—"I repente me gretely inasmuch as they were crystynde"—but he is reassured that his act is excusable by a "good man" who tells him, "Nay, repente you nat . . . for they were nat crystynde" (2:997.24–27).

Yet, as important as adherence to Christianity appears to be in these instances, an examination of the *Morte Darthur* in comparison with other late medieval chivalric works—and here I'm referring both to romances and to more didactic works—reveals that there is little that shows religious piety or devotion in the text, particularly in the all-important early, formative stages of the community, when Arthur creates the Round Table and issues directives, correctives, and rules to his knights. While the community of Malory's work measures time in terms of the church calendar year, holy feast days are subsumed within the project of chivalry; they are primarily important in that these moments in the liturgical calendar provide the occasion for a knightly gathering, at which some marvel is sure to appear that will propel the Round Table knights out on a quest. Many of Malory's sources—including the Prose *Lancelot* and, of course, the *Queste del Saint Graal*—specifically describe a knight's foremost duty as the protection of Holy Church. For example, in the Prose *Lancelot* the Lady of the Lake explains a knight's duties to a young Lancelot thus:

> Chevaliers fu establis outreement por Sainte Eglize garandir, car
> ele ne se doit revanchier par armes ne rendre mal encontre mal; et
> por che est a che establis li chevaliers qu'il garandisse chelui qui

tent la senestre joe, quant ele a estéferue en la destre. Et sachiés que au commenchement, si com tesmoigne l'Escripture, n'estoit nus si hardi qui montast sor cheval, se chevalier ne fust avant, et pot che furent il chevalier clamé. (21a, 11).[9]

[Above all, knighthood was established to defend the Holy Church, for the Church cannot take up arms to avenge herself or return harm for harm; and this is why knights were created: to protect the one who turns the other cheek when the first has been hit. Know, too, that in the beginning, according to the Scriptures, no one but knights dared to mount a horse—a cheval, as they said—and that is why they were called horsemen, or chevaliers.][10]

In the *Morte Darthur*, neither the Lady of the Lake nor anyone else makes such a claim.

The comparative absence of religion is made particularly clear in the Pentecostal Oath. The Round Table knights who participate in this annual ritual pledge

> never to do outerage nothir mourthir, and allwayes to fle treson, and to gyff mercy unto hym that askith mercy, uppon payne of forfiture of their worship and lordship of kynge Arthure for evirmore; and allwayes to do ladyes, damesels, and jantilwomen and wydowes socour: strengthe hem in hir ryghtes, and never to enforce them, upon payne of dethe. Also, that no man take no batayles in a wrongefull quarell for no love ne for no worldis goodis. So unto thys were all knyghtis sworne of the Table Rounde, both olde and yonge, and every yere so were they sworne at the hyghe feste of Pentecoste.   (1:120.17–27)

These seem to be fairly straightforward chivalric values, generally unremarkable for what they emphasize. What *is* striking is what is missing from this oath: Malory's sources and other contemporary chivalric literature all emphasize devotion to God as among the most important of a knight's duties. For example, in Malory's major source for the Tale of King Arthur, the *Suite du Merlin*, the Round Table is explicitly connected to the Grail Quest:

> Et sachiés que leans estoient avoit .iii. manieres de tables. La premiere, la Table Ronde. De celle estoit compains et sires le roy Artus. L'autre table estoit apellee la Table des Compaignons Errans. Et ce estoient ceulx quit aloient aventure querant et actendoient a estre compaignons de la Table Ronde. Ceulx de la table tierce estoient ceulx qui de la court ne se remuoient et qui ne se mectoient pas es queste ne les aventures . . . Et estoient ceulx chevalier apellés les chevaliers moins prisiés. A celle table . . . s'assist Parceval, comme ci qui encor ne se prisoit de riens . . . Et lors y advint une merveille qui

fut puis tenue a miracle . . . [la damoyselle qui oncques ne menti] dist a Parceval: "Sergent Jhesu Christ, virge chevalier et nect, laisse cest siege ou tu t'assies et vien seoir deles le Siege Perilleux, car cel-lui t'a Dieu octroyé, car tu es digne d'estre uns des plus souverains chevaliers de la Queste du Sainct Graal."[11]

[Know that there were three kinds of tables there. The first was the Round Table. King Arthur was lord of this one. The second table was called the Table of the Errant Companions, those who went seeking adventure and waited to become companions of the Round Table. Those of the third table were those who never left court and did not go on quests or in search of adventures. . . . These knights were called the less valued knights. At this table . . . Perceval sat down, for he was not yet valued for anything. . . . Then a marvel happened . . . [the mute maiden] said to Perceval, "Servant of Jesus Christ, pure, virgin knight, leave this seat where you are sitting and come sit next to the Perilous Seat: God has granted it to you, for you're worthy to be one of the chief knights in the quest for the Holy Grail."][12]

This passage makes clear that one of the Round Table's major enterprises will be the pursuit of the Holy Grail; Malory severs this explicit link early in the text, removing any suggestion of the spiritual or religious from the formation of the Round Table Order. Thus, when the Grail does appear in Arthur's court, initiating the Grail Quest, the difference of this knightly enterprise from all others is much more dramatic because it is so distinctly unlike any other challenge presented to the Arthurian community.

In addition to the emphasis on devotion to God in the *Suite du Merlin* and other romances like the Prose *Lancelot*, didactic manuals of knighthood such as Ramon Llull's *Libre del ordre de Cauayleria* and Geoffroi de Charny's *Livre de chevalrie* stress the spiritual aspect of knighthood. William Caxton's 1484 translation of Llull's text maintains this emphasis: "Offyce of a knyght is thende and the begynnynge / wherfore began the ordre of chyualrye. . . . The offyce of a knyght is to mayntene and deffende the holy feyth catholyque / by whiche god the fader sente his sone in to the world to take flesshe humayne in the gloryous vyrgyn our lady saynt Mary."[13] In the *Morte Darthur*, such spiritual devotion is largely absent, eclipsed by more secular chivalric concerns. Or, to put it another way, Malory's depiction of knighthood isn't particularly religious, because knighthood *is* the religion.

Given this primarily secular representation of knighthood, Malory's choice of the French *Queste del Saint Graal* as the source for his Grail Quest narrative is striking, especially since more secular versions of this story were available to him. For example, Malory scholars know that he had the Prose *Tristan* and its

Grail narrative at hand, yet he chose to set this text aside and take up the more spiritually and allegorically oriented *Queste* instead.[14] Indeed, given that the rest of the *Morte* focuses so emphatically on the more earthly aspects of knighthood, Malory's decision to use *this* text is particularly significant. While some scholars have argued that Malory "secularizes" his telling of the Grail narrative,[15] most agree that he retains the spiritual focus and orientation of his source and that such a move deliberately recalibrates the landscape of the quest.[16] I have argued elsewhere that one explanation for this choice was Malory's desire to test the Pentecostal Oath—which appears to be his own creation—and his personal view of what ideal knighthood would look like.[17] In other words, he sets the oath in motion early in the text and then examines it in various knightly contexts to see how well it functions; after deploying it through hundreds of pages of earthly chivalric adventures, Malory examines its utility in the spiritual and allegorical world of the Grail Quest. Therefore, the more religious source offers the greatest contrast to the code of secular chivalry enacted in the swearing of the Pentecostal Oath. Prior to the Grail Quest, the text has emphasized the importance of service to ladies and the acquisition of knightly reputation through skilled performance in combat and tourney; in the Grail Quest, these hitherto crucial elements of chivalry become relatively unimportant.

The Grail Quest demands knights eschew both knightly fellowship and female presence, two elements that have been absolutely essential in establishing and maintaining knightly identity. Thus, Nacien the hermit tells the Grail Quest knights that "none in thys queste lede lady nother jantillwoman with hym, for hit ys nat to do in so hyghe a servyse as they laboure in" (2:869.1–2); later, when Sir Uwain asks Sir Galahad if he may "beare hym felyshyp," a common, expected, and welcome request in the pre-Grail Quest world, Galahad answers: "that may ye nat, for I must go alone, save thys squyre shall bere me felyship" (2:879.11–13). The world of the Grail Quest is markedly different from the knightly landscape of the rest of the *Morte Darthur*.

Christianity in Malory, it seems, is contradictorily both incredibly important and relatively insignificant. The figures of Galahad and Palomides most clearly demonstrate the Arthurian community's complicated relationship to religion.

The (Non) Christian Knight: Galahad and Palomides

An examination of Palomides and Galahad in tandem reveals the shaky foundation on which the chivalric community is founded; although they stand at opposite ends of the spectrum of Christian identity within the *Morte*, both knights threaten the Arthurian society with their religious identities—Galahad in his effortless near-saintliness and Palomides with his hard-fought and -won conversion. That two such different enactments of Christian faith could both threaten the *Morte*'s community reveals the instability of the knightly ideal that the text constantly asserts as fundamental to the maintenance of the chivalric society.

The problem posed by the religious identities of both Palomides and Galahad is perhaps most suggestively limned in Malory's inability to find words to describe an experience each knight has. For example, in the Book of Sir Tristram de Lyones, after the first day of the tournament at the Castle of Maidens, the Saracen knight Palomides is alone in the woods, bewailing his recent defeat in the tournament: "'I, wofull knyght, sir Palomydes! What mysseadventure befallith me . . . ?' And than he gate his swerde in hys honde and made many straunge sygnes and tokyns, and so thorow the rageynge he threw hys swerd in that fountayne. Than sir Palomydes wayled and wrange hys hondys, and at the laste, for pure sorow, he ran into that fountayne and sought aftir his swerde" (1:528.29–529.1). Following his initial verbal outburst, Palomides's despair becomes so overwhelming that he is reduced to making bizarre gestures, unable to verbalize his anguished position. Palomides's inability to articulate what he is feeling—even as soliloquy, a mode particularly associated with the Saracen knight—paired with the narrator's striking inability to describe exactly the "straunge sygnes and tokyns" that he makes, suggest Palomides's radical difference from the other knights encountered in the *Morte Darthur*. The difference suggested by the disordered nature of his behavior points to Palomides's status as Other. No other knight in Malory's text displays such extremes of emotion in this particular way;[18] many knights weep or lament, but none is reduced to mere gesticulation as Palomides is. His otherness, his strangeness, is arguably the result of his split personality as the Saracen who is christened "in [his] harte" (2:666.26); his religious identity is inextricable from his knightly identity, as the text constantly reminds us. Although other Saracens populate the pages of Malory's text, Palomides stands apart from them just as he remains distinct from those Christian knights to whose faith he converts. Peter Goodrich has noted this distinction, arguing that "Malory's treatment of Saracens depends upon his crusading-era literary sources and his personal awareness of Ottoman Turk incursions into Europe. *Except for Palomides*, his Saracens develop typical orientalist functions" (emphasis added).[19] Whether he is compared to Saracens or Christians, Palomides is always Other.

An incident surprisingly similar to Palomides's "strange sygnes and tokyns" occurs when the narrator attempts to describe the triumphant moment when Galahad at last beholds the Holy Grail. At the castle of Corbenic, a holy man commands Galahad to approach an altar to see "that thou hast much desired to se" (2:1034.20). Galahad complies, but what he sees apparently can only be rendered indirectly, in terms of the young knight's reaction: "And than he began to tremble ryght harde whan the dedly fleysh began to beholde the spirituall thynges. Than he hylde up his hondis towarde hevyn and seyde, 'Lorde, I thanke The, for now I se that that hath be my desire many a day. Now, my Blyssed Lorde, I wold nat lyve in this wrecched worlde no lenger, if hit myght please The, Lorde'" (2:1034.21–27). Like Palomides's "straunge sygnes and tokyns" the experience cannot be fully and accurately described; it is ineffable, linguistically inexpressible, perhaps even invisible to worldly eyes that have been focused on the kind of questing, tourneying, and rescuing of damsels that builds honor and reputation for the majority of Malory's text.

After his vision of the Grail, his request is granted, and Galahad is taken up to heaven; at the end of *his* series of adventures, Palomides's status as "good Saracen knight" is seemingly converted to simply "good knight" with his literal conversion to Christianity through baptism. Both of these moves would appear to strengthen, rather than weaken, the Arthurian social order—Galahad's transcendence reflects honor and glory on his knightly order, and Palomides's conversion asserts the hegemony of the Christian ideal for those who belong to the Round Table. This, however, is not the case: in the aftermath of both events, the text demonstrates an anxiety about the intersection and overlap of chivalric and religious ideals.

While the community expresses a preference for knightly agents who are Christian, Galahad's strident Christianity casts a shadow on Arthur's court; his arrival at court coincides with the commencement of the Grail Quest, in which the rules of knighthood that have served the community so well up to this point are insufficient and inappropriate. The only knight who is able to negotiate the spiritual terrain of the search for the Grail with ease is Galahad; in his success he continually reminds the other knights of their shortcomings. The other two successful Grail Quest knights—Bors and Perceval—are certainly accounted respectable knights prior to the Grail Quest, but they are almost never listed in the pantheon of Arthur's greatest knights, which usually includes Lancelot, Tristram, Lamorak, and Palomides.[20] Significantly, three of these four greatest knights of Camelot do not even participate in the Grail Quest, and Lancelot, the *primus inter pares* of the Round Table Order, has only qualified success in this endeavor.[21]

In his focused pursuit of the Grail and rejection of fellowship and romantic love, Galahad threatens the community founded primarily upon exactly those two components of chivalric behavior. In the early parts of the Grail book, he consistently rejects any companionship. For example, after Galahad saves Perceval from twenty men at arms, Perceval tries to detain him, crying, "Fayre knyght, abyde and suffir me to do you thankynges" (2:909.34). Ignoring Perceval, Galahad characteristically departs: "ever sir Galahad rode fast, that at the last he past oute of hys syght" (2:910.1). Later, however, he admits Perceval and Bors into his company. His fellowship with them is sometimes accidentally knightly, as when the three fight to save Perceval's sister from the blood-letting that she later allows (2:1000–1004), but in general they unite in services increasingly resembling the Mass, like the holy meal they share with King Pelles at Castle Corbenic (2:1029–30). Throughout the Grail book, Galahad devotes his life, brief as it is, solely to the spiritual, culminating in his request for his holy death, which is granted (1:1034–35). Clearly, if Arthur's knights could follow his lead, the Round Table would cease to exist. In his holy dedication, he subverts the earthly ideals of Arthur's court.

Similarly, Palomides's split personality as both Christian and pagan troubles the Arthurian society.[22] As the outsider who wants in, a figure of otherness who aspires to sameness and inclusion, Palomides challenges the idealized homogeneity of knightly Arthurian ideals. The other knights' ambivalence toward Palomides and other Saracen knights—distaste and fear often mingled with admiration of their exploits and concern for the state of their souls[23]—speaks to the community's dual identification of itself as the center of both Christian and chivalric excellence. The Round Table attracts the best knights of the world, regardless of their religious affiliation, but it would prefer that those knights be baptized. As Isolde says while watching Sir Tristram and Sir Palomides fight one another: "Alas! that one I loved and yet do, and the other I love nat, that they sholde fyght! And yett hit were grete pyté that I sholde se sir Palomydes slayne, for well I know by that the ende be done sir Palomydes is but a dede man, bycause that he is nat crystened, and I wolde be loth that he sholde dye a Sarezen" (1:425.8–13).

Palomides recognizes the activities that help define one as a legitimate member of the knightly community—questing, knightly fellowship, devotion to ladies—and pursues them eagerly. He seeks Tristram's companionship and Isolde's love, lamenting when he loses both: "For I have bene in sir Trystrams felyshyp this moneth and more, and wyth La Beall Isolde togydyrs. And, alas! . . . unhappy man that I am, now have I loste the felyshyp of sir Trystram and the love of La Beall Isolde for ever" (2:770.13–17).[24] Although there is little evidence of Palomides's pagan self—indeed, when he appears in the text for the first time he is already on his way toward Christian baptism—he is almost always identified in terms of his alterity: "Sir Palomides the Saracen" (1:316.27, 343.24, 385.10, 2:687.24, 739.11, etc.).[25] The threat posed by his religious identity is made plain at the Tournament at Surluse when Arthur, responding to Palomides's great feats of prowess, exclaims, "A, Jesu! . . . this is a grete dispyte that suche a Saryson shall smyte downe my blood!" (2:663.7–8). His religious identity—even as he rejects it—pressures the Arthurian community. Even when he is made a member of the Round Table Order, his previous identity as a Saracen can never be overwritten; it constantly undermines the unified, homogeneous ideal of knighthood demonstrated from the earliest pages of the text through the Grail Quest and beyond.

The challenge that Palomides presents to the chivalric community of the *Morte Darthur* is most clearly demonstrated through a comparison of Malory's treatment of the Saracen knight with that of his main source for Palomides's character, the Prose *Tristan*. As Goodrich has rightly pointed out, in comparison with his sources, "Malory deemphasizes the fullness of Palomides's conversion and assimilation to the Round Table."[26] Although the Grail Quest in Malory begins just moments after Palomides's baptism, the newly Christian knight does not participate; although he participates in the activity of questing by following the Questing Beast, he never captures or kills it; and although he has demonstrated that romantic love is the primary engine that drives him to perform knightly feats of prowess, no lady ever grants him her love. As Bonnie Wheeler claims, "Sir Palomydes . . . penetrates the chivalric world, adopts its strategies and shares its values. But he is forever doomed by his 'almost' status."[27] Donald L. Hoffman agrees, noting that "the difficulty of Palomides' situation . . . is that he is simultaneously included and excluded, simultaneously irrelevant and essential."[28]

Although there are other Saracens who inhabit the pages of Malory's text—most notably Palomides's father and brothers, but also the Roman-allied warrior Priamus[29] and the king of Libya—none of them achieves the status and renown of Palomides, none occupies the narrative space that Palomides does, and none desires full membership in the Round Table order as desperately as Palomides does. The figure of Palomides—who is both Other (a Saracen) and Same (a Round Table knight)—disrupts the fantasy of wholeness and inclusiveness that undergirds the organizational scheme of Arthur's kingdom, in the same way that Galahad's spiritual perfection does:[30] Lancelot's son, too, is both Other (a perfectly devout, chaste Christian) and Same (a Round Table knight). Just as Galahad gives an intense performance of Christian knighthood while in pursuit of the Holy Grail, Palomides goes to extremes to prove his right to belong to the Arthurian community. As Goodrich puts it: "Since Palomides desires to belong, he becomes hyperaware of the chivalric conventions of membership in King Arthur's culture, and a self-conscious overachiever of them."[31]

Palomides occupies a position that is as different, and at the greatest possible distance, from the Arthurian social order while still maintaining the possibility of eventual acceptance into that order. This becomes clear through a comparison of Palomides with another insider/outsider, Sir Tristram, his rival for the love of La Beale Isolde.[32] Tristram is the greatest of all Cornish knights, but Malory's text constantly reminds us that Cornish knights are far inferior to those of Arthur's court: "hit is seldom seyne . . . that ye Cornysshe knyghtes bene valyaunte men in armys" (1:398.25–26); "for as yet harde I never that evir good knyght com oute of Cornwayle" (2:488.12–13); "ye knyghtis of Cornwayle ar no men of worshyp as other knyghtes ar" (2:581.28–29); "For I wyste nevir good knyght com oute of Cornwayle but yf hit were sir Trystram de Lyones" (2:555.20–22). As this last statement suggests, Tristram is the only specimen of Cornish knighthood considered fit to join the Round Table, in the same way that Palomides becomes the only converted Saracen deemed a welcome recruit. Tristram and Palomides are continually found in one another's company as both rivals and fellows. By virtue of his frequent proximity to the Saracen knight, Tristram becomes more Same, more like the other Round Table knights, while Palomides is simultaneously rendered less so. The Cornish Tristram may be different from the other Round Table knights, but he is not *as* different as the yet-to-be-converted Saracen Palomides.

In his prowess, love for Isolde, and competition-fellowship with Tristram, Palomides shares the knightly qualities of the Round Table. However, as a Saracen he is nonetheless different from those who are Same. In his pursuit of baptism, on the other hand, he is also different from those who are Different. The "problem" of Palomides is seemingly resolved in his baptism; at that moment, he ceases to be a contradiction in terms—the noble non-Christian knight—and becomes a full-fledged member of the knightly order. Or so it seems. Tellingly, although he does appear later in the *Morte Darthur*, from the moment of his baptism Palomides never again occupies the substantial narrative space that he claims in the Book of Sir Tristram—he fades into the background. Even as the Round Table technically embraces him as one of its own, it simultaneously pushes him away to the outer orbit of the Arthurian social order. For the rest of the narrative, he endlessly pursues the Questing Beast, who wanders the far reaches of Arthur's land, drifting in and out of the narrative space that should now, for Palomides, be Home, but instead remains ever and always Away.

Like Palomides, Galahad also threatens the ideal of unity upon which the Round Table is founded. As the most successful Grail Quest knight he finally "completes" the Round Table when he takes his seat in the Siege Perilous. Ironically, his spiritual superiority to the other knights is what threatens that wholeness. That his arrival at court coincides with the commencement of the Grail Quest is not accidental; that quest will scatter and sunder the fellowship as knights blunder into a spiritual and allegorical landscape so different from that to which they are accustomed. Defeat for the majority is all but assured. Galahad is, as son of Lancelot and achiever of the Grail, the insider who belongs outside that knightly brotherhood which is generally so preoccupied with secular chivalric activity.

The saintly, aggressively virginal,[33] and—to put it bluntly—perfectly boring Sir Galahad is the only knight who will truly achieve the Grail. His success seems to be based on his being the most unknightlike of knights according to the standards of Malory's Arthurian community, largely eschewing service to ladies and knightly companionship. Raised away from the court in the sacred space of a convent, he is knighted there by his father just moments before the Grail Quest begins. He comes to court, then, as a fellow to those knights already present and takes his place in the Siege Perilous, which has been empty until this moment (2:853–55). The order of the Round Table is for the first and last time complete, unbroken, and unified with his arrival, but it is so because Galahad has seemingly come to court only to participate in the Grail Quest. In an ironic move, this quest will break and scatter the fellowship as no other adventure has done.

Galahad's behavior on the quest differs from typical knightly activity. For example, he sets off not yet fully armed, acquiring the accessories of knighthood along the way; he also manages to defeat seven wicked brothers in combat without killing even one of them, for which he is praised (2:887–88). When Gawain and other knights of Arthur's court encounter these same wicked brothers and kill them—something that is perfectly acceptable in the pre–Grail Quest world—they are condemned by one of the conveniently met hermits who populate the forests of adventure in this tale. The hermit says to Gawain: "For sertes, had ye nat bene so wycked as ye ar, never had the seven brethirne be slayne by you and youre two felowys: for sir Galahad himself alone bete hem all seven the day toforne, but hys lyvyng ys such that he shal sle no man lyghtly" (2:892.2–6).

While success in the quest for the Holy Grail has little to do with previously accepted standards of knightly reputation or ability, it still is most importantly an adventure that *is available only to knights*. Galahad seems to succeed because of his chastity, reluctance to kill, and all-around spiritual perfection—qualities relatively low on the list of desirable knightly attributes elsewhere in Malory's text—but his participation is impossible unless he leaves the spiritual space of the convent and *becomes* a knight; holy as the Grail is, it is not hermits, or monks, or priests who are charged to seek it, but rather, the agents of a secular community are given the task. Although the greatest of earthly knights, Lancelot, does not achieve the ultimate prize himself, he provides the link that brings the saintly Galahad into the knightly world of the quest and thus makes it possible for a representative of the Round Table to achieve the Grail.

In his perfection, Galahad reflects honor upon his knightly companions, but simultaneously, his presence points up the weaknesses in the other Round Table knights. If Palomides is trying to *close* a gap between himself and Round Table knighthood, then Galahad seems to be trying to create one—stretching to its breaking point the tether that binds him to earthly, secular chivalry. The threat Galahad poses is alleviated at the moment of his death, when he is lifted from the quest, from knighthood, and from the text itself by the most literal of *dei ex machina*. As is the case with Palomides, however, his impact on the Arthurian community can never be undone. When the quest is over and the "remenaunte" of the knights has returned to Arthur's court (2:1045.6), members of the community attempt to return to a state of normalcy. It is not possible, however, for things to go back to the way they were. The Grail Quest, in its focus and outcome, has irrevocably changed the community by insistently and repetitively revealing the flaws and contradictions inherent in the values and code of conduct by which the chivalric society has sought to define and organize itself. The strong contrast between this tale and the rest of the *Morte*, between this knight, Galahad, and his less spiritually perfect fellows, manifests these shortcomings.

Galahad's character undercuts the idea of the religious inclusiveness of the Round Table as suggested by Perceval's aunt in that his Christianity stands as a shining example that none of the other Round Table knights can emulate; Palomides similarly undermines this idea in that the process of his conversion and baptism concerns so many of the members of the Arthurian community. The text deals with both threats not by addressing the issue but rather by pushing these two figures away—sending Palomides after the Questing Beast, and Galahad up to heaven. Both of these figures demonstrate a religious fervor unusual for the text: Palomides in that he continually risks his immortal soul by refusing baptism until he has fought "seven trewe bataylis for Jesus sake" (2:666.28), and Galahad in his spiritual perfection, an ideal that seems ultimately impossible for other knights to attain. These two knights represent the outer limits of religious fervor within the text: Palomides's Christian identity is hard-fought and -won, while Galahad's performance as a Christian knight is the most effortless of all identity performances within the *Morte Darthur*. Both are striking displays of faith—in dramatically different ways—and they point up the flawed and complicated nature of the social ideals upon which Arthur's court is founded.

The conclusion of Malory's Book of Sir Tristram de Lyones links Palomides and Galahad even as it points up the disruptive force each has on the community:

> And than sone afftyr they departed and rode towarde Camelot where that kynge Arthure and quene Gwenyvir was, and the moste party of all the knyghtes of the Rounde Table were there also. And so the kynge and all the courte were ryght glad that sir Palomydes was crystynde.
>
> And at that same feste in cam sir Galahad that was son unto sir Launcelot du Lake, and sate in the Syge Perelous. And so therewythall they departed and dysceyvirde, all the knyghtys of the Rounde Table.
>
> And than sir Trystram returned unto Joyus Garde, and sir Palomydes folowed aftir the questynge beste.   (2:845.16–26)

Galahad's arrival scatters the fellowship, while the newly baptized Palomides simply does not take part in the quest for the Holy Grail. As Donald L. Hoffman asks of this moment, "Is the baptism of the Saracen the beginning of Camelot's apotheosis or the prelude to its decimation? . . . the only moment in the *Morte* that celebrates the Christian dimension of chivalry . . . becomes, in a way, the sunset of that very code."[34]

Lancelot: The Uneasy Christian

The Arthurian community's discomfort with and difficulty in reconciling the chivalric and religious is perhaps best demonstrated by Sir Lancelot's behavior after the Grail Quest. The time that Sir Lancelot has spent with his saintly son causes him to change the conduct that has served him so well up until this spiritual endeavor. After returning home, Malory tells us that "[i]n all such maters of ryght Sir Launcelot applyed hym dayly to do for the plesure of Oure Lorde Jesu Cryst, and ever as much as he myght he withdrew hym fro the company of quene Gwenyvere for to eschew the sclawndir and noyse" (2:1045.24–28). As Lancelot himself confesses while on the Grail Quest, "all my grete dedis of armys that I have done for the moste party was for the quenys sake, and for hir sake wolde I do batayle were hit ryght other wronge. And never dud I batayle all only for Goddis sake, but for to wynne worship and to cause me the bettir to be beloved, and litill or nought I thanked never God of hit" (2:897.17–22). Lancelot's reputation as the "floure of chyvalry" has been driven by his devotion to Queen Guinevere and his desire to achieve great feats of arms to honor her;[35] the quest for the Holy Grail, only made possible and achieved only by Sir Galahad, has called his father's very identity into question, and in its aftermath Lancelot tries to follow a more spiritual chivalry. Ultimately, he fails in his attempts to negotiate between two modes of knighthood: "Than, as the booke seyth, sir Launcelot began to resorte unto quene Gwenivere agayne and forgate the promyse and the perfeccion that he made in the queste" (2:1045.10–12).

The Healing of Sir Urry episode demonstrates just how much the Grail Quest and Galahad's presence have changed both Arthur's community and Lancelot, its greatest knight and representative.[36] Sir Urry has wounds that are cursed to fester and bleed until such time as "the beste knyght of the worlde had serched hys woundis" (3:1145.19–20). Urry's mother brings him to Arthur's court, and Arthur promises to do his best to help him: "And wyte you welle, here shall youre son be healed and ever ony Crystyn man may heale hym" (3:1146.22–24). Arthur significantly emphasizes the religious, Christian criterion, rather than knightly skill or chivalric reputation, and Malory then gives us a sort of last "roll call" of all the nobles of Arthur's realm who each try in turn to heal Sir Urry. Finally, Arthur calls upon Sir Lancelot, who at first resists: "Jesu defende me . . . whyle so many noble kyngis and knyghtes have fayled, that I shulde presume upon me to enchyve that all ye, my lordis, myght nat enchyve" (3:1151.20–23). This statement expresses a humility lacking in Lancelot's character prior to the Grail Quest. Compelled finally by the direct order of his king and a plea from Sir Urry himself, Lancelot agrees to attempt the healing but again expresses his unfitness to do so, no matter how much he might wish to cure the wounded knight: "Jesu wolde that I myght helpe you! For I shame sore with myselff that I shulde be thus requyred, for never was I able in worthynes to do so hyghe a thynge" (3:1152.12–15). As he attempts the healing, Lancelot significantly offers up a *silent* prayer—the public performance of one's abilities so intrinsic to knightly identity in the pre–Grail Quest world would be wrong in this circumstance—and in it, he emphatically denies that his own abilities could have any part in Urry's healing: "'My lorde Arthure, I muste do youre commaundemente, which ys sore ayenste my harte.' And than he hylde up hys hondys and loked unto the este, saiynge secretely unto hymselff, 'Now, Blyssed Fadir and Son and Holy Goste, I beseche The of Thy mercy that my symple worshyp and honesté be saved, and Thou Blyssed Trynyté, Thou mayste yeff me power to hele thys syke knyght by the grete vertu and grace of The, but, Good Lorde, never of myselff'" (3:1152.17–25).

Lancelot's experience with Galahad on the Grail Quest has taught him that there is much more to good knighthood than prowess in combat and service to ladies. His request that his "symple worshyp and honesté" be saved might at first suggest that he is still focused on his secular knightly reputation, but the adjective "symple" is an important qualifier: he is asking that his basic, *human* goodness and honesty—not as the greatest of earthly knights but as one of God's sinning children—be affirmed. Although the healing of Sir Urry suggests that he has learned this lesson, Lancelot is unable to adhere wholly to this new definition of knighthood; at the end of the text, after Arthur's community has been destroyed, he seeks to re-create a courtly society of his own when he says to Guinevere (in a line original to Malory), "yf I had founden you now so dysposed, I had caste me to have had you into myn owne royame" (3:1253.20–22). As Janet Jesmok rightly puts it, "[b]ecause Lancelot's unstable world revolves around Guinevere, he again becomes enmeshed in worldly things after the Grail Quest."[37]

At the end of the text, when Camelot has collapsed, the agents of the community are still struggling with their chivalric identities. Lancelot, the greatest earthly knight, joins a monastery and becomes a priest, but significantly, does so in emulation of Guinevere's entrance into a nunnery: "therfore, lady, sythen ye have taken you to perfeccion, I must nedys take me to perfection, of ryght" (3:1253.17–19). Karen Cherewatuk has pointed out that this seems to be "vocation by thwarted desire, or at best, imitation."[38] Once within the brotherhood of the monastery, he excels in fasting, penance, and prayers, but his inability to break free from the secular chivalric ideals that were the foundation of his career is suggested in his reaction to Guinevere's death; unable to continue as monk or knight, he wastes away and dies:

> Thenne syr Launcelot never after ete but lytel mete, nor dranke, tyl
> he was dede, for than he seekened more and more and dryed and
> dwyned awaye. . . . that he was waxen by a kybbet shorter than he

was, that the peple coude not knowe hym. For evermore, day and nyght, he prayed, but somtyme he slombred a broken slepe. Ever he was lyeng grovelyng on the tombe of kyng Arthur and quene Guenever, and there was no comforte that the Bysshop, nor syr Bors, nor none of his felowes coude make hym, it avaylled not.

(3:1257.1–11)

Yet, although he seems to die of his grief over the loss of the queen, the bishop at his monastery dreams that Lancelot ascends into heaven—"here was syr Launcelot with me, with mo angellis than ever I sawe men in one day. And I saw the angellys heve up syr Launcelot unto heven, and the yates of heven opened ayenst hym" (3:1258.7–10)—and when the monks discover his body, Malory tells us that it emitted the "swettest savour," a phrase often used to describe the holy scent that was considered in many cases an indication of sainthood, and a detail not to be found in Malory's sources.[39]

Perhaps most significant is the lament offered by Lancelot's brother Ector upon the former's death:

> A, Launcelot! . . . thou were hede of al Crysten knyghtes! And now I dare say . . . thou sir Launcelot, there thou lyest, that thou were never matched of erthely knyghtes hande. And thou were the curtest knyght that ever bare shelde! And thou were the truest frende to thy lovar that ever bestrade hors, and thou were the trewest lover, of a synful man, that ever loved woman, and thou were the kyndest man that ever strake wyth swerde. And thou were the godelyest persone that ever cam emonge prees of knyghtes, and thou was the mekest man and the jentyllest that ever ete in halle emonge ladyes, and thou were the sternest knyght to thy mortal foo that ever put spere in the reeste.   (3:1259.9–21)

Here Ector identifies his brother as the best of Christian knights but eulogizes him in purely secular chivalric terms.[40] The contradictory use of the adjective "Christian" as a descriptor of a knight who has excelled in every knightly quest *except* the most spiritual, the quest for the Holy Grail, here embodies the vexed relationship between religious and courtly ideals that plagues Malory's Arthurian community. Even after Arthur's kingdom has collapsed, the tensions that helped precipitate that collapse are still in play.

Surprised by Faith

Throughout Malory's text, the Round Table has at various times identified chivalric prowess and Christian virtue as fundamental elements in its structure, only to discover that these two ideals are often—but not always—mutually exclusive.

The lack of a clearly defined relationship between these two ideals creates much of the confusion as Arthur's knights struggle to adhere to a high standard of knighthood. While one might expect that non-Christian figures like Palomides pose a threat to the wholeness of the Round Table, what is surprising is to discover that Galahad presents a similar—perhaps even more pronounced—danger to the knightly ideal of Camelot.

Palomides seems to have done everything right in order to become a fully accepted member of the Round Table, yet he is not; as Jacqueline de Weever has succinctly put it: "Inclusion in Arthur's circle, conversion to Christianity, prowess in knighthood, experience of *fin amour*: even taken together, these are not enough to resolve the challenges he represents."[41] Even at the very end of the text, when he takes a respite from his endless pursuit of the Questing Beast to ally himself with Lancelot in the final battle, his reward again emphasizes his marginality: he is given lands in Provence, at the far reaches of Lancelot's territory. He is still the most Other among fellows.[42] Galahad, likewise, seems in many ways the ideal chivalric agent; he leaps into the text fully formed as the perfect Christian knight and succeeds in the Grail Quest with little struggle. Yet, he challenges the model of Arthurian knighthood by resisting romantic love and fellowship with other knights.[43] Lancelot's experience perhaps best demonstrates the vexed relationship between chivalry and faith: the greatest knight of the world, he fails on the Grail Quest; he commits adultery with Guinevere in violation of the promise he makes on that most holy enterprise, but God still grants him the ability to heal Sir Urry; he joins a monastery only because Guinevere refuses to become his lady, yet once a monk, excels in fasting and prayer, dying a saintly death. An examination of these three figures reveals the crisis of conflicting ideals always lurking at the edges of the *Morte Darthur*. Engaging Malory's text in terms of its treatment of religion helps makes those threats plain.

NOTES

I would like to thank D. Thomas Hanks, Jr., for encouraging me to participate in this volume, and Janet Jesmok for her keen editor's eye. Their comments and critiques have vastly improved this essay; all flaws that remain are, of course, my own.

1. Brewer, "'[H]oole book,'" p. 58.

2. The list of scholarly works discussing the tension between Christianity and chivalry is quite lengthy; in addition to many of the essays that appear elsewhere in this volume, two recent articles—Grimm, "Sir Thomas Malory's Narrative of Faith," and Sweeney, "Divine Love or Loving Divinely?"—deal with this issue.

3. To be accounted a "worshipful" knight in Malory's text, prowess in combat and honorable behavior must exist together. Lisa Robeson has pointed out that "[a]s often as the adjective *worshipful* is used in Malory . . . there are quite a few examples of knights who are of high birth and excellent prowess who are nevertheless not deemed *worshipful*" ("Women's Worship," p. 109).

4. I have made a similar argument in *much* abbreviated form in "The (Non)-Christian Knight in Malory."

5. Stuhmiller, "*Iudicium Dei, iudicium fortunae*," p. 456.

6. Malory, *Works of Sir Thomas Malory*, 3rd rev. ed. In this paper, all quotations from Malory's text come from this edition and will be noted parenthetically by volume, page, and line numbers.

7. For example, Sir Palomides's killing of Sir Corsabryne (2:666) and Sir Galahad's killing of unbaptized knights while on the Grail Quest (2:997), both of which I discuss below.

8. For Palomides's status as both insider and outsider as analyzed in terms of postcolonial theory, see my "Postcolonial Palomides."

9. All citations of the French Prose *Lancelot* are to *Lancelot: Roman en Prose du XIIIème siècle*, ed. Micha, 7:250.

10. *Lancelot-Grail*, 2:59.

11. *La Folie Lancelot*, ed. Bogdanow, pp. 90–91.

12. *Merlin Continuation*, p. 86.

13. Llull, *Book of the Ordre of Chyvalry*, p. 24. See also Charny, *Book of Chivalry of Geoffroi de Charny*, ed. Kaeuper and Kennedy.

14. For more on this, see in particular Mahoney, "Truest and Holiest Tale," and Riddy, *Sir Thomas Malory*, pp. 113–15. I also discuss the significance of this in chap. 4 of my *Gender and the Chivalric Community*.

15. The first and foremost of these scholars is Vinaver, the first editor of the Winchester Manuscript. Tolhurst discusses Vinaver's influential reading of the Grail Quest and other scholars' responses to it in great detail elsewhere in this volume.

16. As Mahoney contends: "the Quest still signifies, for Malory, a completely different order of adventure from the rest of the *Morte Darthur*" (introduction to *Grail: Casebook*, p. 41). See Tolhurst's discussion of this issue in this volume.

17. See my *Gender and the Chivalric Communty*, esp. chaps. 1 and 4. I argue that "Malory's Grail Quest critiques the ideal of knighthood upon which the chivalric society is predicated, problematizing the heteronormative gender scheme that renders masculine knightly identity intelligible to the Arthurian community. For example, although some maidens are encountered by the Grail Quest knights . . . the typical character of the mediating quest maiden is strikingly absent from the grail narrative . . . the Tale of the Sankgreall offers a critique of the Arthurian community through its revelation of the importance of kinship and its radical revision of chivalric gender relations" (p. 146).

18. Wheeler discusses the emotional complexity and interiority of Palomides in "Grief in Avalon."

19. Goodrich, "Saracens and Islamic Alterity," p. 10.

20. Gareth might also be included in this list of knights, but he retires to a secondary position in the text after his Tale, returning to it at the last as a reluctant (and unarmed) guard at the proposed burning of Guinevere.

21. Malory has altered Lancelot's Grail Quest experience so that he is a semi-success rather than a complete failure. See Hanks's discussion in this volume.

22. In recent years the character of Palomides has begun to receive significant critical treatment. Grimm has argued that Palomides's character is important in that he reflects in microcosm the structure of Malory's Tristram section ("Love and Envy of Sir Palomides"). Lynch contends that the "contradictory career of Palamides [*sic*] perfectly displays the conflict between the competitive basis of chivalry and its myth of collectivity" and that he is a "figure whose potential as a psychological subject eventually comes to challenge and

complicate the norms of Malory's narrative" (*Malory's Book of Arms*, p. 109). Other recent treatments of Palomides include Dulin-Mallory, "'Seven trewe bataylis for Jesus sake'"; Goodrich, "Saracens and Islamic Alterity"; Hoffman, "Assimilating Saracens"; Roland, "Arthur and the Turks"; Wheeler, "Grief in Avalon."

23. The Roman War section in particular presents an emphatically negative attitude toward Saracens, one that remains in place for much of the text, no matter how much some of the knights admire the exceptional Sir Palomides. For example, when the Saracen Sir Corsabryne is killed by Sir Palomides in combat and his body emits a "stynke," he is specifically buried in the woods because of his status as a "paynym" (2:666.13–16); when Tristram fights Palomides so that Palomides can "check off" his seven battles for Jesus's sake, Tristram explains that he does so in order that Palomides will be christened, renouncing the paganism that he and Galeron see as "grete pyté" (2:843.1–5); when Palomides smites down Sir Lancelot's horse in the tournament at Lonezep, Malory's account of the scene seems to suggest that other knights see a connection between Palomides's status as Saracen and such dishonorable conduct: "Than was the cry huge and grete, how sir Palomydes the Saresyn hath smyttyn down Sir Launcelots horse" (2:739.10–11); the crusading impulse to "make warre upon the Saresyns" is used by King Mark as a ploy to help advance one of his nefarious plots (2:677.30–33); Mark's brother Bodwyne is forced to confront an invading force of "myscreauntys Sarezynes" (2:633.5). There are many other examples, but these all serve to make the point that the status of "Saracen-ness" is suspect throughout the *Morte Darthur*.

24. Mongan has claimed that "on several occasions Palomides' behavior is determined as much by his feelings for Tristram . . . as by his love for Isolde" ("Between Knights," p. 76).

25. Dulin-Mallory has succinctly listed the components that define Palomides's character: "his incessant suit for the hand of Isolt, his pursuit of the Questing Beast, his position at the Round Table below Lancelot, Tristram, and Lamorak as fourth best knight in the world, his identity as a Saracen, and his determination to fight seven battles for Christ before his baptism" ("'Seven trewe bataylis for Jesus sake,'" p. 167).

26. Goodrich, "Saracens and Islamic Alterity," p. 17. See also Cooper's discussion of Palomides in "Book of Sir Tristram de Lyones."

27. Wheeler, "Grief in Avalon," p. 71.

28. Hoffman, "Assimilating Saracens," p. 49.

29. Although Priamus is usually treated as a Saracen by scholars discussing his character, it should be noted that he is never explicitly identified as such in Malory's text. He does seek to be christened (1:230–31) and receives his christening after taking Arthur's part in battles (1:241.8).

30. I have discussed Palomides and his insider/outsider status at greater length in "Postcolonial Palomides."

31. Goodrich, "Saracens and Islamic Alterity," p. 18.

32. I have argued this point at greater length in "Postcolonial Palomides."

33. The phrase is borrowed from Shichtman, "Percival's Sister," p. 13.

34. Hoffman, "Assimilating Saracens," p. 57.

35. For a full discussion of this aspect of Lancelot's identity formation, see my *Gender and the Chivalric Community*, esp. chaps. 2 and 4.

36. This episode has been the subject of much critical debate among scholars; a quick summary of the various major argumentative strands is in Anderson, "'Ein Kind wird geschlagen.'" Hanks, Holbrook, Tolhurst, and Whetter also discuss this episode in essays elsewhere in this volume.

37. Jesmok, "Rhetoric, Ritual, and Religious Impulse," p. 93.

38. Cherewatuk, "Saint's Life of Sir Launcelot," p. 67.

39. Cherewatuk, "Saint's Life of Sir Launcelot," p. 63.

40. Hanks has argued in a personal communication for an interpretation of the word "godelyest" as "Godliest" rather than "goodliest," a reading that makes of Ector's eulogy a more intentional synthesis of religious and chivalric values. See also Tolhurst's discussion of "godelyest" in the *Middle English Dictionary* in her essay in this volume. The occurrences of forms of "godelyest" or "goodly" in the *Morte* strongly suggest that Malory used these forms to denote the quality of being "best" rather than religious, but it is interesting to note that the form of the word that Hanks argues means "Godliest" only appears once in Malory's text, and thus, one could read this occurrence as a unique expression of the idea of "Godliness." See the entries for these word forms in Kato's *Concordance to the Works of Sir Thomas Malory*.

41. de Weever, "Saracen as Narrative Knot," p. 7.

42. Hodges has made this point compellingly in a recent paper, "Lancelot in the North: Borders and Geography of Rebellion," presented at the 42nd International Medieval Congress, Kalamazoo, MI, May 10, 2007.

43. Although he does have an interaction with Perceval's sister, that interaction criticizes rather than affirms the model of knightliness demonstrated by figures like Lancelot. See my *Gender and the Chivalric Community*, chap. 4, for a fuller discussion of this scene. See also Hoffman, "Perceval's Sister" and Shichtman, "Percival's Sister."

Slouching towards Bethlehem: Secularized Salvation in *Le Morte Darthur*

Fiona Tolhurst

Malory the Secularizer?

Although P. J. C. Field has concluded that Malory drew upon at least four Grail romances as he composed his Tale of the Sankgreal, this conclusion in no way undermines the scholarly consensus that Malory based his Grail story on the French Vulgate Cycle's *La Queste del Saint Graal*.[1] Both Eugène Vinaver and his successors in studying *Le Morte Darthur* have explored the possible meanings of Malory's translation of *La Queste*, particularly his simultaneous compression of it to just over one-third of its original length and retention of every significant narrative episode.[2] Some scholars interpret this abbreviated quest as remaining faithful to the Christian content of the thirteenth-century work while others interpret it as secularized—a function of Malory's tendency to stress chivalric ideology over Christian doctrine throughout *Le Morte Darthur*.[3] In the first group are Charles Moorman, who argues that Malory "is always careful to keep, usually in summation, the religious core of the argument presented," and Richard Barber, who notes how, when describing the Grail ceremonies, "Malory follows the French almost word for word, abbreviating slightly but never interfering with the central theological imagery."[4] Also in this group is Dhira B. Mahoney, who, like a good number of her colleagues, concludes that "the Quest still signifies, for Malory, a completely different order of adventure from the rest of the *Morte Darthur*."[5]

Nevertheless, the second group includes a large number of scholars who echo Vinaver, particularly in interpreting Malory's omission of some of the theological context of the Grail Quest as evidence of secularization.[6] Many members of this second group accept and build upon Vinaver's conclusion that Malory's "one desire seems to be to secularize the Grail theme as much as the story will allow" (3:1535).[7] These scholars tend to see Malory's quest as a means of measuring knightly prowess and of increasing the glory—or at least the number of opportunities for earning glory—of Lancelot and his companions of the Round Table. Vinaver eloquently encapsulates this perspective in his comment that Malory's "attitude may be described without much risk of oversimplification as that of a man to whom the quest of the Grail was primarily an *Arthurian* adventure and who regarded the intrusion of the Grail upon Arthur's kingdom not as a means of contrasting earthly and divine chivalry and condemning the former, but as an opportunity offered to the knights of the Round Table to achieve still greater glory in *this* world" (3:1535). Since his conclusions define so precisely *Le Morte Darthur*'s relationship to its French source for the Grail Quest, it is easy to agree with Vinaver that Malory substituted Arthurian values for Christian ones because he saw the quest as an intrusion upon the Arthurian story, and therefore did his best to secularize the quest as much as possible.

Nevertheless, an episode-by-episode comparison of *La Queste del Saint Graal* and Malory's Tale of the Sankgreal confounds the seemingly neat categories of "Christian" and "secular."[8] Certainly, *Le Morte Darthur* significantly compresses the spiritual adventures of Perceval, Bors, Lancelot, and Galahad—severely truncating their tutorials in spiritual perfection. However, if Malory had regarded the Grail Quest as an "intrusion" upon the Arthurian world, he could have omitted whole episodes of the quest, abbreviated all the episodes more drastically, or eliminated discussion of their theological significance. Furthermore, if Malory had found the quest bothersome, why would he have woven the issue of salvation into the fabric of his "hoole book of kyng Arthur and of his noble knyghtes of the Rounde Table" (3:1260.16–17)? The deficiencies of Vinaver's characterization of *Le Morte Darthur*'s quest narrative become evident through analysis of Malory's references to Christian morality; explicits requesting the aid of God, Jesus, or readers; and conflation of earthly and spiritual chivalry. In addition, Malory's accounts of the conversion of Sir Palomides, the healing of Sir Urry, and the conversion and death of Lancelot confirm that his retelling of the Grail Quest is part of a larger project: to model secularized salvation for his late fifteenth-century audience.

Several contributors to this volume, along with other Malorians, have highlighted passages that seem to indicate Malory's traditional Christian morality and his faith in intercessory prayer,[9] but even these passages either clash with the apparent messages of other episodes in *Le Morte Darthur* or frustrate the scholarly desire for a clearly definable degree of Christianness. Three well-known passages that center on Christian standards of morality present significant interpretive challenges for scholars: the often-cited definition of "vertuouse love" (3:1119.30) as it existed in Arthur's day (3:1119.14–1120.13); the pivotal episode of the healing of Sir Urry, in which Lancelot fervently prays to God that he might heal this knight (3:1152.20–25) and then Arthur and his companions thank God and the Virgin Mary for Lancelot's success (3:1152.33–35); and the interpolation into the Book of Sir Tristram de Lyones of both a reference to prayer—"all maner jantylmen hath cause to the worldes ende to prayse sir Trystram and to pray for his soule"—and Malory's response to it: "Amen, sayde sir Thomas Malleorré" (2:683.2–4).

The "vertuouse love" passage articulates the most "Christian" of moral standards but remains fiendishly difficult for scholars to reconcile with other textual data.[10] Undoubtedly, Malory distinguishes between "unstable love" and "stabylité" (3:1119.15, 16), entirely in keeping with traditional church teachings encouraging the devotion of spouses to conjugal love and that of monastics to the love of God. In addition, he defines "vertuouse love" as Christian in two senses: it is Christ-centered since it requires honoring God first and one's lady second (3:1119.28–29), and it produces love affairs that can go on for "seven yerys" without "lycoures lustis" requiring their consummation (3:1120.4). Nevertheless, although the "vertuouse love" passage is consistent with the author's later avoidance of discussing the circumstances of Lancelot's capture in the queen's chamber (3:1165.10–13), its implication that Lancelot and Guinevere's love is virtuous clashes spectacularly with other episodes in *Le Morte Darthur*. For example, only a few hundred lines after suggesting that Arthur's queen and greatest knight embody true love, Malory opens his Knight of the Cart sequence by retaining his French sources' insistence that this relationship was consummated, and in an apparently lustful fashion: "So, to passe uppon thys tale, sir Launcelot wente to bedde with the quene and toke no force of hys hurte honde, but toke hys plesaunce and hys lykynge" (3:1131.28–30). The passion of this consummation is so great that the hero neither tends to his wound nor sleeps (3:1131.29–32). Furthermore, while Malory's verbal tap-dancing later in the plot sequence enables him to avoid describing the lovers in bed together in the queen's chamber, it also reveals the awkwardness of trying to purify his favorite knight: "For, as the Freynshe booke seyth, the quene and sir Launcelot were togydirs. And whether they were abed other at other maner of disportis, me lyste nat thereof make no mencion, for love that tyme was nat as love ys nowadayes" (3:1165.10–13).

The other two well-known passages likewise present interpretive challenges because their degree of Christianness is difficult to discern. The healing of Sir Urry presents a quintessentially Christian moment: Lancelot humbly asks God for aid and then receives the gift of healing despite his possible unworthiness. Nevertheless, this passage presents interpretive challenges: Why exactly does Lancelot succeed here? Does God bless him because he is, as Arthur believes, the best knight in the world? Or does God do so because Lancelot behaves so humbly and reverently here—despite his failings at other moments in the narrative? Furthermore, why exactly does Lancelot weep "as he had bene a chylde that had bene beatyn" (3:1152.36)? Because he feels unworthy? Grateful? Ashamed? These interpretive cruxes have produced a wide range of readings, only some of which attribute Christian meaning to the healing of Urry.[11] The aforementioned reference to prayer in the Tristram section is also overtly Christian but opens up various interpretive possibilities. It inserts into the tale of the second-best earthly knight an acknowledgment that gentlemen the world over should pray for Tristram, but that moment is at odds with mainstream critical dogma that Tristram's function in *Le Morte Darthur* is to provide an exemplar of flawed, earthly chivalry.[12] Malory's "Amen" (2:683.4) further complicates matters by not only aligning him with those praying gentlemen but also suggesting that he wishes to purify Tristram here just as he purifies Lancelot in other episodes. However, this passage leaves open the question of how Christian Malory's version of the Tristram character is.

Malory's explicits, because they give more direct access to his voice than the narration itself, can be interpreted as evidence of the author's Christian beliefs.[13] Nevertheless, even a brief examination of them requires Malorians to provide specific definitions of the terms "Christian" and "secular," for a phrase using Christian language in a conventional manner is not necessarily proof of Malory's sincere devotion to Christ. For example, Malory's statement at the end of the Tale of King Arthur that "this was drawyn by a knyght presoner, sir Thomas Malleorré, that God sende hym good recover. Amen" seems to be specifically Christian in expressing the hope, and perhaps the faith, that God will aid the author (1:180.21–23), although what form Malory's "recover" might take is open to interpretation. Two of the word's common meanings, release from prison and recovery or extrication from a difficult situation (such as imprisonment for treason), have a secular focus; however, the word's cousin-noun *recoverer* can connote salvation.[14] Because writing a book of Arthurian romance could earn him such "recover," Malory is more likely to have in mind here a change in his earthly fortunes, but the Christian element remains. Similarly ambiguous are Malory's request, at the end of the Tale of Sir Gareth of Orkney, to his readers to pray "that God sende hym good delyveraunce sone and hastely" (1:363.19–20) and his reference to himself at the end of the Book of Sir Tristram as "sir Thomas Malleorré, knyght, as Jesu be hys helpe. Amen" (2:845.29–30). Admittedly, "delyveraunce" has the primary meaning of release from prison and suffering, but it can also connote justice or facing the Last Judgment.[15] Because "delyveraunce" could entail salvation and/or release from prison and "as Jesu be hys helpe" is a common figure of speech, the cultural mores of a traditional Christian are palpable here, but specific beliefs are not. Furthermore, both Malory's explicit to the Tale of the Sankgreal describing how this true tale has been recorded by "sir Thomas Maleorré, knyght. O Blessed Jesu helpe hym thorow Hys myght! Amen" and his plea to Christ as "le Shyvalere Sir Thomas Malleorré, Knyght" who must report the death of Arthur—"Jesu, ayede ly pur voutre bone mercy! Amen"—could likewise reflect either personal faith in the salvific power of Jesus, or cultural norms in late medieval England, or both (2:1037.11–13; 3:1154.17–19).

Malory's final explicit also has both secular and Christian connotations, but it tempts readers to apply the term "culturally Christian" to it. In it the knight-author asks gentlemen and gentlewomen to pray for him while he is alive so that God will send him "good delyveraunce" (3:1260.23) and, when he is dead, to pray for his soul—with "delyueraunce" again invoking earthly and/or heavenly aid (3:1260.20–24). In addition, by asking his social peers—not priests or hermits—to pray for him, Malory tips the balance toward earthly over heavenly concerns. He then ends his "hoole book" with references one might term culturally or conventionally Christian: this book "was ended the ninth yere of the reygne of Kyng Edward the Fourth, by Syr Thomas Maleoré, Knyght, as Jesu helpe hym for Hys grete myght, as he is the servaunt of Jesu bothe day and nyght" (3:1260.25–29). Malory positions himself in secular terms—using regnal year rather than anno domini—but then ends with conventional Christian references to Jesus's aid and to serving him day and night. Although these last two references mark Malory as a person immersed in the Christian culture of late medieval England, they do not necessarily make him a devout Christian. Moreover, the reference to serving Jesus "day and nyght" might simply be a convenient means of achieving internal rhyme. If this phrasing is merely convenient, then the author's Christianity could be cultural rather than religious.

However, to apply the term "culturally Christian" to *Le Morte Darthur* is inadequate and potentially misleading because it suggests that Malory lacks interest in the issue of salvation. What is needed instead is language that encapsulates Malory's struggle to clear a path toward salvation for worldly knights, like himself, to follow. Therefore, I use William Butler Yeats's image of the "rough beast" that "slouches towards Bethlehem to be born" in an optimistic sense to capture the awkward movements toward salvation of two less-than-perfect males.[16] The first is Malory's Lancelot, who manages to "slouch" toward the position previously occupied by *La Queste*'s Galahad. The second is Sir Thomas Malory himself, who manages to "slouch" toward political, and perhaps spiritual, rebirth through the Winchester manuscript of *Le Morte Darthur*, the extant version closest to what the author composed.[17] Malory's Arthuriad makes possible, and appears to have as its primary goal, the rebirth of Lancelot within a fictional world that blurs *La Queste*'s clear line between earthly and spiritual chivalry so completely that Lancelot becomes a salvific figure—one who heals Sir Urry and later transforms the surviving Round Table fellowship into a spiritual community, following King Arthur's apparent death. Malory's retelling of the Grail Quest gives Lancelot a spiritual rebirth, one which facilitates his full rehabilitation as a hero of Arthurian legend. Furthermore, through his explicits, Malory also attempts to "slouch" toward a rebirth. Both near the beginning of *Le Morte Darthur*—as he concludes the Tale of Sir Gareth of Orkney (1:363.18–21)—and at the very end of it (3:1260.20–29), the author asks for his readers' prayers. The former explicit asks them to pray for his "delyveraunce sone and hastely" (1:363.20) and the latter for his "good delyveraunce" while he lives and for his soul after he dies (3:1260.22–24). Such prayers could help the author move toward both political rebirth—through release from prison—and salvation. In several other explicits, Malory asks for the aid of God or

Jesus: for that of God at the end of the Tale of King Arthur (1:180.15–25) and for that of Jesus at the end of the Book of Sir Tristram (2:845.29–30, 846.4–5), the Tale of the Sankgreal (2:1037.13), the Healing of Sir Urry (3:1154.19), and the Dolorous Death and Departing Out of This World of Sir Launcelot and Queen Guinevere (3:1260.27–29). The fact that these invocations appear in key transitional passages in the "hoole book" suggests that the author cares deeply about his own salvation.[18] Should Malory receive the requested aid of the Almighty, he could undergo a spiritual transformation akin to Lancelot's and achieve salvation.

In short, then, the image of "slouching" toward salvation captures the essence of Malory's Christian aesthetic: a sometimes-awkward attempt to reconcile conflicting Arthurian sources such as the French *Queste*, which idealizes monastic asceticism, and the *Alliterative Morte Arthure*, which revels in earthly battles. Consequently, a useful term to describe Malory's theological approach is secularized salvation: it reflects both his strong interest in earthly life and his concern that knights of the world achieve salvation. Secularized salvation allows both Lancelot and Malory to enter heaven as good earthly knights and lovers, sins confessed, but with loyalties to king and lady made compatible with the demands of Christian practice in late fifteenth-century England.[19]

The Case of the Quest: Malory's Model of Secularized Salvation

Catherine Batt notes that religious experiences among the medieval English gentry varied widely in their "intensity and engagement," so she cautions against assuming anything about Malory's religion based on his status as a gentleman.[20] Although scholars cannot know the depth of Malory's religious conviction, his Arthuriad suggests that Malory was an orthodox follower of the Christian church whose daily life as a knight caused him to focus on how God's power had shaped the lives of Arthur and his knights of the Round Table, as well as how God's power could improve Malory's earthly lot.[21] Malory's version of the Grail Quest develops a French source that "is, above all, a glorification of idealized knighthood" in which only Galahad embodies the chivalric perfection that makes him worthy to receive a beatific vision; as a result, the Vulgate Galahad defines that vision "in essentially chivalric terms, 'daring' (*hardemenz*) and 'prowess' (*proeces*)."[22] Given this chivalric grounding for *La Queste*'s spirituality, Malory can then expand upon it—enabling him to narrow the huge gap between spiritual and earthly lifestyles in his primary source by carving out a theological middle ground. This middle ground is *Le Morte Darthur*'s particular brand of secularized salvation, one that honors Christian imagery and expressions as well as the idea of a spiritual hierarchy but finally collapses the distance between Galahad's and Lancelot's levels within that hierarchy.[23] By examining Malory's method of translating the monastic theology of *La Queste*, readers discover that Vinaver's characterization of *Le Morte Darthur*'s Grail Quest narrative is inadequate and therefore misleading.

Some passages in the Tale of the Sankgreal fit Vinaver's definition of secularization because they decrease the amount of theological detail, detracting from the theological significance and richness of *La Queste*. These passages favor plot and character development over doctrinal explication. For example, as he condenses the Vulgate account of the Tree of Life, Malory omits the long introduction about Adam and Eve's fall into sin and subsequent punishment (*Queste* 210–12/67; 2:990); the explanation of the distinction between spiritual virginity (a lack of carnal desire as well as of carnal relations) and physical virginity (a lack of carnal relations) (*Queste* 213–14/67–68; 2:990);[24] and the account of Adam and Eve's misery at their exile and shame at the thought of copulating as well as of the comfort they receive from God (*Queste* 214–15/68; 2:990). Malory likewise heavily condenses the hermit's homily regarding Lancelot's being harder than stone, more bitter than wood, and more barren than a fig tree—omitting his source's use of the parable of the talents to develop the portrait of Lancelot as an ungrateful servant of God (*Queste* 67–70/23–24; 2:897.35–898.35). By decreasing the proportion of theological material in these episodes, Malory to some extent secularizes his source.

Nevertheless, Vinaver's characterization of Malory as viewing the Grail as an "intrusion ... upon Arthur's kingdom" (3:1535) requires correction, for Malory does not secularize out of any apparent distaste for the French *Queste* and edits his source at least partially out of a desire to clarify the narrative. Malory is never overtly critical of his French source, and he appears to have great reverence for it given his preservation of all the significant episodes in the Grail Quest sequence— including their theological explications by spiritual advisors.[25] In fact, Malory repeats both the plot sequence and many details from his source. He retains the sequence of events initiating the quest (*Queste* 1–12/3–6; 2:853–63); the tournament celebrating the coming of the Grail (*Queste* 13–14/7; 2:864.5–33); the Grail's appearance at Arthur's court (*Queste* 15–16/7; 2:865.27–866.2); all of the adventures and visions that Perceval, Lancelot, Bors, Galahad, Gawain, and Hector experience while on it (*Queste* 26/11–62/82; 2:873–1020); and the series of episodes leading up to the death of Galahad and the disappearance of the Grail and Lance (*Queste* 262/82–279/87; 2:1021–37). By following his primary source so closely, Malory suggests that he accepts the Grail Quest as an essential part of the Arthurian story, making Vinaver's characterization of it as an "intrusion" doubtful. In addition, some of Malory's condensing appears to be motivated by a desire to simplify the Vulgate's plot. He omits nonessential details such as Arthur's accompanying his knights a short distance as they set out (*Queste* 25/10; 2:872.17–21) and several of the many details in the story of King Mordrain (*Queste* 83–87/28–29; 2:908.14–909.2). By omitting *La Queste*'s long-winded account first of King

Crudel's persecution of Joseph of Arimathea and his son Josephus, then of King Mordrain's freeing Josephus from prison (*Queste* 83–87/28–29), Malory focuses squarely on the key issue: Mordrain offended God but is waiting for Galahad to heal him. Such revisions make Vinaver's position difficult to accept. Furthermore, some of what Vinaver calls secularization is more likely revision for theological clarity. For example, when Malory truncates the explication of Perceval's vision of the ladies who ride the lion and serpent respectively, he sharpens the theological focus in the episode by encapsulating a long lecture about New Law versus Old Law in about twenty lines of dialogue (*Queste* 101–4/33–34; 2:915.6–25). Malory's tendency to clarify his source text, whether or not theology is involved, reveals Vinaver's description of Malory's revision of *La Queste* to be a misleading oversimplification.

The second deficiency in Vinaver's description of the Tale of the Sankgreal's relationship with its primary source is the claim that Malory's "one desire seems to be to secularize the Grail theme as much as the story will allow" (3:1535). The situation is, in fact, more complex than that: at times the author retains or adds secular details and at others retains or adds Christian ones. When Malory tells of how Galahad repairs the broken sword (*Queste* 266/83–84), his phrasing preserves the French source's secular detail that Bors should get the sword because it could not be put to better use than serving a good and valiant knight: "for hit myght no bettir be sette, for he was so good a knyght and a worthy man" (2:1027.28–29). However, when retaining King Arthur's concern that many of his knights will die on the Grail Quest as well as Lancelot's response that it would be more honorable to die on the quest than to die in any other way (*Queste* 17/8; 2:867.10–12), Malory augments the episode by making the king's expression of concern more dramatic than in the Vulgate. By having his Arthur feel that the dissolution of his beloved fellowship of the Round Table has "nygh slayne" him (2:866.20), Malory adds a secular detail. In other cases, Malory either preserves or expands Christian details. He preserves most of the Vulgate's lengthy histories about the shield the white knight sends to Galahad (*Queste* 32–35/12–13; 2:879.19–881.21) and the bed Solomon's wife designed (*Queste* 223–26/70–71; 2:992.28–994.16)—despite their minor contributions to plot advancement. In addition, the pattern of his omissions supports my claim that Malory decreases the status gap between Galahad and the other knights, not Vinaver's claim that Malory systematically replaces Christian content with Arthurian. More significantly, Malory feels free to add details to Christian elements of his story. He inserts Galahad's responses to Perceval's sister's tale about the broken sword (2:989.31–32; 2:990.15) and adds the suspension of two swords over the bed Solomon's wife uses to transmit sacred history (*Queste* 210/67; 2:990.17). It is misleading, therefore, to say that Malory is a translator whose primary goal is to excise theological content.

The third deficiency in Vinaver's description of how Malory responds to *La Queste del Saint Graal* is his claim that the author regarded the Grail Quest sequence as "an opportunity" for knights "to achieve still greater glory in *this* world" because he was "primarily concerned with 'erthly worship', not with any higher purpose" (3:1535). *Le Morte Darthur*'s presentation of Lancelot suggests instead that Malory viewed the quest as a means for Lancelot to gain glory in heaven as well as on earth through a secularized version of spiritual chivalry. The pattern of Malory's revisions reveals his "higher purpose": to make Lancelot—the French text's example of the failings of earthly chivalry—less problematic and more praiseworthy, thereby implying that a man engaged in secularized spiritual chivalry has God's favor. For example, as Malory recasts *La Queste*'s conclusion to its second Lancelot sequence, he raises the status of earthly chivalry through its well-known embodiment. The author makes the hero's failings less problematic by omitting the Vulgate Lancelot's reply to the recluse in which he states that if he should fall into mortal sin in the future, despite the lessons she and a holy man have provided, he will be the sinner worthiest of blame (*Queste* 145/47). Malory then gives Lancelot's status as the best earthly knight positive connotations through several revisions. First, he changes the recluse's rather generic wish, that God prevent the knight's backsliding out of pity, to a more sympathetic reminder: "Beware of everlastynge payne, for of all erthly knyghtes I have moste pité of the, for I know well thou haste nat thy pere of ony erthly synfull man" (2:934.21–23). Next, Malory compresses *La Queste*'s account of Lancelot's travel to a beautiful valley, eliminating the French text's references to his praying twice and revising the knight's crossing of the river. Instead of crossing because he has faith in God and trusts him to keep him safe (*Queste* 145–46/47; 2:934.25–29), Malory's Lancelot simply "in the name of God . . . toke hit [the river] with good herte" (2:934.28–29). This revision combines with Lancelot's response to the loss of his horse—"than he toke hys helme and hys shylde, and thanked God of hys adventure" (2:935.3–4)—to present this man as the embodiment of Malory's secularized version of spiritual chivalry. Together these revisions make Lancelot a Christian knight whose behavior is more manly and less monkish than his French counterpart's, but one who sincerely desires to achieve salvation and apparently deserves to do so.

A brief examination of how Malory begins and ends his version of the Grail Quest provides a snapshot of his theological compromise. His version of the Grail's appearance at the court of King Arthur elaborates upon the Vulgate account of Galahad's ancestry, in which Lancelot's son "descends on both sides from kings and queens and is of the highest lineage," by having Guinevere explain that "he ys of all partyes comyn of the beste knyghtes of the worlde and of the hyghest lynage: for sir Launcelot ys com but of the eyghth degré frome Oure Lord Jesu Cryst, and thys sir Galahad ys the nyneth degré frome Oure Lorde Jesu

Cryst. Therefore I dare sey they be the grettist jantillmen of the worlde" (*Queste* 20/9; 2:865.7–12). Through the queen's words, Malory links Galahad to both earthly and spiritual bloodlines while using a plural pronoun to blur the Vulgate's clear dividing line between father and son: "*they* be the grettist jantillmen of the worlde." When the Grail appears and "the grace of the Holy Goste" descends (2:865.21), Malory adds a detail that blends chivalric brotherhood with individual Christian identity: "Than began every knyght to beholde other, and eyther saw other, by their semyng, fayrer than ever they were before" (2:865.21–23).[26] In this moment, the Holy Ghost gives to each knight a glow that enhances his appearance; this glow could signify either how God's grace amends the Round Table, or how each man sees the other more positively than before when he sees with God's eyes (as each man would see if he were free from sin), or both. By retaining but not interpreting the moment at which the Grail's presence strikes the knights dumb, Malory creates a theological middle ground—suggesting either their sinfulness or their awe, or both.

As Malory restates his French source's conclusion in which Bors returns to Arthur's court and the king's clerks record the Grail adventures that Bors relates (*Queste* 279–80/87), he again offers readers access to a compromise between his source's monastic standard of perfection and a worldly standard. Malory's Bors reports not just the adventures of the Grail he has witnessed (*Queste* 279/87) but rather all "the hyghe aventures of the Sankgreall such as had befalle hym and his three felowes, which were sir Launcelot, Percivale and sir Galahad" (2:1036.16–19). Thus, Malory refuses to follow his source in placing Galahad in a separate category. Furthermore, the final scene of the Tale of the Sankgreal, one which he adds to his source text, includes a moment of fellowship that blends earthly and spiritual chivalry so thoroughly that readers struggle to decipher its meaning. Because Lancelot pledges to Bors that he will always be ready to "do for you and for yours" and while they live they "shall never departe in sundir," and then Bors echoes this pledge (2:1037.2, 5–6), readers might conclude that the Grail Quest has forged a bond between Lancelot and Bors—one which founds a spiritual fellowship. This conclusion is reasonable given that Bors has just reminded Lancelot "to remembir of thys unsyker worlde" (2:1036.28). Therefore, by embracing Bors Lancelot could signify his internalization of Galahad's teachings. Nevertheless, since Malory's account of the quest ends not with Galahad's reminder to Lancelot sent through Bors but instead with Lancelot's and Bors's pledge of fellowship (2:1037.1–7), readers might instead conclude either that, after the quest, the man who succeeded on it (Bors) is finally no different from the one who succeeded only partially (Lancelot), or that earthly fellowship finally matters more to these men than serving God. Moreover, as he develops his Grail Quest narrative, Malory makes many small-scale revisions to his source text that conflate—rather than sharply distinguish between—earthly and spiritual chivalry. Using such revisions, Malory makes Perceval and his aunt, Galahad, and Bors more earthly than in his source text.

Perceval and his aunt become less otherworldly than their French counterparts because Malory makes the familial bond seem more important than their devotion to God. He underscores the aunt-nephew bond by having her love Perceval more than any other knight (2:905.10–12) rather than just "molt" [much/ dearly] (*Queste* 72/25), and by having nephew and aunt meet the morning after Perceval's arrival—without the delay caused in the Vulgate account by Perceval's attending Mass (*Queste* 72/25; 2:905.15–16). Malory continues to deemphasize monastic values when Perceval leaves his aunt sooner than he does in the French source, making possible the omission of the Vulgate sequence in which they spend the evening discussing the necessity of his remaining a virgin (*Queste* 80/27). This revision enables Malory to narrow the distance between the earthly knight (Lancelot) and his spiritual peers (Perceval and Galahad) through two means: he avoids the topic of virginity that categorizes the knights in the French *Queste* so neatly, and he omits Perceval's aunt's pronouncement that Lancelot is condemned to fail on the Grail Quest because of his "eschaufement de char et par sa mauvese luxure [fleshly ardor and evil debauchery]" (*Queste* 80/27; 2:907). In keeping with this pattern of revision, Malory omits most of the hermit's explanation of Perceval's temptation by the lady of the black ship (*Queste* 113–15/37–38; 2:920.3–12) and omits Perceval's realization that his elderly advisor is the living bread (*Queste* 115/37; 2:920). These changes allow Malory to avoid dwelling upon either Perceval's near loss of his virginity or the Grail knight's thigh wound that so graphically represents it. Later on, when Bors rejoins Perceval and Galahad for the end of the quest, Malory omits the knights' comments about how much they desire to see the Grail (*Queste* 265–66/83) but retains their joy at finding one another again—refocusing the episode on chivalric fellowship rather than on the holy object they seek (2:1027.4–7). Such amendments to his French source reconcile the earthly and spiritual drives of the successful Grail-knights in Malory's book and prepare for Lancelot's joining that group.

Like Perceval and his aunt, Galahad becomes more earthly because Malory omits much theological background connected to the Vulgate's presentation of Galahad as a second Christ. Malory heavily abbreviates the explanation Perceval's aunt gives regarding the spiritual significance of three tables—those of the Last Supper, the Holy Grail, and King Arthur—and of the red heraldic arms of Galahad; as a result, he integrates Galahad into a spiritualized but still secular Round Table community rather than into an unearthly Grail community (*Queste* 74–79/25–27). First, he omits from this sequence any mention of the table at which Jesus sat with his apostles, or of the Grail Table (2:906–7). Next, he amends the description of the Round Table to give it spiritual significance, expanding its description as signifying the "rowndnes of the worlde" to encompass "the rowndenes signyfyed by ryght" (*Queste* 76/26; 2:906.16–17). Malory then retains his source's description of the fellowship of the Round Table as making its members, whether from a Christian or non-Christian land, think themselves more fortunate than if they possessed either the whole world (*Queste*-author) or half the world (Malory)—perhaps because it fits nicely with his vision of the Round Table as creating community (*Queste* 76–77/26; 2:906.17–21). Finally, Malory not only secularizes the meaning of Galahad's garments but also puts Galahad's magnificence into a chivalric context. In *Le Morte Darthur*, Perceval's aunt simply states that Galahad is worthy to wear the color red instead of discussing the theology of Galahad's wearing the color of fire and his Christlike entry into a closed room (*Queste* 78/27; 2:906.11–12).[27] Then, where *La Queste* links Jesus and Joseph of Arimathea to the Good Knight (Galahad) and dubs Galahad both "mestre [master]" and "pastor" to Perceval, *Le Morte Darthur* stresses that—through miraculous power—Galahad cannot be defeated in battle: he "hath no peere, for he worchith all by myracle, and he shall never be overcom of none erthly mannys hande" (*Queste* 78/27; 2:906.12–14). These revisions secularize the corresponding material from *La Queste* by shifting all the significance that the French source reserved for three tables onto the Round Table and repositioning it in a secularized setting. Their effect is to conflate earthly with spiritual chivalry so that knights—especially Lancelot—can achieve glory in this world and the next.

Other revisions further blend earthly and spiritual chivalry by modifying both Lancelot and Bors; consequently, Lancelot's earthly strengths can help to make him worthy of salvation. When a hermit addresses Lancelot, he does not define the knight as spiritually inferior to his son Galahad but rather stresses his extraordinary gifts as an earthly knight: "And thou ought to thanke God more than ony othir man lyvyng, for of a synner erthely thou has no pere as in knyghthode nother never shall have. But lytyll thanke hast thou yevyn to God for all the grete vertuys that God hath lente the" (2:930.14–18). Malory then creates a fictional world in which earthly gifts help knights earn salvation, using a more earthly Bors. First, Bors's words blend earthly chivalry into spiritual when he characterizes the Grail Quest as a means of achieving "much erthly worship" (2:955.9), and then "a religious man" explains that a successful Grail-seeker "shall be the beste knyght of the worlde and the fayryst of the felyship" (2:955.2, 12–13). It is significant that this description of the Grail-seeker can apply to both Galahad and Lancelot. Later, when Bors rescues a maiden from rape, he does so because she appeals to his loyalty to King Arthur as well as his loyalty to God (2:961.5–12), whereas the *Queste*-author has the maiden invoke Bors in the name of God alone (*Queste* 175/56). Based on this pattern of revision, readers might reasonably conclude that, for a knight who hopes to enter heaven, reputation in the secular world and loyalty to secular authority are just as important as service to God.

Malory's creation of a secularized version of spiritual chivalry becomes even more palpable when a holy man reminds Lancelot that his sin will make him as able to see the Grail as "a blynde man that sholde se a bryght swerde" (2:927.14) but soon thereafter stresses the knight's relative success: "yet shall ye se hit more opynly than ever ye dud" (2:928.5–6).[28] Malory's theological compromise is most evident, however, in his recasting of the end of the Grail Quest sequence in which Lancelot joins Bors as an eyewitness to the Grail adventures and receives validation as a Grail knight: "And whan they had etyn the kynge made grete clerkes to com before hym, for cause they shulde cronycle of *the hyghe adventures of the good knyghtes. So whan sir Bors had tolde hym of the hyghe aventures of the Sankgreall such as had befalle hym and his three felowes*, which were sir Launcelot, Percivale and sir Galahad and hymselff, *than sir Launcelot tolde the adventures of the Sangreall that he had sene. And all thys was made in grete bookes and put up in almeryes at Salysbury*" (2:1036.13–22, my emphasis). Thus, Lancelot joins Perceval, Bors, and Galahad as a member of the spiritual elite.[29] This is a moment for which Malory has prepared his readers by asserting, at the end of the Tale of King Arthur, that four knights would achieve the Holy Grail (1:180.9–10).[30] In addition, Malory has even the most spiritual of knights, Galahad, mark himself as a participant in earthly chivalry through his pledge to Perceval's sister, "Damesell . . . ye have done so muche that I shall be your knyght all the dayes of my lyff" (2:995.30–31). Perceval's aunt confirms Galahad's earthly ties by hailing him as the "beste knyght of the worlde!" (2:893.7). Malory is, therefore, not secularizing in Vinaver's sense of decreasing his source's theological content. Instead, he is reconciling chivalric and Christian values by transforming that theological content. By modifying—not eliminating—the spiritual values of his source, Malory achieves two goals: the conflation of earthly and spiritual chivalry and the compression of the hierarchy of Arthurian knights.

Compressing the Spiritual Hierarchy of *La Queste del Saint Graal*

In order to compress the spiritual hierarchy of Arthur's top knights, Malory must redeem his Lancelot. Malory's gradual elevation of Lancelot—a man who has been willing to serve his ladylove "in ryght othir in wronge"—to the position of "hede of al Crysten knyghtes" suggests a willingness to shift the monkish Christianity of the French *Queste* toward a more practical, secularized theology (2:1058.31–32, 3:1259.9–10). Malory's emendations create a Galahad significantly less singular and ethereal than the Vulgate one. This program of revision entails humanizing Galahad, lessening the flaws of Galahad's companions on the Grail Quest, and elevating Lancelot.

As the quest begins, Lancelot is already inching toward Galahad's position at the top of the Arthurian hierarchy because Malory makes Galahad more earthly, carefully linking son to father. While the *Queste*-author presents Galahad as handsome but stresses how his innocence makes him capable of great deeds (*Queste* 2–3/3), Malory focuses on the young man's appearance rather than his spiritual state in order to liken him to an earthly knight (2:854.29–30). In addition, Malory's Galahad possesses the title "the Hawte Prynce"—one consistent with his noble birth in Lancelot's line (*Queste* 7–8/5; 2:860.11)—and delights Lancelot as "hys sonne" rather than as the knight he dubbed (*Queste* 9/5; 2:861.13).[31] Malory's Guinevere reinforces this close tie between son and father when she expresses her interest in Galahad as the product of both his father's nobility and Pelles's daughter's deception (2:862.2–7), not as the knight who will end the adventures of the Wounded King (*Queste* 10/6). Later on, Malory again reinforces Galahad's close tie with his earthly father, both through a hermit who reminds Lancelot of Galahad's begetting on the daughter of King Pelles and through his own omission of background information connected to Mordrain that might distract readers from the father-son relationship (*Queste* 134–38/44–45; 2:930.11–14, 21–25).

Malory also decreases the spiritual gap between Galahad and his companions on the Grail Quest through further omissions and alterations, ones that make Galahad less of a second Christ. Malory humanizes Galahad by replacing the Vulgate's statement that only "qui Diex l'a destiné [God's chosen one]" should be "tant hardiz [so impudent]" as to touch the shield meant for Galahad (*Queste* 34/13; 2:881.9–11) with the secularized claim that "never shall no man beare thys shylde aboute hys necke but he shall repente hit" (2:881.9–11). He also omits the Vulgate's labeling Galahad as a second Christ after he drives the devil out of a tomb (*Queste* 38/14; 2:882.28–35) as well as its description of the knights' swearing an oath on relics before departing for the quest—an oath Galahad swears first (*Queste* 22–23/9–10; 2:871–72). Malory further humanizes Galahad by omitting the Vulgate sequence in which an unfeeling Galahad insists on leaving Meliant behind—despite Meliant's initial objection—to pursue the more important task of seeking the Grail and by adding the Good Knight's explanation of his departure as necessary to pursue the quest like the "many good knyghtes [who] be fulle bysy aboute hit" (*Queste* 44/16; 2:886.4–7).

Malory even makes his Galahad part of a team of equals. In the sequence in which Galahad, Perceval, and Bors slaughter the knights of Castle Carcelois, Malory has each knight win his own horse—making them into three equals—where the Vulgate has Perceval and Galahad win their own horses and then one for Bors, thus underscoring the superiority of virgins (*Queste* 230/72–73; 2:996.24–29). Then, Malory has his three knights achieve a joint triumph in just a few lines (2:996.30–997.2) rather than replicate his source's comparison of Galahad to a supernatural force: "Car Galaad fet tiex merveilles et tant en ocit qu'il ne cuident mie que ce soit hons mortieux, mes anemis qui laienz se soit embatuz por aus destruire [Galahad had accomplished such amazing feats and had killed so many men that the others felt he was not human but the devil himself who had rushed in to destroy them]" (*Queste* 230/73). When the three companions fight at the leprous lady's castle, Malory again modifies his source in order to bring

Galahad closer to the level of his companions—despite echoing *La Queste*'s characterization of him as a monster on the battlefield (*Queste* 238/75; 2:1001.21–26). Whereas the Vulgate describes Galahad's forcing the enemy to retreat with the aid of Perceval and Bors, Malory makes the two knights integral to the victory. First, he omits the image of Galahad driving the enemy and praises Perceval and Bors directly, saying "hys two felowis holpe hym passyngly well"; then, he uses the construction "and so *they* helde their journey [i.e., their work in the battle] everych inlycke harde tyll hit was nyghe nyght" to create a cause-and-effect connection between Perceval and Bors's aid and the victory (*Queste* 238/75; 2:1001.26–28). Malory's emendations create a character significantly less singular and ethereal than the Vulgate Galahad.

As Malory gently shifts Galahad lower on the spiritual ladder, he shifts the other knights higher. Gawain, the Vulgate's exemplar of how *not* to seek the Grail, becomes less blameworthy for his failure to do penance. While the Vulgate Gawain simply states that he cannot bear to suffer penance (*Queste* 55/19), Malory's Gawain excuses himself. He says, "I may do no penaunce, for we knyghtes adventures many tymes suffir grete woo and payne"—suggesting that he does his penance on the field (2:892.19–20). The hermit's response, "Well," appears to express assent, as does his holding "hys pece" afterwards (2:892.21).[32] Neither the holy man nor the narrator overtly criticizes the knight. Later on, Gawain echoes his Vulgate counterpart when he excuses himself for refusing another hermit's instruction, pleading time constraints: "and I had leyser I wolde speke with you, but my felow sir Ector ys gone and abithe me yonder bynethe the hylle" (*Queste* 161/52; 2:949.10–12). Although the hermit Nacien tells Gawain, "Well . . . thou were better to be counceyled," again there is no overt criticism from either the holy man or the narrator of Gawain's departure (2:949.13–14). However, Malory's omissions make both of these decisions seem more reasonable than they do in his source text. Since the first holy man neither tells Malory's Gawain to repent and make amends to God nor falls silent when he realizes Gawain will not listen (*Queste* 55/19; 2:892), the knight appears to depart with the hermit's blessing. Later, Gawain leaves the hermit Nacien having successfully asserted the importance of the chivalric fellowship: he does not, as in *La Queste*, indirectly acknowledge his wrongdoing by promising to return as soon as possible for a private conversation with the hermit (*Queste* 161/52; 2:949.12). Malory further improves Gawain's standing by having the knight ask Nacien to receive his confession rather than just advise and instruct him (*Queste* 155/50; 2:945.30–31). These small-scale revisions raise Gawain's status considerably through reconciling spiritual and earthly fellowship in *Le Morte Darthur*.

Like Gawain, Perceval and Bors improve under Malory's pen. While the Vulgate Perceval tends to be rather slow in his theological processing (*Queste* 112–15/37) and despairs easily, Malory's Perceval is more even-tempered. The Vulgate

Perceval reacts to losing Galahad's trail by fainting, wanting to die, and begging a squire to kill him and thus end his suffering (*Queste* 89/30); Malory's Perceval, however, expresses "sorow oute of mesure" (2:910.20) but does not faint or seek his own death (2:910.13–20). Later on, Malory retains the scene in which Perceval bemoans his error of nearly sleeping with the lady of the black ship and punishes himself with a thigh wound but reins in the Vulgate Perceval's histrionics (*Queste* 110–12/36; 2:919.10–26). Malory's not-so-bright knight does *not* believe he will die of shame and guilt, desire to die, lament naked, let himself bleed all day, or pray all night for forgiveness. Although Malory has his knight faint with shame at the white ship's approach (2:919.26–27), his Perceval does not proclaim he will die without the comfort of the Holy Spirit (*Queste* 112/36). By being less volatile than his French counterpart, Malory's Perceval becomes a useful role model for the author's contemporaries.

Bors, in contrast, is already the most competent of Galahad's companions in the Vulgate Grail Quest, but Malory's revisions remove what minor flaws he had. Both *La Queste* and *Le Morte Darthur* make it clear that Bors cannot rescue Collgrevaunce, but Malory's presentation of that fact improves Bors's image. In both versions of the episode, Bors feels anguish at the thought of either his brother Lionel or Collgrevaunce dying (*Queste* 191/61; 2:972.6–11). However, whereas the *Queste*-author stresses that Bors cannot move because he is in terrible pain (*Queste* 191/61), Malory more directly excuses Bors for failing to rescue Collgrevaunce: "he had nat so much myght to stonde one foote" (2:972.12–13). In addition, Malory makes Bors seem manlier by revising *La Queste*'s reference to his struggle to stand up before retrieving and donning his helmet; in *Le Morte Darthur*, Bors simply "arose and put on hys helme" (*Queste* 192/61; 2:972.27–28). Furthermore, Malory gives Bors a speech in which he first takes the moral high ground by charging Lionel with the murders of two innocent men and then asserts his manliness: Bors states that he fears God's wrath much more than he fears his brother and asks God to "shew His myracle" (29) upon them both (2:973.23–31). Malory even ensures that Lionel forgives Bors "gladly" and has Bors leave the abbey where he has lodged without stealing away at an awkwardly early hour, as he does in the Vulgate account; as a result, the author removes any doubts readers might have regarding Bors's perfection (*Queste* 194/62; 2:974.17, 18–20).

In order to complete the compression of *La Queste*'s spiritual hierarchy, Lancelot—with Malory's aid—becomes his son's rival in spiritual excellence. As Stephen C. B. Atkinson has observed, Lancelot is the only one of Malory's Grail knights "who begins to interpret events before they are explicated by an expert" and who manages to "describe at length his own spiritual condition in the sort of speech otherwise reserved for hermits and priests."[33] Even before the Grail adventures begin, Malory gives his Lancelot more dignity than his Vulgate counterpart by having him speak like a prophet. In both texts, Lancelot tells Arthur the same information—that he will not touch a sword he is unworthy to possess, that whoever fails in his attempt to draw it will receive a wound, and that on this day the Grail adventures will begin (*Queste* 5–6/4; 2:856.21–27). However, Malory's knight possesses the dignity of a prophet for three reasons. First, Malory has Lancelot reply to Arthur "full sobirly" rather than in a "toz corouciez [distraught]" manner (*Queste* 5/4; 2:856.20). Second, Malory makes Lancelot's speech more powerful by removing Arthur's interruptions, thereby transforming the knight's replies into a prophet's pronouncement. Third, when Malory recounts the episode in *La Queste* in which a lady tells Lancelot that he cannot call himself the world's best knight and he pledges not to claim that title again (*Queste* 12–13/7), Malory's lady encourages a humbler Lancelot to continue to consider himself a great knight. Malory adds not only the knight's humble words, "I know well I was never none of the beste," but also the lady's correction of them: "[y]es ... that were ye, and ar yet, of ony synfull man of the worlde" (2:863.28–31). Her labeling Lancelot the best of sinful men prepares for Ector's description of him, in the closing lines of the "hoole book," as "the trewest lover, of a synful man, that ever loved woman" and "the godelyest persone that ever cam emonge prees of knyghtes" (3:1259.14–15, 17–18).

While the *Queste*-author portrays Galahad as superior to Perceval, Bors, and especially to Lancelot (*Queste* 137–38/45), Malory presents Lancelot as the best of sinful knights while making him seem less sinful than his French counterpart. By minimizing the humiliation his favorite knight receives, Malory deemphasizes Lancelot's sins. The knight receives neither the admonitions of a hermit that underscore Galahad's superiority to his father (*Queste* 116–17/38; 2:925) nor those of another hermit that label Lancelot a failure on the Grail Quest (*Queste* 123/40) and then reduce the knight to tears—first by reminding him of his sullied virtue and then by likening him to the inappropriately dressed wedding guest in the Gospel of Matthew (*Queste* 123–28/40–42). Malory further narrows the gap between Lancelot and his son by having the hermit who interprets Lancelot's vision of his ancestors stress not Galahad's superiority but his father's goodness: "And thou ought to thanke God more than ony other man lyvyng, for of a synner erthely thou hast no pere as in knyghthode nother never shall have" (2:930.14–16; cf. *Queste* 137–38/45). If Malory's superlative adjective "godelyest" (3:1259.17) means "godliest" rather than "goodliest," then the gap between Galahad and Lancelot narrows still further.[34]

In later episodes, Malory continues to compress the spiritual hierarchy through revisions that give Lancelot both lineal and spiritual proximity to God. To the aforementioned description of Galahad as a descendant of the world's best knights and noblest family (*Queste* 14–15/7), Malory has Guinevere add the information that Lancelot is eight degrees removed from Jesus Christ and Galahad nine; this addition makes Lancelot and his son the greatest gentlemen in the world but puts Lancelot lineally closer to the Lord than Galahad (2:865.9–12).[35] By changing Vulgate details that increase the distance between Lancelot and his Lord, Malory presents Lancelot as less spiritually troubled than his French counterpart. Malory not only decreases Galahad's shame at the circumstances of his conception—so "sir Galahad was *a lityll* ashamed"—but also minimizes the damage to Lancelot's reputation when discussing his affair with Guinevere (*Queste* 20/9; 2:870.1, my emphasis). Malory omits the entire episode in which a squire berates Lancelot for his sinful love of Guinevere, tells him he is the world's worst knight and has lost heaven, and finally reduces Lancelot to tears when the hero realizes he is doomed "unless God's mercy was very great" (*Queste* 117–18/38–39; 2:925). Furthermore, Malory makes Lancelot's sin an impediment to his success on the Grail Quest that "hyndryth" and "shamyth" him (2:896.7) rather than the cause of both his failure on the quest and his consequent despair (*Queste* 61–62/21; 2:896.5–9). In a similar bit of editing, Malory omits the Vulgate's parable of the gold coins that condemns Lancelot as a bad servant who has separated himself from God (*Queste* 63–64/21–22; 2:896–97). Malory also avoids dwelling upon his favorite knight's sexual transgressions: he does not use Lancelot as an example of how debauchery costs a knight his chance to finish the Grail Quest, as his source does (*Queste* 80/27; 2:907.19), and he nearly eliminates the French text's extended criticism of Lancelot's sinfulness in the dead monk episode (*Queste* 118–28/39–42; 2:927.12–31). In addition, Malory has a good man conclude his brief chastising of Lancelot by saying that if it were not for the knight's sin "ye were more abeler than ony man lyvynge" (2:927.15–16). Elsewhere, too, rather than focusing as the Vulgate does on Lancelot's weak spiritual grounding, Malory underscores his potential for spiritual growth: if Lancelot lives as cleanly as he has promised to do, he will have "more worship than ever [he] had" (2:897.30–31). In short, Malory gives his Lancelot spiritual proximity to God.

Having elevated Lancelot's spiritual position, Malory can make perfunctory the great knight's two fervent prayers for protection against backsliding, reducing them to a few lines (*Queste* 130/42, 131–32/43; 2:928.15–17). Malory reinforces Lancelot's ameliorated position by having Nacien acknowledge Lancelot's "unstablenesse" (2:948.27) but then present him as a spiritual role model: Lancelot has made a commitment to forsake sin, would have been "nexte to encheve hit [the Grail] sauff sir Galahad" (26) if it were not for that fault, and will die a holy man (*Queste* 160–61/51–52; 2:948.20–29). Malory reinforces Lancelot's position again when Galahad kneels in order to receive Lancelot's blessing (2:1012.18).[36]

Malory's modifications to the end of the Grail Quest likewise improve Lancelot's position within the spiritual hierarchy. First, Malory omits the Vulgate's labeling of knights who failed on the quest as shamed (*Queste* 262/82; 2:1020.20–25) and gives Lancelot the knowledge that only one of the successful questers will return to Arthur's court, again making him a prophet (*Queste* 262/82;

2:1020.33–34). Then, Malory ends his Tale of the Sankgreal not with Bors alone reporting the adventures of the Grail but instead with Bors fulfilling his promise to greet Lancelot—before greeting Arthur and his court—on behalf of Galahad and Perceval (2:1036.23–26). Consequently, Malory's Lancelot becomes an honorary Grail companion by recounting Grail adventures (*Queste* 279/87; 2:1036.19–20) and exchanging pledges of loyalty with Bors (2:1036.33–1037.7). Both Lancelot's "truste to God" that Galahad's prayer for his father's continued spiritual health will "avayle" him and Galahad's earlier statement to his father that "[s]ir . . . no prayer avaylith so much as youres" reinforce Lancelot's lofty position in *Le Morte Darthur* (2:1036.31–32, 1014.1–2). By the end of Malory's Grail Quest, readers will probably agree with Lancelot's self-assessment: "no man in thys worlde have lyved bettir than I have done to enchyeve that I have done" (2:1018.5–6). Lancelot's transformation makes the Grail Quest sequence pivotal in Malory's development of the concept of secularized salvation, a fact that further undermines Vinaver's claim that Malory saw it as an "intrusion" upon the Arthurian world.

Lancelot's Ascent in the Context of the "hoole book"

In keeping with its focus on raising Lancelot's spiritual status is *Le Morte Darthur*'s melding of spiritual concerns with secular ones from the end of the Book of Sir Tristram de Lyones to the end of the "hoole book." In particular, the baptism of Palomides and the healing of Sir Urry demonstrate the efficacy of Malory's brand of secularized Christianity. By positioning the baptism of Palomides (a non-Christian) and his assimilation into Arthurian society at the end of the long Tristram section, Malory prepares readers for Lancelot's later integration into the group of knights that achieves access to the Holy Grail (2:845.5–20). This episode also demonstrates how earthly considerations often trump heavenly ones in *Le Morte Darthur* because Palomides might be said to convert to Christianity as penance for offending Tristram. The Saracen's offer to receive baptism immediately follows his recognition that he has vexed and caused bodily harm to Tristram, and he asks Tristram—rather than God—for forgiveness (2:844.19–845.1).[37] Tristram then gives himself both spiritual and earthly authority through his response to Palomides: "all my evyll wyll God forgyff hyt you, and I do" (2:845.6–7). At the baptism itself, Tristram tells the suffragan what he and Palomides desire, an act that makes Tristram—often interpreted by scholars as an all-too-earthly knight—a spiritual mentor of sorts, and then Palomides travels to Camelot where King Arthur, Queen Guinevere, and all the Round Table knights who are present rejoice in his baptism (2:845.16–20). As Dorsey Armstrong has noted, Palomides receives baptism into the Round Table fellowship and Christianity simultaneously since for Malory the two are inextricably linked.[38] By shaping Tristram into a spiritual mentor, despite the Saracen's more perfect devotion to love and chivalry,

Malory connects the Book of Sir Tristram to the "hoole book" while preparing for Lancelot's ascent to a spiritual position just below Galahad's.[39]

As one of the few episodes in *Le Morte Darthur* original to Malory,[40] the healing of Sir Urry indicates the author's attitudes toward spirituality and salvation while moving Lancelot up the ladder of perfection. It gives Lancelot a moment of spiritual connection with and blessing from God that counterbalances his significant lapses in faith, such as when he joins the weaker party "in incresyng of hys shevalry" instead of seeking the side of right or trusts his sword rather than God to protect him from the lions guarding the Grail castle (2:931.25; 2:1014.16–18). In the Urry episode, Lancelot resists obeying Arthur's command that he attempt to heal this man (3:1151.24–30). However, validating Malory's conflation of the Round Table fellowship with the Christian community, Arthur overcomes that resistance by asking Lancelot to search Urry's wounds "to beare us felyshyp, insomuche as ye be a felow of the Rounde Table" (3:1151.32–33). Despite his secular motive, when Malory's favorite knight prays devoutly for the power to heal, it is granted to him: Urry's wounds heal immediately after Lancelot touches them (3:1152.18–32). Harry E. Cole has discussed this episode as representative of "the common-sense approach to goodness that the entire 'Book of Sir Launcelot and Queen Guinevere' captures."[41] One aspect of this "common-sense approach" is Lancelot's miracle that reflects late medieval Christianity in England, with its "continuing and indeed growing commitment to corporate Christianity."[42] This miracle also reflects how "[t]he healing mediated by the saint restored more than health to the sick: it restored them to the community of the living."[43] "Saint" Lancelot's healing restores Urry to the life of an active knight, with strikingly secular results: Urry becomes one of the two best jousters in a tournament Arthur organizes, and then a knight of the Round Table (3:1153.7–21). Urry, like Lavayne, appears to be "irresistibly drawn to [Lancelot] as the ideal knight."[44] After Lavayne and Urry share success in the tournament (3:1153.14–19) and entry into the fellowship of the Round Table (3:1153.19–20), the two knights strengthen their secular bond, first through Lavayne's marriage to Urry's sister and then through their shared devotion to Lancelot (3:1153.25–26). Both men then serve Lancelot continually and do great deeds at Arthur's court (3:1153.25–31). The Urry episode, therefore, situates Lancelot as the source of miracles on earth after the death of Galahad, and it prepares readers for the final sequence of events in *Le Morte Darthur* during which Lancelot becomes the center of a new spiritual community and earns salvation. Through this and other episodes, Malory transforms Lancelot into a spiritual as well as secular anchor for Sirs Urry and Lavayne, and eventually into the spiritual center of the community that coalesces at the end of Malory's book. This transformation makes Lancelot the spiritual center of *Le Morte Darthur*.[45]

As I have argued elsewhere, Lancelot achieves salvation at the end of Malory's "hoole book" by following Guinevere into monastic life, but he enters that life because of their earthly love.[46] Like many members of the medieval gentry, Lancelot chooses to become a monk (and, departing from common practice, a priest) late in his life, but unlike them he does so to prove his loyalty to his earthly love—not because he converts.[47] Having refused the queen's suggestion that he return to his homeland and marry another woman, declaring "for I shall never be so false unto you of that I have promysed," Lancelot decides to remain true to Guinevere by embracing her new lifestyle: "But the same desteny that ye have takyn you to, I woll take me to, for to please Jesu, and ever for you I caste me specially to pray" (3:253.3–6). By making "Guinevere's manner of life . . . a substitute for Guinevere herself," Lancelot can practice a secularized version of monasticism.[48] His final words reveal that Lancelot's salvation will result from his devotion to both Guinevere and Jesus: he states he will become a monk both to keep his promise to his queen and "for to please Jesu," but then he tells Guinevere that he will pray "specially" for her—making her the focus of his newfound Christian practice. Therefore, Lancelot earns salvation both despite and because of his earthly love for the queen.[49] Only through his devotion to the queen does Lancelot advance to the next stage of his spiritual journey, taking "hym to suche perfeccion" that first Bors and then seven other knights enter monastic life because "they had no lust to departe but toke such an habyte as he had" (3:1255.1–2). The fact that these knights take Lancelot as their role model in penance suggests that Guinevere's former lover is the heart of this monastic community.

Lancelot gains heaven, and what appears to be sainthood, through devotion to both his God and his queen. He obeys God's command that he earn "remyssyon of his synnes" (3:1255.15) by burying Guinevere, and then he proves his devotion to the dead queen by "grovelyng on the tombe" (8) she shares with Arthur and starving himself to death (3:1257.1–9). The Lord's gift to Lancelot of a vision regarding Guinevere's death, which he receives three times in one night, is one sign that Lancelot has become venerable (3:1255.14–21). Soon afterwards, the knight's salvation becomes apparent, first in the bishop of Canterbury's dream in which he sees Lancelot escorted to heaven by angels (3:1257.35–1258.10) and then in the state of Lancelot's corpse: it wears a smile and, like a saint's, exudes "the swettest savour aboute hym that ever they felte" (3:1258.16–17). Lancelot also receives memorials consistent with his image as one who has gained access to heaven through both earthly and spiritual perfection. First, Ector's threnody defines him as the best knight, lover, and sinful man who ever lived (3:1259.9–21); then, Lancelot's companions respond to the hero's death, as Ector does, with "wepyng and dolour out of mesure" (3:1259.22)—suggesting that they mourn not only the priest whose death and entry into heaven should be a source of joy but also the great knight whom the world has lost. The manner of Lancelot's death and the responses to it constitute the most powerful expression of Malory's brand of secularized salvation.

Lancelot's lasting spiritual impact on his companions becomes palpable when several knights return to their homes and "there they al lyved in their cuntreyes as holy men" (3:1260.3–4). In addition, Malory notes that "the Frensshe book" tells of how Bors, Ector, Blamour, and Bleoberis went to the Holy Land, fought "many batayles upon the myscreantes," and "there they dyed upon a Good Fryday for Goddes sake" (3:1260.7–8, 14–15). This new set of holy companions displaces the successful Grail knights as Malory defines them: Perceval, Bors, Galahad, and Lancelot. It is noteworthy, however, that Lancelot inspires some knights to live holy lives in the day-to-day world and others to become soldiers of God and martyrs—providing two spiritual life-paths for his Round Table companions. In this way, Malory reinforces the central message of *Le Morte Darthur*: that there is more than one path to heaven. The fact that Bedivere ends his days as a hermit while other knights serve God as soldiers, though more spiritual ones than they were before, provides a final glimpse of Malory's vision of secularized salvation (3:1259.32–33, 1260.7–10). Lancelot's role here in creating a spiritual path for earthbound men is the final product of Malory's gradual elevation of Lancelot so that he can rival, and finally displace, Galahad as the spiritual center of the Arthurian legend. The knights' seeking the company of Lancelot in the book's closing pages parallels their seeking the company of Galahad during the Grail Quest, and that quest is emblematic of Lancelot's displacing his son by the end of *Le Morte Darthur*.

Although C. David Benson has argued that in the last two tales of *Le Morte Darthur* "what replaces it [sexual desire] is only superficially Christian,"[50] such a dismissal of the complexity of Malory's approach to Christian theology ignores Lancelot as the embodiment of a powerful, though secularized, vision of Christianity. Malory has not rejected his thirteenth-century literary model of salvation but rather has revised it to make it relevant to late medieval knights and ladies. *Le Morte Darthur* models late medieval Christian values that are anchored in this world but reflect the compatibility of earthly and heavenly achievements—in both the Grail Quest sequence and the "hoole book." It carefully reshapes the story of the quest so that Lancelot can glide to heaven on the path the Vulgate Cycle authors found, but Malory cleared, for him. By marking Lancelot for spiritual success throughout his book and altering the spiritual hierarchy of *La Queste* to raise Lancelot's status, Malory makes his favorite knight the embodiment of a secularized brand of salvation. This version of salvation does not, however, sacrifice theological depth: as Felicity Riddy notes, "Malory, for all his demystification of the Grail, has a much stronger awareness than Hardyng of the inwardness of the religious experience that it represents and the spiritual meanings it might be made to bear."[51] Malory's transformation of his French sources does not diminish the spiritual focus of the Arthurian story; instead, it tailors and enriches that focus so that it can affect his late fifteenth-century audience as powerfully as the Vulgate Cycle affected its thirteenth-century one.

Malory's Practical Christianity and Its Consequences

Because Malory had lived through the end of the Hundred Years' War, his level of nationalistic enthusiasm was lower than that of the English chroniclers of the previous generation.[52] Nevertheless, Malory offers a means for himself and his readers to move beyond such pessimism by using the Vulgate Cycle as his primary source for his Grail Quest narrative. *La Queste del Saint Graal*'s version, unlike the one he had available in the prose *Tristan*, was the "earlier version of the story [that] was purer, less adulterated by the wider chivalric narrative of the prose *Tristan*."[53] Therefore, it probably appealed to him as representing the purer days of England's early medieval past—familiar to readers of Malory's discussion of "love nowadayes" (3:1120.1, 9) in contrast to "the olde love" (3:1120.2–3), which he calls "vertuouse" (3:1119.30). Given that the Vulgate version is exceptional in its focus on spiritual chivalry, Malory's Grail Quest is in the tradition of "the Grail romances [that] are not religious works, but secular and chivalric: they do not pretend to be devotional."[54] If Richard Barber is correct that the author of the Vulgate *Queste* was "a chivalric enthusiast bold enough to add a spiritual dimension unparalleled in any other romance," Malory might have been attracted to this "hybrid" text and then followed its example of adding a spiritual dimension, one he felt appropriate for his own generation.[55] Malory's awareness of *L'Estoire del Saint Graal* in which "the appearances of the Grail have been interspersed between secular, chivalric adventures" could likewise have shaped his treatment of the Grail story.[56] Perhaps Malory's aim as he reconciled French sources (*L'Estoire del Saint Graal*, the Vulgate Cycle, the Post-Vulgate Cycle, the prose *Tristan*) with English ones (the *Stanzaic Morte Arthur* and the *Alliterative Morte Arthure*) was to create a compromise version of the Grail Quest—one that relaxes the strict monastic standard of the Vulgate *Queste* but treats the Grail as integral to the Arthurian world.[57]

Malory's revision of *La Queste del Saint Graal* reveals his practical brand of Christianity, one that makes the demands of Christian practice compatible with those of chivalric and political practice. Malory's theological middle ground between the absolute moral standard of thirteenth-century monasticism and the flexible one of earthly chivalry emerged naturally from his grappling with ideological clashes within contemporary literature and culture. As a late fifteenth-century reader, Malory probably knew that mainstream works such as *Mirk's Festial* and *The Pricke of Conscience* make no mention of the Grail or of the quest it inspired[58] and that "the normal attitude of the Church to the stories about the Grail . . . was to studiously ignore them."[59] Since the Grail story was not central to church doctrine, Malory could modify this legend to appeal to the members of the aristocracy and gentry who made up his audience. However, no fifteenth-century Christian could have been unaware of the Grail legend that John of Glastonbury had promulgated in his *Chronicle of Glastonbury Abbey*, according to which Joseph of Arimathea—thirty-one years after Christ's Passion—had brought Christianity to Britain.[60] Malory's omission of a full account of Joseph of Arimathea from his Grail Quest narrative could have resulted from pessimism about the state of fifteenth-century chivalry in England, from skepticism of Glastonbury Abbey's claim to the oldest Christian heritage in Western Europe, and/or from a desire to present the majority position of the authors of medieval Grail narratives. Nevertheless, his discussion of the Grail itself reflects sensitivity to the religious sensibilities of his day. Although Malory follows popular English legend when he connects the Grail to the Holy Eucharist through its receiving "parte of the bloode of Oure Lorde Jesu Cryste, which Joseph off Aramathy brought into thys londe" (1:85.24–25), he judiciously avoids the highly controversial issue of the nature of the Eucharist. Since Lollards had questioned church teaching about it and the church had responded by burning as heretics those with unorthodox beliefs about the meaning of the sacred meal, Malory avoids a potential accusation of heresy by abbreviating the rituals in the final Grail scene so that he does not include details that "could have been understood as an interpretation of the Eucharist."[61]

The theological middle ground *Le Morte Darthur* inhabits is also a product of developments in English Christian practice from the fourteenth century up to the Reformation.[62] Like his fellow English Christians who gained prayers of intercession for themselves and their loved ones in exchange for contributions to their parish churches,[63] Malory asks a community of fellow knights and their ladies for prayers of intercession in exchange for his literary contribution. Through such intercession, he hopes to gain "unity in salvation" with his fellow knights although, as a prisoner, he is dead to the world.[64] Furthermore, his blending of earthly and spiritual chivalry is entirely consistent both with the mixing of ecclesiastical and secular hierarchies in the Corpus Christi processions that developed during the fourteenth century and with the "increasing access to and interest in types of spirituality previously confined to the monastery" that the wealthy and literate gained during the fifteenth and sixteenth centuries.[65] Malory's focus on the mortality of individual knights and on the Round Table as an inspiration to true chivalry parallels how "the thought of mortality was endlessly harnessed by preachers and dramatists, not to call people away from social involvement but to promote virtue and sociability in this world."[66] Malory's willingness to reshape the Vulgate Cycle's Grail Quest narrative is likewise consistent with English religious culture in the fifteenth and sixteenth centuries that was "rooted in a repertoire of inherited and shared beliefs and symbols, while remaining capable of enormous flexibility and variety."[67] That culture produced an "enormously varied" but "massive and growing literature in English designed to instruct and edify the laity and to provide the simple clergy with material for their preaching and teaching."[68]

Malory's practical Christianity is most evident, however, in the preface that his contemporary William Caxton wrote for his book. Caxton's opening sentence eloquently summarizes how Malory's editor—and most likely Malory as well—understood practical Christianity. It specifies key tenets of this faith: that earthly conquests are an essential part of kingship, the story of the Grail is an integral part of the Arthurian story, and King Arthur himself is an exemplar of Christian life:

> After that I had accomplysshed and fynysshed dyvers hystoryes as wel as of contemplacyon as of other hystoryal and worldy actes of grete conquerours and prynces, and also certeyn bookes of ensaumples and doctryne, many noble and dyvers gentylmen of thys royame of Englond camen and demaunded me many and oftymes wherfore that I have not do made and enprynte the noble hystorye of the Saynt Greal and of the moost renomed Crysten kyng, fyrst and chyef of the thre best Crysten, and worthy, kyng Arthur, whyche ought moost to be remembred emonge us Englysshemen tofore al other Crysten kynges.   (1:cxliii.1–11)

Caxton encourages practical Christianity by urging readers to embrace *Le Morte Darthur* as an educational tool whether or not they choose "to gyve fayth and byleve" to all that is in Malory's book: echoing Romans 15.4, Caxton reminds them that "al is wryton for oure doctryne, and for to beware that we falle not to vyce ne synne, but t'exersyse and folowe vertu" (1:cxlvi 10, 11–13). Since his editor interpreted *Le Morte Darthur* as an aid to developing the moral virtue that could earn people "good fame and renommé in thys lyf" and "everlastyng blysse in heven," Malory's intention might well have been to educate the laity about how to lead good lives as members of a chivalric society (1:cxlvi. 14–15, 16). Malory's having a hermit remind Gawain that he should have embraced "knyghtly dedys and vertuous lyvyng" supports this conclusion (2:891.31–32).

Caxton's desire that readers approach *Le Morte Darthur* having accepted that the tales might not be completely true and their heroes might not be perfect Christians is consistent with what Malory as author needs from those same readers: practical and compassionate morality. If Malory has successfully convinced the ladies and gentlemen of late fifteenth-century England that Lancelot was the greatest of sinful men, there is hope for him too. Caxton's generous interpretation of *Le Morte Darthur* suggests that—for readers of Malory's day—his Lancelot successfully "slouched" his way to Bethlehem, despite his sins, and Malory himself "slouched" his way into his audience's good graces despite his imprisonment for treason. Although readers today cannot know whether Sir Thomas Malory reached his spiritual Bethlehem, they can take comfort in the fact that he reached his literary one.

NOTES

I gratefully acknowledge Helen Cooper for helping me to locate several studies of medieval spirituality cited here; the staff of The Rossell Hope Robbins Library at the University of Rochester for bibliographical aid; D. Thomas Hanks, Jr., Janet Jesmok, and K. S. Whetter for their generous responses to earlier versions of this paper; and D. Thomas Hanks, Jr., for encouraging me to write it.

1. Field, "Malory and the Grail," pp. 147, 145–46.

2. All references to Malory's text will be to Malory, *Works*, ed. Vinaver, 3rd rev. ed. All quotations from Malory's text come from this edition and will be noted parenthetically by volume, page, and line numbers. All references to the Vulgate Cycle's *La Queste del Saint Graal* will be first to *La Queste* and then to *Lancelot-Grail*. I quote the translation for ease of reading except where comparative analysis requires attention to the phrasing of the French text. Parenthetical citations will refer first to *La Queste*, then to Malory's *Le Morte Darthur*.

3. Hynes-Berry, in "Tale 'Breffly Drawyne Oute of Freynshe,'" argues that Malory's version of *La Queste* "cannot be accurately described either as a translation or as an abridgement" and judges it to be "a genuinely original work" (p. 93). Stephen Atkinson, in "Malory's Lancelot," takes the position that "Malory follows the French source closely, although he makes countless alterations, many of them subtle but most, significant" (p. 131).

4. Moorman, "Tale of the Sankgreall," p. 187; Barber, *Holy Grail*, p. 219.

5. Mahoney, "Introduction," *Grail*, p. 41. Hodges's position is similar to Mahoney's: "Although condensing his French source, Malory respects the theological material and, if anything, heightens the Grail's connection to the Eucharist" ("Making Arthur Protestant," p. 194). Richard Barber, however, disagrees with Mahoney: "The Grail adventure is one more of the marvels of Arthur's time, even if it does lead to a wholly spiritual conclusion: and when Lancelot attempts to achieve the Grail, Malory emphasizes his relative success rather than his complete rejection at the last and crucial moment" (*Holy Grail*, p. 218). Boardman likewise views the Grail Quest as just "another narrative call to adventure on the way to the tragic conclusion," and he argues that the quest has little impact on "that conclusion" ("Grail and Quest," p. 129).

6. For a full exploration of *Le Morte Darthur* as a secular text, see Whetter's contribution to this volume.

7. For scholarship that builds upon Vinaver's assertions about Malory's Grail Quest, see C. David Benson's "Ending of the *Morte Darthur*," Larry D. Benson's *Malory's "Morte Darthur,"* Cole's "Forgiveness as Structure," and Whitehead's "Lancelot's Penance."

8. Vinaver notes that the text Malory used is not among the extant manuscripts of *La Queste del Saint Graal* and suggests that it was probably "more closely related to [the] lost common original" of the two groups of extant manuscripts (3:1534).

9. For a full analysis of Malory's book in a traditional Christian context, see Beverly Kennedy, "Malory's Lancelot," as well as the essays by Cherewatuk, Hanks, and Holbrook in this volume.

10. Olsen fully analyzes the "vertuouse love" passage in this volume.

11. Anderson summarizes the range of interpretations that the healing of Sir Urry has received in "'Ein Kind wird geschlagen'" (p. 46). Boardman, in contrast, interprets this miracle as "a direct result of Lancelot's self-effacing prayer" ("Grail and Quest," p. 128).

12. Fries, in "Malory's Tristram as Counter-Hero," characterizes Tristram as "the catalystic [*sic*] embodiment of that immoderation in sex and arms destined to overwhelm the

Arthurian world" (p. 613), and, in "Indiscreet Objects of Desire," explores Tristram's "deceit and disregard of chivalric values" (p. 101). Hanks, in "Malory's *Book of Sir Tristram*," argues that Malory presents Tristram and Isolde as involved in "a great love distinctly tarnished at the edges" (p. 25).

13. See, for example, Hanks in this volume.

14. *The Middle English Dictionary* offers several meanings for the noun *recover(e)*: (a) 'Recovery from illness, injury, poverty, misfortune, etc., relief'; (b) 'release from imprisonment, deliverance'; (c) 'help, succor; a way out of a dangerous situation, means of extrication from a distressing situation'; and (d) 'treatment or cure of a sick man, remedy for wounds' (R.1 [1984], p. 244). For the noun "recoverer," it offers these meanings: (a) 'Relief from suffering or from the pain of hell; recovery; also salvation'; (b) 'shelter, safety; also safekeeping'; and (c) 'help, succor' and possibly 'hope for aid' (R.1 [1984], p. 247).

15. *The Middle English Dictionary* gives the following primary meanings for the noun *deliveraunce*: (1 a) the 'Act of freeing (from pain, disease, sin, danger, etc.), saving, rescue; being freed, escape, deliverance'; (1 b) 'release from an obligation'; (2 a) 'The release of a prisoner; freeing from captivity or bondage'; (2 b) 'ransoming'; and (2 c) 'clearing a prison to bring the prisoners to trial'; also figuratively connected with the idea of 'Judgment Day' (D.2, pp. 943–44).

16. Yeats, "Second Coming," lines 21–22.

17. In his introduction, Vinaver notes that "while the manuscript is neither Malory's own 'copy' nor the one used by Caxton, it is at least as reliable as Caxton's text and quite independent of it" (Malory, *Works*, 1:cii).

18. Readers of Vinaver's edition will note that most of Malory's transitions between stories lack the rhetorical force of the ones just cited, and some are so gradual that they do not create clear boundaries. See Malory, *Works*, 1:56.3–7, 1:92.16–20, 1:120.28, 1:132.26–30, 1:152.29–31, 1:247.3–9, 1:287.27, 1:441.1–4, 1:451.29–31, 2:476.23–25 and 481.1–3, 2:523.1–6, 2:545.1–4, 2:572.26–27, 2:633.1–4, 2:648.16, 2:670.28–31 and 675.1–2, 2:711.1–4, 2:722.26–27 and 727.1–5, 2:769.1–2, 2:791.1–4, 2:833.9–11, 2:872.27–30, 2:899.13–14, 2:920.16, 2:935.5–6, 2:949.20, 2:975.20, 2:1005.25, 2:1020.35, 2:1060.3–6 and 1065.1–2, 2:1098.14–22, 3:1114.29–32, 3:1140.11–13 and 1145.1–5, 3:1183.1–5, 3:1205.22–23 and 1211.1–4, 3:1221.14–18 and 1227.1–4, and 3:1249.1–4.

19. Evans has discussed Malory's blending of secular and Christian chivalry in "Camelot or Corbenic?," pp. 256–59. Radulescu, in "'Now I take upon me the adventures to seke of holy thynges,'" describes Malory as having "a pragmatic understanding of religious experience" based upon an analysis of Lancelot's Grail adventures and the Urry episode (p. 285).

20. Batt, *Malory's "Morte Darthur,"* p. 134.

21. The assumption that Malory was an orthodox and traditional Christian is one that Duffy's research indirectly supports when he notes that early publishers, including Caxton, printed religious literature that was "overwhelmingly traditional and orthodox" (*Stripping of the Altars*, p. 78).

22. Barber, *Holy Grail*, p. 157.

23. Of course, Malory was not the first Arthurian tale-teller to draw the Quest of the Holy Grail into the world of secular chivalry. As Barber notes in *The Holy Grail*, there is both Heinrich von dem Türlin's *Diu Crône* [The crown], which makes the Grail Quest "simply another adventure," and the prose *Tristan*, which focuses on stories of heroes in the context of the Round Table and on "Tristan as the exemplar of chivalrous love" (pp. 187, 200).

24. E. Jane Burns notes in her translation of *La Queste* that the text makes a distinction

between *virginitez* 'virginity' and *pucelages* 'maidenhood', with *pucelages* indicating a state of physical virginity but *virginitez* indicating the absence of any desire for carnal relations (*Lancelot-Grail* 4:68).

25. Hynes-Berry, in "Tale 'Breffly Drawyne Oute of Freynshe,'" offers an example of how carefully and respectfully Malory uses his French source (p. 93).

26. Moorman, in "Tale of the Sankgreall," interprets the Grail's appearance here as underscoring "the civil strife of the Round Table," explaining how "[u]nder the light from the Grail, the incivility and internal dispute are forgotten for the moment" (p. 203).

27. "Wyte you well," seyde she, "that this ys he, for othirwyse ought he nat to do but to go in rede armys" (2:906.11–12).

28. Boardman notes that Malory must emphasize Lancelot's success on the Grail Quest in order to succeed as a translator: "Malory's larger structure depends on displaying and valuing the success of Lancelot even as a 'synful man' of prowess in the World of Arthur" (Grail and Quest," p. 128).

29. Stephen Atkinson has noted that Malory's Gawain groups Lancelot with Perceval, Bors, and Galahad ("Malory's Lancelot," p. 140, citing *Works* 2:941.19–20).

30. Field interprets Malory's identification of Pelleas as one of the four successful Grail knights as the product of his confusion of Pelleas with Perceval, and Malory's turning three successful knights into four as the result of "unconsciously promoting his favourite knight Launcelot, who hangs between success and failure in Malory's own Grail story and in his source"; however, within the context of Malory's other modifications of his primary French source, it seems more likely that these preparations for the later spiritual promotion of Lancelot are products of conscious choice ("Malory and the Grail," p. 146).

31. As Vinaver notes, this title of "Hawte Prynce" could have resulted from Malory's confusing Galahad and "Galehoult li Haut Prince," who appears in both the prose *Lancelot* and the prose *Tristan* (3:1546, note for 2:860.11).

32. "Well" is a word whose meaning varies greatly. Although in some contexts it connotes agreement or assent, in others it can introduce an objection. *The Middle English Dictionary* notes that "well" can be "used to initiate an utterance, acknowledgement, or a response, usually with reduced semantic force and sometimes perhaps conveying acquiescence, skepticism, or concession"; see "wel (adv)," sense 17. (a), W.1 [1999], p. 258.

33. Stephen Atkinson makes the first observation in reference to Lancelot's understanding of his suffering defeat and capture at the hands of the white knights ("Malory's Lancelot," p. 139, citing Malory, *Works* 2:932.16–18) and the second in reference to Lancelot's speech at 2:896.1–9 ("Now I Se and Undirstonde,'" pp. 104–5).

34. Although Vinaver construes the word "godelyest" as goodliest, it is also possible to construe it as "godliest" since *The Middle English Dictionary* notes that both *godli* (short *o*) and *godli* (long *o*) can be spelled "gode-" (G.2 [1963], p. 211).

35. Hodges interprets Queen Guinevere as "clearly misunderstand[ing] Galahad's significance," but her statement is entirely in keeping with the practical Christianity that Malory presents ("Making Arthur Protestant," p. 210).

36. Stephen Atkinson discusses the significance of Galahad's kneeling before Lancelot, a detail Malory adds to the story ("Malory's Lancelot," pp. 142–43).

37. "I requyre you, my lorde, forgyff me all that I have offended unto you! And thys same day have me to the nexte churche, and fyrste lat me be clene conffessed, and aftir that se youreselff that I be truly baptysed" (2:844.33–845.1).

38. Armstrong, in *Gender and the Chivalric Community*, notes how Palomides "is already always on his way to baptism" when readers meet him and how Malory makes

the "significant move" of "using the more spiritually oriented *Queste del Saint Graal* as his source" for the Grail sequence (p. 143).

39. Owen and Owen argue that the Book of Sir Tristram de Lyones has a structure consistent with Malory's narrative patterns in his "hoole book" and that "[m]ost of the so-called ramblings and digressions in the Tristram section" contribute to a book that "weaves together a number of narrative and thematic motifs" ("Tristram in the *Morte Darthur*," p. 16).

40. Most scholars agree with Mann, in "Malory and the Grail Legend," that the Urry episode "has no counterpart in the French source" (p. 219). However, Robert L. Kelly, in "Wounds, Healing, and Knighthood," contends that "there is solid evidence that the prose *Lancelot* episode [of the knighting of Lancelot] was the model of Malory's tale of Urry" (p. 175).

41. Cole, "Forgiveness as Structure," p. 40.

42. Duffy, *Stripping of the Altars*, p. 131.

43. Duffy, *Stripping of the Altars*, p. 189.

44. Parry, "Following Malory," p. 154.

45. See Jesmok in this volume. For a discussion of how Malory's Lancelot "succeeds in great part in participating in Holiness," see Morris ("From Malory to Tennyson," pp. 88–90).

46. Tolhurst, "Once and Future Queen," pp. 304–7.

47. Given Duffy's assertion that "*the* defining doctrine of late medieval Catholicism was Purgatory" (*Stripping of the Altars*, p. 8), Malory's choice of focusing on Lancelot's anguished struggle to embrace monastic life after a lifetime of sin must have had a more powerful emotional impact on his fifteenth-century readers than it has on readers today. Therefore, Malory's tale of Guinevere's and Lancelot's salvation would have had particular appeal to late medieval readers.

48. Parry, "Following Malory," p. 168.

49. Whitehead, in "Lancelot's Penance," asserts that Malory's Tale of the Death of King Arthur builds upon *La Mort le Roi Artu* but "perverts the message, by allowing two things to remain while all else changes: the power of human affection and the remembrance of the past," both of which are evident in Lancelot's "bitter self-reproach" and "grovelling on the queen's tomb" (pp. 112–13). However, Whitehead does not explore the issue of salvation in Malory's retelling.

50. C. David Benson, "Ending of the *Morte Darthur*," p. 234.

51. Riddy, "Chivalric Nationalism," p. 407.

52. Riddy, "Chivalric Nationalism," p. 410.

53. Mahoney, "Truest and Holiest Tale," p. 382.

54. Barber, *Holy Grail*, p. 115.

55. Barber, *Holy Grail*, p. 159.

56. Mahoney, "Introduction," *Grail*, p. 25.

57. Lacy aptly describes Malory's relaxing the moral standard of his primary French source: he "lowered the standard of purity required for success" on the Grail Quest ("From Medieval to Post-Modern," p. 121).

58. See *Mirk's Festial* and Rolle, *Pricke of Conscience*.

59. Barber, *Holy Grail*, p. 170. Wood likewise notes the silence of the church regarding the Holy Grail, but she cautions that it is "just silence, and not evidence of an institution fearful of powerful heretical secrets" ("Holy Grail," p. 180).

60. John of Glastonbury, *Chronicle*, pp. 2–3.

61. Barber, *Holy Grail*, p. 220.

62. For a full exploration of the development of late medieval Christian practice in England, see Duffy, *Stripping of the Altars*.

63. Duffy, *Stripping of the Altars*, pp. 334–37.

64. Duffy, *Stripping of the Altars*, p. 337.

65. Duffy, *Stripping of the Altars*, pp. 43–44, 3.

66. Duffy, *Stripping of the Altars*, p. 303.

67. Duffy, *Stripping of the Altars*, p. 3.

68. Duffy, *Stripping of the Altars*, pp. 62, 61.

Malory's Secular Arthuriad

K. S. Whetter

In the final scenes of *Le Morte Darthur* Sir Thomas Malory records how the few remaining Round Table knights depart Arthur and Guinevere's tomb for Joyous Garde, where they meet Ector and inter Lancelot's body; shortly thereafter, Bors, Ector, Blamour, and Bleoberis depart England altogether for the Holy Land. "And there," says Malory, "they dyed upon a Good Fryday for Goddes sake" (3:1260.14–15).[1] Taken out of context like this, such an ending certainly seems to offer a deeply Christian conclusion to "The Hoole Book of Kyng Arthur and of His Noble Knyghtes of the Rounde Table" (3:1260.16–17). This final scene, however, is still only one of many, and when measured against the events and emphases of the "hoole book" it may well take on a different meaning. Furthermore, even within this scene the setting in the Holy Land should not blind us to the fact that the knights are once again knights of this earth, not religious hermits as they had been for the period between Arthur's and Lancelot's deaths. While the knights were assembled at Arthur's grave their horses had roamed free (3:1255.8–9), but this is significantly no longer the case in the final scene. Far from showing a conclusive departure from earthly chivalry, then, the ending of the *Morte* actually indicates a return to it.

This scene of the knights' return to chivalric action is Malory's invention and typifies his focus on secular chivalry and secular fellowship,[2] for throughout the *Morte Darthur*, including the Grail Quest, Malory continually valorizes earthly deeds in order to aggrandize and memorialize the secular fellowship of Round Table knights. Such memorialization reveals Malory's secular rather than Christian focus and narrative. I shall accordingly argue that the thematic coherence of the *Morte Darthur* that the Unity Debate did so much to elucidate includes a unifying focus on the glory and tragic destruction of a very earthly institution. The destruction of the Round Table, moreover, is not proof of the vanity of earthly living or divine punishment for sin, merely a tragic fact of life. Malory's focus on the importance of secular Arthurian chivalry is best illustrated through an examination of: (1) secular aspects of the Grail Quest; (2) the importance of scenes from throughout the *Morte* that incorporate religious language for secular ends; (3) episodes that emphasize the importance of the earthly companionship of the Round Table; (4) the Healing of Sir Urry; and (5) the very earthly motivation of the final community gathered around Arthur's grave. All of these ideas and episodes, of course, blend into one another and should not be considered rigidly separated.

1. The Critics and Secular Aspects of the Quest

It is well known and often remarked that Malory follows his "auctorysed" (3:1260.8) French book much more faithfully in his Tale of the Sankgreal than anywhere else in the *Morte Darthur*: Eugène Vinaver established that "Malory's *Tale of the Sankgreall* is the least original of his works. Apart from omissions and minor alterations, it is to all intents and purposes a translation of the French *Queste del Saint Graal*."[3] Vinaver made this claim in his first edition in 1947, and it was repeated in the second and third editions. P. J. C. Field concurs, stating authoritatively that the "Vulgate *Queste del Saint Graal* . . . is the only source where [Malory] begins at the beginning and relates all the episodes in the same order through to the end, sometimes word for word."[4] An equally often remarked corollary of this faithfulness to the source is that Malory likewise adopts the Christian sentiment and religious rigor of the French book, and that he does so both in the Grail Quest and throughout the *Morte* as a whole. Charles Moorman, for instance, claims that Malory "always preserves the core of the French book's doctrinal statements" and argues at length that the Grail section accurately reflects Malory's views of the *Morte*'s narrative and theme as a whole.[5] C. S. Lewis similarly takes pains to show the essentially Christian nature of both Arthurian chivalry and its Malorian narrative, and Felicity Riddy and Raluca L. Radulescu each see the *Morte*, and especially Malory's Grail Quest, as reflecting and reinforcing orthodox late medieval piety.[6] Many of the contributors to this book argue along lines similar to one or the other of these interpretations. The Christian view gains considerable support from Malory's explicit to the Grail Quest and its expression of a mindset that might well be thought to contain a markedly reverent Christian tone: "Thus endith The Tale of the Sankgreal that was brefly drawyn oute of Freynshe—which ys a tale cronycled for one of the trewyst and of the holyest that ys in thys worlde—by Sir Thomas Maleorré, Knyght. O Blessed Jesu helpe hym thorow Hys myght! Amen" (2:1037.8–13). Regardless of whether or not one sees this last line as a sincere and penitential reflection on Malory's own sin,[7] an inevitable conclusion of the Christian reading of the *Morte Darthur* is that the Grail Quest represents a spiritual and critical test of Lancelot and the Round Table fellowship, a test that most of the knights obviously fail and that both highlights previous sins and foreshadows the post-Grail sinful decline of the fellowship. Hence Moorman's statement that "Lancelot . . . represents the sins which are to lead to the destruction of this society," or Lewis's claim that Lancelot fails both in the quest and even in the Healing of Urry, where Lancelot's tears are said to represent his awareness "of his illicit love" and the "failing" of the entire Round Table.[8]

Against such readings, Vinaver maintains that Malory is really concerned "to secularize the Grail theme"; although Malory is faithful to the basic plot of his source, he is translating the letter rather than the spirit, thereby bringing it in line with Arthurian rather than celestial chivalry.[9] Furthermore, as the dashes in Vinaver's presentation of the explicit to the Sankgreal make clear, the "truest and . . . holiest" comment could well be Malory's apostrophe on the Vulgate *Queste* rather than an assessment of his own version of the Grail story. It has even been speculated that "truest and . . . holiest" refers not to Malory's narrative or source but to the man for whom he wrote, Henry VI.[10] As the varied but inconclusive attempts by scholars to establish Malory as either Lancastrian or Yorkist reveal, there is not enough evidence to support or deny this speculation, but even if Malory *is* characterizing his own Grail quest this way, the Tale of the Sankgreal is far more secular than its source. This secular tone is apparent even in the mouth of one of the elect Grail knights, for Bors states that Galahad's attaining the Siege Perilous betokens the winning of "grete worship" (2:861.15–16), and that whoever wins the Grail "shall have much *erthly* worship" (2:955.9; my emphasis).[11] As I have remarked in a different context, it is significant that the hermit to whom he is speaking in the latter instance does not contradict him.[12] Likewise, the hermit who admonishes Lancelot to repent his sins also urges him "to sew knyghthode" and perform deeds of earthly prowess (2:899.5). Lancelot had shortly before this conversation expressed concern "never to have worship more" (2:895.31–32) because of his failures in the Grail Quest, but the words of Bors and the hermit reveal that a focus on earthly worship and glory is perhaps not so misguided after all. Indeed, as Jill Mann emphasizes, Malory's presentation of adventure in the Sankgreal is "consistent with that of the rest of his work."[13] And elsewhere in the *Morte* Lancelot can invoke God to celebrate combat and the winning of worship, exclaiming happily during the adventures that first establish his earthly fame, "God gyff hym joy that this spere made, for ther cam never a bettir in my honde" (1:278.4–5). In marked contrast to the Vulgate *Queste*, then, Malory's juxtaposition of Christian and secular values continually valorizes rather than condemns earthly chivalry.

I therefore contend that Malory throughout the *Morte Darthur* downplays any reverently Christian theme in favor of a notably secular concern not merely with the affairs of this world rather than (preparation for) the next but specifically with earthly fellowship and its very earthly tragedy. This is the case before, during, and after the Grail Quest. I am treating "secular" and "Christian" as to some extent opposing values here, principally because in the final analysis the medieval Christian view demands a renunciation of sin that, by definition, involves a partial or total renunciation of earthly concerns and earthly love.[14] Hence the marked superiority of celestial over earthly chivalry in the Vulgate *Queste*. Even in Malory Galahad asks Bors to warn Lancelot to "remembir [hym] of this worlde unstable" and keep his distance from earthly affairs (2:1035.8–12, 1036.27–28). The religious reading of the *Morte*, then, ultimately demands that characters and readers turn their backs on Camelot and look to heaven: such is the example provided by Galahad and Perceval, each of whom actively seeks to depart this world in favor of the next. Similarly, Lancelot's complete failure in the Vulgate *Queste* and qualified failure in Malory's Sankgreal are each made the consequence of his inability to renounce earthly affairs. As I shall discuss later, even Guinevere ostensibly turns to heaven in the wake of Arthur's death. In contrast, while the secular reading does not necessarily question the instability of this world, neither does it condemn it, and I suggest that Galahad's opposition of secular and celestial living in no way represents the majority of Malory's characters—nor Malory himself.[15]

Of course, Arthur and his knights frequently manage to combine both celestial and earthly values and concerns, especially in the overlap of Christian and chivalric virtues. It is, however, ultimately the earthly or secular view that matters to most characters (as well, it seems, as to Malory himself), not the Christian one.[16] I shall return to this later, but it is significant that in the Grail Quest's final scene appear two passages not in Malory's source. One is Bors's delivery of Galahad's warning that Lancelot should "remembir [hym] of thys unsyker worlde" (2:1036.28). This might be thought to confirm the Christian and celestial reading were it not for the fact that the passage is followed by the second original statement, in which Lancelot and Bors vow never to be separated in the future (2:1036.33–1037.7). We are thus forced to question whether this world *is* unstable and, even if it is, whether this justifies renouncing it. For in contrast to Galahad and Perceval, Lancelot and Bors do not turn their backs on this world or on Arthurian chivalry. On the contrary, Lancelot and Bors both return to Camelot and each vows to "never departe in sundir whylis [their earthly] lyvys may laste" (2:1037.5–6). Their returns, their reunion, and their vows undermine the supposed superiority of celestial fellowship by revealing an explicit desire to embrace and maintain *earthly* companionship and love.[17] It is no doubt for this reason that one of the two tales in the Arthuriad in which the word *fely-shyp* appears most often is in fact the Sankgreal.[18] Thus, by closing the Sankgreal with this conversation and vow between Bors and Lancelot, Malory modifies the celestial focus of the Vulgate *Queste* to emphasize instead that the human and secular fellowship of the Round Table is a society good in itself, worthy of preservation.[19]

2. Secularizing Religion

I noted above that the Christian reading of the *Morte Darthur* often focuses on the supposedly sinful failings of Arthur and his knights, linking the destruction of the Round Table to the sins of its champions and exemplars. One of the earliest scenes in the Arthuriad that is often invoked to support a Christian condemnation of earthly chivalry is Arthur's incestuous union with Morgawse. In the aftermath of this affair Merlin informs Arthur that God is angry with him (1:44.16–30); many critics take this as confirmation that Arthur's eventual violent demise is a (deserved) punishment for incest, a consequence of the sinful failings of the Round Table as epitomized by Arthur's lechery in this scene and by Lancelot and Guinevere's own affair elsewhere.[20] Such an argument is, however, far truer of Malory's French source for this tale than it is of his English adaptation. That source is the *Suite du Merlin* from the Post-Vulgate *Roman du Graal*, and "Seule la Post-Vulgate [*Roman*] établit un *rapport direct* entre le péché d'Arthur et sa mort."[21] Although I am not suggesting that God or Merlin condones the incest, Malory's Merlin says explicitly that God is angry because this act will secure the destruction of the kingdom: "ye have gotyn a childe that shall destroy you and all the knyghtes of youre realme" (2:44.17–19). Merlin does reiterate God's anger and desire to punish Arthur for his "fowle dedis" (2:44.26–27), but this is much less condemnatory than the *Suite*'s clear castigation of Arthur as "dyables et anemis Jhesucrist."[22] Malory devotes more attention to suggesting that it is the actions of the son, not the sins of the father, that secure Arthur's death. Moreover, despite repeated critical claims about Arthur's punishment, neither Merlin nor Malory makes any mention of God's wrath hereafter. One might object, of course, that such mention is unnecessary: the Round Table *is* destroyed, and such destruction ably illustrates God's wrath and Arthur's sin. But as ever with Malory, things are not always as they seem, and however logical this objection might be, its interpretive validity is considerably undermined by what Malory *does* emphasize. What Malory emphasizes is that Arthur shall have "a worshipfull dethe" which contrasts with Merlin's own "shamefull dethe" (2:44.28-30). This is far from the explicit denunciation of sin found in the *Suite*. Arthur's worshipful death in the Arthuriad thus reveals that Malory's primary focus is on the *earthly consequences* of the incest (the destruction of the fellowship and the realm), not the initial sinful act and not any potential divine punishment.

Malory's Arthuriad thus records and laments the glory and tragic destruction of a very secular institution. That institution and its exemplars, moreover, are not destroyed exclusively or even predominantly owing to sinful moral failure. The final destruction of the Round Table fellowship is instead the consequence of a complex interplay of good and bad characters, good and bad intentions, fate and free will; even sheer "unhappy" (3:1236.29) chance plays a role in Malory's version of events.[23] Human weakness does occur, I argue, but Malory does not condemn such weakness as Christian or moral failure. Rather, the destruction of the realm in Malory is given earthly motivations such as Mordred's eventual rebellion and Lot's bitterness because Morgawse happens to be his wife as well as Arthur's one-night incestuous lover; but in each case the motivations are earthly honor and rivalry, not divine wrath. Once again we can clarify this interpretation by comparison with the source. In the *Suite du Merlin* Lot opposes Arthur because of the supposed death of Mordred in the May Day slaughter,[24] but Malory changes the motivation, stating explicitly that "because that kynge Arthure lay by hys wyff and gate on her sir Mordred, therefore kynge Lott helde ever agaynste Arth-ure" (1:77.5–7). Likewise, although the archbishop reminds us of Arthur's incest as he castigates Mordred's attempt to wed Guinevere (3:1227.29–1228.17), the reminder is tangential and the "condemnation [is] of Mordred, not Arthur."[25]

All of this helps to indicate that God is not always where we think in the *Morte Darthur*. Elsewhere in this volume Karen Cherewatuk focuses on the sig-nificance of religious funerals in the *Morte*, and D. Thomas Hanks, Jr., analyzes Malory's entreaties that his readers pray for his soul, but it is important that God is frequently invoked in far less Christian contexts. Thus various knights "pray to God [to] sende" themselves or their peers "honoure and worshyp" (1:164.6–7). More emphatically, Arthur swears early in the story to be so revenged on Morgan le Fay "that all crystendom shall speke of hit" (1:157.8–10) and swears by God at the end that he would be revenged on Mordred if he could (3:1236.19–21). Gareth similarly vows by God and the Order of Knighthood to avenge the kid-napping of his dwarf (1:330.13-16), and Lancelot in the queen's apartment prays "Jesu Cryste, be Thou my shylde and myne armoure" (3:1167.5–6) before single-handedly defeating fourteen knights at close quarters, thereby achieving his great-est feat of individual combat. Lancelot's language is Christian—but his actions and adulterous love are not.[26] It is crucial that this scene follows the Grail Quest and that Lancelot is victorious, for his presence in the queen's apartment, whether they are in bed or no, serves as a reminder and symbol of the lovers' markedly human relationship; his escape is equally physical, equally earthly.[27]

Like Malory's Healing of Sir Urry (discussed below), the scene in Guine-vere's apartment reminds us of, but also mitigates and supersedes, Lancelot's par-tial failure in the Grail Quest because of his love of the queen. As he claims when he returns Guinevere to Arthur, he managed single-handedly to defeat the four-teen knights only because "the myght of God" was with him (3:1197.21–24). In these and other cases throughout the *Morte*, then, Malory juxtaposes secular and Christian language and values to reveal that the *Morte* is, at the very least, both secular *and* Christian.[28] For if the "myght of God" is with Lancelot in this instance so too is the body of Guinevere, whose love continues to inspire him. As the *Morte* draws toward its tragic climax, moreover, Malory does not choose to illustrate the inadequacies of secular values and characters, including human love; rather, he celebrates them and laments their passing in ways that valorize secular institutions, emotions, and characters. This is especially true of his elegiac aggrandizement of the Round Table fellowship.

This scene in the queen's apartment where the lovers face their accusers hearkens back to the same commingling of secular and religious in the Knight of the Cart and the episode where Lancelot defends Guinevere against charges of adultery in trial by combat with Melleagaunt. The formal combat of the cart episode itself implicitly echoes the opening of the Book of Sir Launcelot and Queen Guinevere, where Malory records how Lancelot attempts to evade the slander of Aggravaine by applying "hym dayly to do for the plesure of Oure Lorde Jesu Cryst" by championing all manner "of ladyes and damesels ... [i]n all such maters of ryght" (2:1045.10–28). Lancelot is not entirely pure "in his prevy thoughtes" (2:1045.13) about Guinevere, but he is innocent where these other ladies are concerned, and so he continues to achieve victory. He is less innocent in the Knight of the Cart, the one place in the entire narrative where we see the lovers *in flagrante* and arguably the only occasion in the *Morte* where the idea that "God woll have a stroke in every batayle" is explicitly invoked,[29] for when Lancelot chastises Melleagaunt for entering the queen's chamber uninvited, Melleagaunt warns Lancelot: "I rede you beware what ye do; for thoughe ye ar never so good a knyght, as I wote well ye ar renowmed the beste knyght of the worlde, yet shulde ye be avysed to do batayle in a wronge quarell, for God woll have a stroke in every batayle" (3:1133.24–28). Lancelot admits "God ys to be drad!" (3:1133.29), but neither Melleagaunt's nor Lancelot's invocation of God is rubricated in the Winchester Manuscript at this point (fol. 441v), whereas the knights' names are continually highlighted throughout the narrative, including several times on this folio alone. Manuscript rubrication thus helps to reinforce Malory's human focus by constantly highlighting Arthur, his knights, and their deeds, as well as the predictable outcome of the combat: despite Melleagaunt's rhetoric and the idea—commonly accepted in medieval literature and life both—that in trial by combat God will secure victory for the righteous rather than the strong, Lancelot is victorious.

Beverly Kennedy, Keith Swanson, and Jacqueline Stuhmiller all argue for the prominence of trial by combat in the *Morte*, and all give different accounts of just how many such trials there might actually be in the text. I do not have space in this essay for a detailed study of trial by combat, but it is telling that Stuhmiller herself admits that Malory seems "far more interested in the combats themselves than in the legal processes that were supposed to instigate and regulate them."[30] What I wish to emphasize further is that in the Knight of the Cart episode Lancelot has just committed adultery with the queen and so is also technically guilty of treason (just as Guinevere has obviously likewise committed adultery and is likewise guilty of treason). His victory over Melleagaunt thus runs contrary to the very idea of trial by combat overseen by God. Although it is true that Malory has arranged this scene so that Lancelot is in fact fighting on the side of justice with an ostensibly true oath—the queen did not sleep with any of the injured knights originally captured by Melleagaunt—Malory also makes clear, and readers are well aware, that Lancelot's "vindication of Guenevere is . . . achieved by contentious means, and any notion of divine intervention to uphold absolute justice is severely attenuated."[31] In other words, Malory is not interested in the legal or religious ramifications of this scene, nor does he wish to present the lovers as guilty; rather, he uses the scene to emphasize that human love, the secular chivalry of the Round Table, and the earthly nobility or worthiness of the principal Arthurian characters are capable of standing on their own merits. Even Stuhmiller, who does argue for a certain prominence of trial by battle in the *Morte*, maintains, rightly I think, that "Malory takes care to *secularize* the theoretically sacred process of trial by battle."[32] Lancelot's manipulation of the oaths involved in trial by combat is proof of this. This secularization of trial by battle, moreover, has significant textual and thematic consequences. Most importantly for my purposes, and contrary to the Vulgate and Post-Vulgate views that the fall of the Round Table is due to sinful failures such as lechery or adultery, Lancelot and Melleagaunt's battle reveals just how far Malory goes to avoid presenting the lovers as sinful. Instead, he repeatedly suggests that human feelings and secular characters are valid and *worthy* subjects even with their human weaknesses and human sins: hence Lancelot's victory over Melleagaunt, hence the Healing of Urry, hence the statement, original to Malory, that Guinevere "was a trew lover, and therefor she had a good ende" (3:1120.12–13). Malory *is* concerned with the fall of Arthurian civilization, but not due to Christian sin or failure. Camelot falls because all human endeavor ultimately falls, but a secular reading of the *Morte* acknowledges that, for Malory, such a collapse is not a sinful failure but a tragic fact of life. Indeed, the tragedy is made all the more poignant by the essential *worshipfulness* of its participants. Such worship, moreover, is entirely secular.

3. Earthly Fellowship and the Round Table

Malory accentuates the secular nature of the *Morte* by emphasizing the glory of the earthly, chivalric brotherhood, and one way in which he does this is by revealing the love and comradery amongst its members. Judson Allen argues that Lancelot loves the "society of the Round Table" as much or more than he loves Guinevere.[33] Lancelot's lament when exiled from Camelot and England testifies (as Allen observes) to his love of the Round Table fellowship (3:1201.9–22), but it is equally true that he regularly fights in disguise against those fellows to aggrandize himself and his ladylove. Arthur, too, might be said to love the fellowship as much as the queen, famously bemoaning the imminent destruction of the Round Table by exclaiming, "much more I am soryar for my good knyghtes losse than for the losse of my fayre quene" (3:1184.1–3). This has proven to be a problematic, even an irritating passage for modern readers, and Arthur has accordingly been castigated for privileging homosocial over heterosexual bonds;[34] but it is worth remembering that the passage is original to Malory and asking ourselves why he added it.[35] I suggest that the real point is not Arthur's supposed dismissal of Guinevere but rather a profound expression of sorrow for the loss of what was an ideal knightly fellowship.[36] He is not proving that he never loved Guinevere or that she is merely a (female) commodity to be valued only in good times; he is instead saying that the destruction of the Round Table fellowship and all that the Round Table knights have worked to achieve makes the loss of even a queen—even if that queen is Guinevere—pale in comparison. He mourns, quite explicitly, an *earthly* fellowship, one whose destruction both characters and audience deeply regret.

Arthur makes a similar lament at the outset of the Grail Quest: "'Now,' seyde the kynge, 'I am sure at this quest of the Sankegreall shall *all ye* of the Rownde Table departe, and nevyr shall I se you agayne *holé togydirs*, therefore ones shall I se you *togydir* in the medow, *all holé togydirs*! Therefore I wol se you *all holé togydir* in the medow of Camelot, to juste and to turney, that aftir youre dethe men may speke of hit that such good knyghtes were here, such a day, *holé togydirs*'" (2:864.5–12; my emphases).[37] Moorman observes how the corresponding passage of the French book completely lacks Malory's plangent sorrow, and that this effect is achieved in large measure through the repetition of "holé togydirs." Yet for Moorman the peace and comeliness that the Grail immediately casts over the company is proof of the superiority of the celestial and Christian themes that, he says, Malory shares with his source.[38] This, however, is far from self-evident. Malory's secular memorializing of the knightly fellowship is in fact explicit in Arthur's concern that "men may speke of" the Round Table company after the knights' deaths. There is, moreover, little to suggest that Arthur has improperly read the signs or that Malory himself is favoring a Christian over a secular focus. It is well known that Malory's originality extends to reversing the French portrayal of Arthur as an unwise and enfeebled king, and this more positive characterization of Arthur suggests that Arthur's assessment of the Grail Quest is correct. In this sense we are meant to share rather than censure Arthur's very human *and* secular lament for the fading of the fellowship. So it is that the "holé togydirs" refrain and the accompanying somber and sorrowful tone echo throughout the close of the Arthuriad. One instance is Arthur's lament for the loss of the fellowship over his queen, noted above. Another comes in the Winchester Tournament in the Book of Sir Launcelot and Queen Guinevere, where Arthur recalls the Grail tournament by promising Guinevere that "thys seven yere ye saw nat such a *noble felyship togydirs* excepte the Whytsontyde whan sir Galahad departed frome the courte"

(2:1065.17–19; my emphasis). This is a straightforward celebration rather than lament, but we are meant to contrast the fellowship here with the departed fellowship of the Grail and to recall Arthur's earlier sorrow for those knights (including Galahad) who would not return. The narrative context of the Winchester Tournament and readers' awareness that Lancelot and Guinevere's affair is in danger of becoming public knowledge also render Arthur's words somber as well as celebratory: we know, even if he does not, that soon the fellowship will vanish because its members will destroy one another. The final evocation of the "holé togydirs" refrain occurs in the final explicit and in a phrase that is very likely Malory's title for his tragic story: "Here is the ende of the hoole book of kyng Arthur and of his noble knyghtes of the Rounde Table, that whan they were *holé togyders* there was ever an hondred and forty" (3:1260.16–19; my emphasis).

It is thus significant that even Malory's version of the establishment of the Round Table and its oath emphasizes the importance of secular chivalry and institutions. In the Vulgate *Merlin* and Post-Vulgate *Suite du Merlin* the Round Table is presented as a religious institution whose inauguration and code prefigure the arrival of the Grail. Malory rejects this, for his fellowship and table are more earthly and human; not only does he then create his own Round Table oath which, we are told, is reiterated at each Pentecost feast (1:120.25–27) but its "precepts convey no hint of religious piety, no promise of mystical experiences."[39] What it does emphasize, by association and origin, is the idea of the secular brotherly fellowship of Round Table knights.[40]

Of course, Christian and chivalric ideals sometimes commingle; the similarity of Arthur's sentiments in religious (Tale of the Sankgreal) and earthly contexts (the Morte Arthur proper) emphasizes the possible interconnection of these two spheres of the *Morte*. Certainly there is congruence in Arthur's laments for the Grail's disruption of knightly fellowship at the outset of the Tale of the Sangreal and in the aftermath of Lancelot's rescue of the queen in the Morte Arthur proper (Vinaver's final tale, sometimes also called Death of Arthur). Theoretically, medieval literature and society both reveal considerable potential overlap between Christian and chivalric values.[41] Malory might thus be balancing secular and Christian sentiments in culturally specific ways suggested by Fiona Tolhurst elsewhere in this volume. Repeatedly in the *Morte Darthur*, however, Christian and earthly-chivalric values or duties conflict. Such conflicts are not restricted to Christian and chivalric obligations in the *Morte*, but they are part of the earthly tragedy. And Malory, like Arthur, is more concerned with the dissolution of secular chivalry, with the "High Order of Knighthood" and its human exemplars and consequences, than with Christian morality:[42] thus Malory's emphasis on the worshipfulness of the principal characters and the fact that the honor and love of Lancelot, Guinevere, Arthur, and Gawain all contribute to the tragic destruction of the Round Table. One must recall the uniqueness of Arthur's sorrow at the beginning of the Grail adventure,[43] for it suggests that the sundering of fellowship, whether through civil war or religious ecstasy, is equally negative and equally human and earthly in its consequences.

The secularity of Arthur's realm and the prominence of fellowship in the *Morte* are further apparent in the words of Perceval's aunt, that "all the worlde, crystenyd and hethyn, repayryth unto the Rounde Table, and *whan they ar chosyn to be of the felyshyp of the Rounde Table they thynke hemselff more blessed and more in worship* than they had gotyn halff the worlde" (2:906.17–21; my emphasis). As Dorsey Armstrong observes, it is striking that such a philosophy of Christian and heathen parity and inclusiveness should occur in the mouth of a religious recluse in the midst of the supposedly orthodox Christian Grail Quest.[44] What is even more striking for my purposes, however, is the palmary importance the passage gives to secular worship and fellowship, especially to the *union* of worship and human fellowship.

In part, this interconnection of secular and Christian in Malory's Arthuriad reminds us of the paramount importance of worship (or glory) in romance, reminds us, as Larry D. Benson argues, that the worshipful performance of "chivalric deeds [is] a religious duty and to fail in their performance is a sin to be avoided at all costs."[45] The earthly glory to be had in the Grail Quest has already been mentioned. Arguably the *Morte*'s most notable example of earthly glory in seemingly Christian contexts, however, comes in the Healing of Sir Urry when Lancelot prays not only for success but also, significantly, "that my symple *worshyp* and honesté be saved" (3:1152.21–22; my emphasis). His words are important, for despite their earnestness we must remember that *worship* and *shame* are entirely secular concepts in the *Morte*: Lancelot is asking for God's grace and Urry's health, but also for (continued) earthly glory.

4. The Healing of Sir Urry

The Healing of Sir Urry, one of Malory's longest original episodes, figures prominently in most critical discussions of Christianity in the *Morte*, including many of the essays in this book. Nonetheless, there is little agreement as to what exactly the episode, and especially Lancelot's tears, signify. Judson Allen observes a seeming dichotomy: "On the one hand, Lancelot is asking that his [earthly] reputation not be compromised by a failure in this crucial test; on the other, he is asking that whatever he is in himself be transformed by the power of God into a greater grace. . . . Even so, . . . what happens when Sir Urry is healed is a grace, not an achievement. It is a gift of God."[46] Thus, the argument continues, for all of his worship and (in all senses of the word) nobility, not even Lancelot can heal Urry by his own merits. His famous weeping might be thought to illustrate just how much he realizes this. Allen consequently suggests that "it is precisely Malory's point that to devote one's self to the achievement of holiness is to leave the society of chivalry—it is an idealism incompatible *in practice* with knighthood."[47] A corollary is that Lancelot has now learned what was so difficult for him to discern in the Grail Quest: that his prowess and success come from God rather than from himself or Guinevere.[48] Such comments suggest that Malory is advocating—as the French *Queste* certainly does—a cessation of and turning away from earthly chivalry, earthly love, and earthly fellowship. I disagree.

As other contributors to this volume remark, there certainly is a concern here and elsewhere in the *Morte* with divine grace and salvation. Both Galahad and Perceval depart this world and its vanities to rejoin the Grail and God (2:1034.10–1036.4); Lancelot is lifted up to heaven by angels (3:1257.36–1258.10); and Guinevere is convinced that "thorow Goddis grace and thorow Hys Passion of Hys woundis wyde, that aftir my deth I may have a syght of the blyssed face of Cryste Jesu, . . . for as synfull as ever I was, now ar seyntes in hevyn" (3:1252.13–17).[49] We may well question the sincerity of Guinevere's repentance, for despite her Christian rhetoric Arthur is now dead and most of the Round Table destroyed: she has few options other than a religious retreat, especially since her love of Lancelot has helped destroy Arthur's realm. This is even more true of Lancelot, whose adoption of religion is (as we shall see below) consequently even less convincing. Lancelot's secular motives further reveal Malory's own secular sympathies and show that Malory is emphatically not dismissing the affairs or the knights of this world. It *is* telling that Lancelot weeps like a child that had been beaten upon healing Urry (3:1152.35–36), but it is even more telling that Malory goes out of his way to create a scene not in his sources in which Lancelot is allowed to be the agent of divine grace and to secure that healing. Lancelot is blessed by God, but he is also manifestly still the most worshipful knight of the Round Table and (as his prayer reveals) he is still concerned with *earthly recognition* of that worship: "Now, Blyssed Fadir and Son and Holy Goste, I beseche The of Thy mercy *that my symple worshyp and honesté be saved*, and Thou Blyssed Trynyté, Thou mayste yeff me power to hele thys syke knyght by the grete vertu and grace of The, but, Good Lorde, never of myselff" (3:1152.20–25; my emphasis). Lancelot's concern with his very secular "worshyp and honesté" is a telling indication that it is not only God's virtue being showcased by the healing. After all, Malory could have had Urry healed earlier by the Grail or by one of the *Morte*'s many hermits or even by the Lady of the Lake. He does not. On the contrary, the great—and original—catalogue of knights that prefaces Urry's healing emphatically reminds us of Malory's true focus: King Arthur and all the knights of the Round Table and their deeds on this earth.[50] The secular memorialization generated by this catalogue is intensified in the Winchester Manuscript by the red rubrication of the knights' names: repeatedly for nearly four complete folios this rubrication individualizes and memorializes "an hondred an ten" (3:1146.33) of the remaining one hundred and fifty surviving members of the earthly fellowship. And while all of the *knights'* names are rubricated in the catalogue—as they are throughout the manuscript— neither Urry's invocation of "God" at the beginning of the catalogue (3:1147.15), nor Lancelot's invocation of the "Blessed Trynyté" at the end (quoted above), nor the "Jesu" of Lancelot's twice-uttered "Jesu defende me" (3:1151.20 and 30) is so rubricated.[51] The rubrication and catalogue, together, celebrate, eulogize, and memorialize the *human* characters and deeds, not the divine. In order to drive home this memorialization Malory extends the catalogue to include the names of dead knights such as Tristram and Alisaundir. Since dead men have even less chance of healing Urry than the living knights who fail the task, the only purpose for their inclusion is not only to emphasize the earthly glory of the Round Table but also to reflect upon its losses and sorrows.[52]

In context, such reflection is not there to suggest we turn from such a fellowship to the joys of heaven: just the opposite. Thus this final catalogue of the Round Table fellowship echoes the unified assembly of knights swearing to follow the Grail. That Grail assembly marks the penultimate occasion in the *Morte* when the court is unified in a single mission, but as we have seen, the emphasis is more on the destruction the Grail quest will cause than on the benefits of celestial chivalry. That destruction is recalled in the Urry catalogue, not only in the mention of those knights still alive but also in the recollection of the deaths of many others. The Healing of Urry, moreover, is the final occasion where the remaining knights are unified in a single mission. That the Urry catalogue occurs at the close of the Book of Sir Launcelot and Queen Guinevere, after the Grail Quest and the return of Lancelot and even Bors to the earthly fold and its affairs, is thus significant. There *is* a marked focus on God's grace in allowing Lancelot to heal Urry, but there is even more a sense of the aggrandizement of Lancelot and his human fellows. As Elizabeth Archibald observes, the Healing of Sir Urry is "an episode invented by Malory and placed at the very end of the penultimate book as a final celebration of the Round Table fellowship."[53] Hence, to my mind, the tears are not merely tears of religious joy but, more importantly, tears of relief:[54] Lancelot has immediately prior to this scene committed adultery and treason with Guinevere, and yet here his earthly worship and love are condoned and celebrated by God, who allows the adulterous but worshipful Lancelot to heal Urry. The characters' focus, not to mention that of Malory himself, is—as always—more on the earthly chivalric ideal and fellowship than on any celestial afterlife. Indeed, Arthur explicitly states that he will attempt the first healing not because he presumes success but rather to unify and participate in the Round Table fellowship (3:1146.24–32). And, when all the remnant of the knights have tried and failed, Arthur similarly and explicitly convinces Lancelot to attempt the healing "nat . . . for no presumpcion, but for to beare us *felyshyp*, insomuche as ye be a *felow of the Rounde Table*" (3:1151.32–33; my emphases).[55] Earthly chivalry may be less than celestial chivalry in the Vulgate *Quest del Saint Graal*, but it is not in the *Morte Darthur:* that is why Malory does not conclude his Arthuriad with the Grail Quest, why he invents the Urry episode, and why Lancelot weeps tears of relief.

That we are meant to compare these various scenes and reach this conclusion is evident in part in the *Morte*'s unity, and especially in the last use of that phrase *holé togydir*, for Malory returns to it in the final explicit and the final rehearsal of the fellowship: "Here is the ende of the hoole book of kyng Arthur and of his noble knyghtes of the Rounde Table, that whan they were *holé togyders* there was ever an hondred and forty" (3:1260.16–19; my emphasis). Malory may commit one of his famous errors here, for elsewhere in the *Morte* there are always one hundred and fifty knights of the Round Table; but the important thing, as P.J. C. Field reminds us, is that Malory gets the *nobility* of the knights correct.[56] That nobility, furthermore, is earthly and entirely human.

As the wording of the final explicit reminds us, the idea, image, and reputation of this earthly fellowship recur throughout the *Morte*. The *Concordance to the Works of Sir Thomas Malory* lists "nearly two hundred entries for 'fellowship' under various spellings" in the *Morte Darthur*, and Malory goes well beyond the examples and wording of his French and English sources and cognates to emphasize and eulogize the idea and ideal of the fellowship of the Round Table.[57] Further, its members are bound together by an entirely laudable human love and secular ideal. Thus, that Lancelot is able to heal Urry after the one occasion in the entire *Morte Darthur* when we do see the lovers in bed together is, suggests Larry Benson, "a sign of divine approval. It is surely a sign that Malory did not make a simple equation between the sin of lust and the fall of the Round Table."[58] Yet it is equally certain that Lancelot and Guinevere's affair is based as much or more on love as on lust. This is, I think, one reason why Malory invents scenes in which both the Maid of Astolat and Lancelot are castigated for their excessively earthly loves, for in each case Malory then allows the lovers successfully to rebut their accusers (2:1092.9–1094.3, 3:1256.21–39).[59] Furthermore, Elaine's insistence that sensual romantic love does not offend God is itself regularly repeated throughout the closing scenes of the Arthuriad.[60] Nowhere is this more evident than in Malory's epitaph on Guinevere, "that whyle she lyved she was a trew lover, and therefor she had a good ende" (3:1120.12–13). We must remember that technically Guinevere's relationship with Lancelot is both adulterous and traitorous. We also remember that the seventh commandment (it would have been the sixth commandment for Malory, following the Vulgate Bible and Augustine and medieval Catholic numeration) enjoins us not to commit adultery. Yet Guinevere is hailed as a true lover and granted a good death. Partly, of course, this testifies to the power of repentance and God's grace. But it also suggests quite strongly that, in the *Morte Darthur*, the affairs of this world, including sexual love affairs, are not necessarily bad. Indeed, not only is "Lancelot's earthly love" of Guinevere said to be the "theme that holds the whole last part of the *Morte Darthur* together"[61] but the Book of Sir Launcelot and Queen Guinevere celebrates that love in a way that supersedes and disproves its ostensible castigation in the Sankgreal. Part of the tragedy of the *Morte* lies in the fact that this love *is* partially responsible for the final destruction, but the tragedy is all the more poignant precisely because this love is ultimately presented as noble rather than sinful.

Yet it is not merely heterosexual love that is celebrated, for Lancelot's groveling sorrow at the tomb of Arthur and Guinevere expresses his love for both queen *and* king (3:1256.29–1257.11). Even the eremitical archbishop is found "grovelynge on all foure" when Bedevere first discovers Arthur's tomb; his grief is not as excessive as Lancelot's, but the parallel is telling, especially since the archbishop—unlike Lancelot—is initially uncertain whether the tomb *is* Arthur's (3:1241.5–1242.20; quotation from 1241.8). Platonic brotherly love is also apparent in the company of those few knights left alive in the fellowship, those few who have gathered at Arthur's tomb in what is clearly an attempt to re-create the fellowship now destroyed.[62] As is the case in the stanzaic *Morte Arthur*, Bedevere, Lancelot, and the rest make a poignant attempt to re-create the Round Table fellowship in their joining one another at Arthur's grave, but they do so only in a macabre imitation of the lost chivalric fellowship that reminds us all the more of what and who it is that they lament.

5. The Earthly Fellowship of Death

As we have seen, Malory's emphasis on the singular importance of the Round Table brotherhood with Arthur as its head establishes the preeminent stature of earthly and human community in the Arthuriad. Lancelot and Bors had earlier been crucial to reestablishing that community after the completion of the Grail Quest; in the wake of Arthur's death Bors is initially absent and Lancelot and Bedevere and the rest can only pretend to reenact the Fellowship. Their fellowship of death is, moreover, a highly secular and lachrymose one. It thus highlights the tragedy of Malory's Arthuriad by reminding us of the sense of waste and loss that the death of Arthur and his knights has generated.

The *Morte Darthur* does occasionally possess a dual focus, mediating between earthly and heavenly concerns. While the focus is at times evenly balanced, the scales nonetheless ultimately tip decisively in favor of earthly matters. Although Field argues that the religious deaths of Lancelot and Guinevere at the close of the Arthuriad create a happy ending of sorts,[63] the destruction of Arthur and his entire realm, emphasized in Malory's final explicit, is not sufficiently palliated by flights of angels heaving "Launcelot unto heven" (3:1258.9). Lancelot, although a prominent figure, is still only one of the "hondred and forty" knights to whose "ende" we have come (3:1260.18–19). And as Lancelot's sorrowful and mortal starving of himself at Arthur and Guinevere's tomb reveals, these deaths are in no way illustrative of a *contemptus mundi* leading either readers or characters to a celestial better world. Indeed, Lancelot's angelic choir mirrors and subverts Galahad's earlier angelic reception into heaven (2:1035.13–16), for Galahad dies having renounced earthly existence, whereas Lancelot dies after excessive "grovelyng" at the tomb of his earthly king and his lover (3:1257.1–12).

Initially, of course, Lancelot and his followers throw off armor and let their horses wander free in what appears to be a thorough dismissal of this world and its affairs. As Lamerok observes, a knight cannot be a knight without a horse (2:667.21–28). Dhira Mahoney accordingly argues that "[a]t the end of the *Morte* a tiny detail suffices to indicate renunciation of the knightly life by Lancelot's seven companions when they follow him into the cloister: 'And soo their horses wente where they wolde, for they toke no regarde of no worldly rychesses' (*Works* [3:]1255.8–9)."[64] I suggest, however, that Bors and his fellows, like Lancelot before them, are simply paying lip service to religion. Lancelot, for instance, seeks out Guinevere in the hope of returning to her arms and to France (3:1251.14–31, 1253.19–22). When she refuses he swears to take upon himself the same habit as she has, begs fruitlessly for a kiss, collapses in grief, then wanders aimlessly till he happens upon Bedevere and the chapel (3:1252.30–1254.6). When he discovers that Bedevere and the archbishop stand vigil at Arthur's tomb, "Launcelottes hert almost braste for sorowe" and he joins them (3:1254.9–15): not to condemn earthly affairs but to lament Arthur's passing and bemoan their secular fates. His motivation is human love, not love of the divine.[65] Malory makes Lancelot's earthly motives and earthly loves abundantly clear by modifying the nature of Lancelot's death: in the sources, Lancelot dies due to the rigors of ascetic living. In Malory's version, he starves himself to death groveling on the tomb of his beloved king and queen. This groveling and sorrowful death reveals both the extent of Lancelot's human loves and the extent to which he completely fails to accept, let alone achieve, the "perfect peace and felicity of eternal life with God" that, according to St. Augustine, supersedes earthly suffering and is essential for the "true Christian" death.[66] Since Bors and his comrades are in turn merely following Lancelot in attempting to re-create the lost fellowship rather than renounce earthly and knightly ways, the ending of Malory's *Morte* similarly presents not a condemnation but a celebration of earthly human fellowship.[67] This is made even more apparent by their actions after Lancelot's death, for Bors and the others forsake the hermitage and return to the world immediately upon his burial. They may die in the Holy Land "upon a Good Fryday for Goddes sake" (3:1260.15), but their horses are significantly no longer roaming free, and the knights are once again knights of this earth, not religious hermits. We are thus reminded that, while Perceval renounced "seculer clothyng" in Sarras, Bors did not, for—crucially—he intended all along to return to Camelot (2:1035.22–30).

It is a literary commonplace that the physical or spiritual isolation of the protagonist(s) leads to tragedy, and it is important to remember that Ector, Bors, and their fellows, like Guinevere and Lancelot before them, all die isolated from the most important community in the *Morte Darthur*, that of King Arthur and the Round Table. The Vulgate and Post-Vulgate cycles suggest that there is a more important community to strive toward, but Malory consistently avoids adopting this view. It is perhaps significant in this context that as a general rule in the *Morte* the only times knights deliberately eschew their horses—as opposed to being knocked off them—is when they have gone out of their wits or act so dishonourably as to seem like they have lost their wits (as do, respectively, Tristram at 2:496.7–9 and Palomides at 1:423.17–23).[68] This may well indicate that Lancelot, Bors, and the rest are wrong in ignoring their secular-chivalric accoutrements at Arthur's grave.

More certainly, Malory's additions to the French *Queste* and its aftermath repeatedly return our attention from Sarras and heaven to the earthly Round Table fellowship. As I have suggested, even the reminder of Galahad's concern with Lancelot's affairs in this unstable world cannot be taken as favoring celestial chivalry over earthly chivalry. Most obviously, the Sankgreal closes with a very secular emphasis on "the permanent severance of Galahad and Perceval from the . . . fellowship,"[69] one which places more focus on earth than on heaven. Similarly, Bors and Lancelot each vow never to be parted from one another again, never to sever that fellowship which has just been cobbled back together in the destructive wake of the Grail. The sundering of this familial company, a microcosm of the Round Table as a whole, leads to near disaster, as at the Winchester Tournament when Bors "by myssefortune" strikes the disguised "Launcelot thorow the shylde into the syde, and the speare brake and the hede leffte stylle in the syde" (2:1072.3–5).[70] We are meant to remember this when Lancelot leaves Bors and his kin on the beach to seek Guinevere, and then chances to go straight from Guinevere to the chapel where Arthur lies buried. These, however, are unusual circumstances, and they only occur after Bors has followed Lancelot into exile and after civil war between first Lancelot and Arthur and then between Arthur and Mordred. Bors, moreover, soon follows Lancelot to the chapel, "and whan syr Bors sawe sir Launcelot in that maner clothyng, than he preyed the Bysshop that he myghte be in the same sewte" (3:1254.32–34). Significantly, the community around Arthur's tomb is repeatedly described in terms of "felowes" and "felyshyp," the same ideas used elsewhere to epitomize Malory's sense of the importance and brotherhood of the *secular* Round Table, and a near-final reminder "of the value of this Arthurian and Malorian ideal."[71]

Bors, then, is clearly motivated by human love and earthly emulation of Lancelot. Lancelot himself turns to religion only out of love for Guinevere, after Guinevere has spurned him and Arthur is denied him by death. Lancelot's other followers similarly join Bors and Lancelot at Arthur's tomb in emulation of Lancelot. All of this reveals secular motivations and themes, not celestial ones. The secular nature of the *Morte* is explicitly announced in Ector's great threnody:

> "A, Launcelot!" he sayd, "thou were hede of al Crysten knyghtes! And now I dare say," sayd syr Ector, "thou sir Launcelot, there thou lyest, that thou were never matched of erthely knyghtes hande. And thou were the curtest knyght that ever bare shelde! And thou were the truest frende to thy lovar that ever bestrade hors, and thou were the trewest lover, of a synful man, that ever loved woman, and thou were the kyndest man that ever strake wyth swerde. And thou were the godelyest persone that ever cam emonge prees of knyghtes, and thou was the mekest man and the jentyllest that ever ete in halle emonge ladyes, and thou were the sternest knyght to thy mortal foo that ever put spere in the reeste."   (3:1259.9–21)

The threnody is Malory's last word on Lancelot and to some extent on the Round Table as a whole, is the final speech in the *Morte*, and is Malory's addition to the sources for the final tale.[72] It is a speech spoken by Lancelot's brother amongst the handful of knights remaining of the once glorious one hundred and fifty members of the Round Table. And it is entirely secular, not religious: as the repetition of *knyght(es)* helps to indicate, Ector (and Malory) emphasizes only Lancelot's abilities as earthly knight and lover. As Michael W. Twomey reveals in his exemplary stylistic analysis of this passage, Ector's entire "speech is enclosed in an envelope structure based on the word 'knight.' . . . Between these unequivocal statements of Lancelot's prowess in combat, the speech depends heavily on a series of striking antitheses focusing on Lancelot's secular and chivalric virtues."[73] Significantly for my purposes, there is no hint of *contemptus mundi*, and the appearance of "synful man" in the center of the lament is not a qualification but a corroboration, reminding us that Lancelot was the greatest of the Round Table knights precisely *because* of his humanity and earthly sins—notably his love for Guinevere.

But the threnody does not just memorialize Lancelot: by reminding us of his earthly achievements and of his profound effect on the rest of the Round Table fellowship it also reminds us of all the other knights for whom Lancelot was the yardstick: Tristram, his only equal in love or combat, whose death is recalled in the Urry catalogue (3:1149.25–1150.6); Gareth, knighted by Lancelot earlier in the *Morte* and later slain by Lancelot's hand (3:1177.31–78.6); Gawain, slain in part through a wound given by Lancelot (3:1230.18–24, 1231.8–23); Lionel, slain searching vainly for Lancelot (3:1254.19–22); and all the remnant, surpassed by Lancelot in the Healing of Sir Urry and subsequently slain in an unhappy quarrel that stinted not till all the best knights of the world were dead. Malory's final explicit accordingly reminds us of the glory of that fellowship "whan they were holé togyders." In this he also recalls the close of the Book of Sir Launcelot and Queen Guinevere, where the catalogue of knights at the Healing of Urry offers a "final reprise of the glories of the Round Table" as well as a roll call of its remaining members.[74] And the Urry catalogue and final explicit both look back to the end of the Sankgreal and another original passage in which Malory emphasizes, not religious devotion, but the earthly fellowship between Lancelot and Bors—and, by association, the entire Round Table that, as Ector's threnody attests, Lancelot epitomizes.

What I wish to emphasize, then, is that we are consistently presented throughout the *Morte Darthur* with a celebratory focus on the *secular* deeds of the very human Round Table knights and a heartfelt lament for their passing. This lament is felt both by readers and characters, for each of the principals dies "look[ing] back at the glories that were in Camelot" rather than "forward to the New Jerusalem."[75] This lament for lost earthly glory, I have suggested of the stanzaic *Morte Arthur*, is more typical of tragedy than romance, and it helps to indicate the poem's mixed tragic-romance genre.[76] The same is also obviously true of Malory's Arthuriad which, even more than the stanzaic poem, constantly mingles romance with destruction and tragedy. It is all the more tragic that Bors, who declined the early entry to heaven that Galahad and Perceval chose and who returned to Arthur's court and Lancelot's company, should at the end be one of those few remaining members of the fellowship vainly attempting to re-create that earthly company by still following Lancelot's orders even after his death (see 3:1260.11–14, especially "so syr Launcelot commaunded").

All of this can indeed appear very religious, as Moorman, Lewis, and many of the contributors to the current volume maintain. But, as so often in Malory, appearances can be deceiving, for the dominant note at the end of the *Morte Darthur* is not religious expiation but a profound sense of sorrow and loss. Stephen Halliwell perspicaciously suggests that tragedy revolves in part around an awareness and "affirmation of . . . what is supremely worth living *for*," and that the accompanying inevitable tragic destruction of such a noble life generates a profound sense of "irreversible loss."[77] Although this comment is made in relation to Plato and classical Greek conceptions of tragedy, Malory's focus on the secular worthiness and destruction of the knights of the Round Table makes it equally applicable to the *Morte*. Indeed, this sense of loss is heightened in Malory's Arthuriad by the constant emphasis on human fellowship and the reminder, in the closing attempts to re-create that fellowship, of precisely what has been lost. In the Vulgate *Queste* "Brotherly love has no place."[78] In the *Morte Darthur*, on the other hand, nothing could be further from the truth. Here, Malory's emphasis on earthly brotherly love and the glory of the Round Table indicates a profoundly secular focus. We should not let the occasional shimmering of the Grail floating past with its procession blind us to the sorrowful and secular tragedy that occurs in Malory's illustration of the destruction of the whole earthly but worshipful fellowship.

NOTES

1. Parenthetical citations are by volume, page number, and line number to Malory, *Works*, 3rd rev. ed. (1990). In my quotations from *Morte Darthur* I do not reproduce Vinaver's various emendation brackets, nor his uniform capitalization of the explicits. I am indebted to D. Thomas Hanks, Jr., for the initial invitation to submit a proposal to the 2005 International Congress on Medieval Studies sessions that inspired this book. I would like to thank all in attendance at that session and the 2006 roundtable for their comments on earlier drafts of this argument. I am especially grateful to Thomas H. Crofts, Fiona Tolhurst, and Michael W. Twomey.

2. For the originality of the scene see Vinaver's commentary and note in Malory, *Works*, 3:1663.n. to 1260.5–15.

3. See Vinaver's commentary in Malory, *Works*, 1st ed. (1947), 3:1521; Malory, *Works*, 2nd ed. (1967), 3:1534; Malory, *Works*, 3rd rev. ed. (1990), 3:1534. All subsequent references to Vinaver's *apparatus criticus* are to the third revised edition.

4. Field, "Sir Thomas Malory's *Le Morte Darthur*," p. 238. See also McCarthy, "Malory and His Sources," pp. 81–82 and 91.

5. Moorman, "'Tale of the Sankgreall,'" esp. pp. 185–92 (quotation at p. 187).

6. Lewis, "English Prose *Morte*," pp. 7–28; Riddy, *Sir Thomas Malory*, pp. 113–38; Radulescu, "Malory and the Quest for the Holy Grail," pp. 327–28 and 333–34.

7. For an exploration of the Christian sentiment of the explicits see Hanks's essay in this volume. Note that, in the Winchester Manuscript version of the text (BL Add. MS 59678), everything from "Thomas" to "Amen" in the current explicit is rubricated in red ink. This accords with the practice throughout the manuscript of rubricating names. Taken out of context, the red ink (like the explicit) appears to emphasize the prayer, but it also emphasizes Malory as author. Furthermore, it is quite possible that, as occurs occasionally throughout the manuscript, Scribe A here simply forgot to switch from red to black after he had written Malory's name: the red highlighting of the prayer may well be an accident after the more standard red highlighting of a name. This possibility is increased by the fact that the remainder of this folio (409r) is blank.

8. Moorman, "'Tale of the Sankgreall,'" pp. 189–95 (quotation at p. 192); Lewis, "English Prose *Morte*," pp. 17–20 (quotations at p. 20).

9. See Vinaver's commentary in Malory, *Works*, 3:1535–37 (quotation at 1535). See also McCarthy, "Malory and His Sources," p. 82.

10. Hardyment, *Malory*, p. 419 and n.

11. In Malory, *Works*, 3:1535 and 1564.n. to 955.9–10, 12, Vinaver also marshals this second example. He adds that the comment is original to Malory and totally "alien to the *Queste*."

12. Whetter, "Warfare and Combat," pp. 175–76.

13. Mann, "Malory and the Grail Legend," p. 209.

14. Mahoney tries to argue that Malory balances the two views, but such balance is largely illusory given the "withdrawal from the world" that she sees as necessary for success in celestial matters ("Truest and Holiest Tale," pp. 123–24). Radulescu likewise attempts to argue for a balance between chivalry and religion in the *Morte Darthur*, but as she herself notes, "Malory consistently subordinates religious values to the chivalric ones" ("Malory and the Quest for the Holy Grail," p. 333). The same argument and same contradiction are evident in Radulescu, "Malory's Lancelot and the Key to Salvation."

15. All the evidence suggests that he did, after all, rob Combe Abbey twice, and twice commit adultery. The arguments of Field, *Life and Times*, have recently been further confirmed and often also fictionalized by Hardyment, *Malory*.

16. Even in medieval society "secular aristocratic ideals, heroic and courtly, which had nothing to do with ecclesiastical ideology, remained basic to chivalry even in its most deliberate mood of religious commitment." I quote Keen, *Chivalry*, p. 57, but see further Kaeuper, *Chivalry and Violence*, especially pp. 47–53.

17. *Pace* Evans, "Camelot or Corbenic," p. 252, who sees Galahad's words of warning as a clear "note of *contemptus mundi*." *Pace* also Radulescu, who considers the message to emphasize sin and encourage penance ("Malory and the Quest for the Holy Grail," p. 337).

18. On the frequency of *felyshyp* see Archibald, "Malory's Ideal of Fellowship," p. 318; and Kato, *Concordance to the Works of Sir Thomas Malory*, s.v. "felyshep," "felyship," "felyshipped," "felyshyp," "felyshyppe," "felyshyppyd," "felysship."

19. Ihle, *Malory's Grail Quest*, pp. 158–60.

20. See, e.g., most of the essays in *Malory's Originality*, esp. Moorman "'Tale of the Sankgreall,'" pp. 189, 191–93; and Rumble, "'Tale of Tristram,'" pp. 166–70.

21. Bogdanow, "La chute du royaume d'Arthur," p. 511; my emphasis: "Only the Post-Vulgate [*Roman*] establishes a *direct connection* between the sin of Arthur and his death."

22. *La suite du roman de Merlin*, vol. 1, §11, p. 8: "devil and enemy of Christ."

23. Cf. Edward Donald Kennedy, "Malory's *Morte Darthur*," pp. 165–69. On multiple causation in the *Morte* see also Lambert, *Malory: Style and Vision*, pp. 158–60.

24. See *La suite du roman de Merlin*, vol. 1, §134, pp. 99–100; Vinaver's commentary in Malory, *Works*, 3:1310.n. to 77.5–7.

25. Edward Donald Kennedy, "Malory's *Morte Darthur*," pp. 164–65.

26. Note further how, in accordance with the rubrication of characters' names throughout the Winchester Manuscript, the *knights'* names in this scene and this folio (452r) are printed in red, but neither Guinevere's use of *God*, nor Lancelot's use of *God*, nor Lancelot's *Jesu Cryste* are so rubricated. Manuscript layout, then, emphasizes human characters and themes, not divine.

27. For a different reading of the episode in Guinevere's chamber, see the essay by Hanks in this volume.

28. For an analysis of Malory's juxtaposing of religious rhetoric with secular themes and actions, see Janet Jesmok's essay in this volume. See also Fiona Tolhurst's argument in favor of Malory's form of "secularized salvation" and "cultural Christianity," also in this volume.

29. There are only ten possible trials by battle in the entire *Morte*, and this one between Lancelot and Melleagaunt is one of the two that best conform to medieval practice. See Eynon, "Use of Trial by Battle," pp. 55–86.

30. Beverly Kennedy, *Knighthood*; Swanson, "'God woll have a stroke'"; Stuhmiller, "*Iudicium Dei, iudicium fortunae*"; quotation at p. 438. This observation seems to undermine her own argument for the prominence of official trials by combat in the *Morte*, as do similar claims at pp. 434, 439–40, 442, 451. See also Swanson and the argument that Malory is skeptical of the validity of providential judgment, emphasizing instead human agency and human prowess. None of these critics makes use of Eynon, "Use of Trial by Battle."

31. Swanson, "'God woll have a stroke,'" p. 167. Cf. Stuhmiller, "*Iudicium Dei, iudicium fortunae*," pp. 449–51. The study of treason in the *Morte Darthur* has undergone a critical resurgence of late. The most insightful of the recent articles is Leitch, "Speaking (of) Treason."

32. Stuhmiller, "*Iudicium Dei, iudicium fortunae*," p. 435; my emphasis. As Vinaver perspicaciously observes, "[t]he technique of fighting, and more particularly of single combat, is Malory's favourite topic" (in Malory, *Works*, 1:xxxiii). On the significance of Malory's presentation of combat see my "Warfare and Combat."

33. Allen, "Malory's Diptych *Distinctio*," p. 243.

34. Finke and Shichtman, "Introduction," pp. 3–4. One might object that Finke and Shichtman generalize their case, overlooking Malory's very real characterization of Arthur's feelings in what is a complex situation, thereby minimizing Arthur's love for both Guinevere and the knightly fellowship.

35. For Malory's originality, see Vinaver's commentary in Malory, *Works*, 3:1634.n. to 1183.27–84.11; Archibald, "Malory's Ideal of Fellowship," p. 325. On the meaning of Arthur's words see further my "Love and Death," p. 110.

36. On Malory's aggrandizement of the ideal of the Round Table fellowship, see Archibald, "Malory's Ideal of Fellowship." Ihle points out how even in the Grail Quest "Malory places a high value on [familial and knightly] earthly brotherhood" (*Malory's Grail Quest*, pp. 132 and 127); this is a marked contrast to the Vulgate *Queste*.

37. See also Arthur's words to Gawain at 2:866.19–868.2 and (in a different context) 3:1230.11–17. As Mann emphasizes, the "fourfold repetition of 'holé togydir(s)' is Malory's own intensification of the single word 'ensemble' in the [Vulgate] *Queste*" ("Malory and the Grail Legend," p. 210).

38. Moorman, "'Tale of the Sankgreall,'" pp. 203–4. For a contrary view, see Ihle's perceptive secular reading of this scene (*Malory's Grail Quest*, pp. 133 and 140–41).

39. Wright, "'Tale of King Arthur,'" pp. 10–12, 36–39 (quotation at p. 39).

40. Cf. Archibald, "Malory's Ideal of Fellowship," pp. 317–18.

41. See Keen, *Chivalry*, esp. pp. 5–6, 12–15, 30–32, 42–43, 44–63. See further n. 16, above, and the convenient overview in Kaeuper and Bohna, "War and Chivalry."

42. Such is the argument of Vinaver in Malory, *Works*, 1:xxix–xxxiv; see also Brewer, "'[H]oole book,'" p. 58.

43. Whitaker, *Arthur's Kingdom of Adventure*, p. 82. The remainder of the sentence is my own.

44. Armstrong, "(Non-)Christian Knight in Malory," p. 30. Armstrong argues further that the inclusiveness of this statement is illusory. I contend that the centrality of fellowship in the *Morte* suggests otherwise.

45. Larry D. Benson, *Art and Tradition*, p. 210.

46. Allen, "Malory's Diptych *Distinctio*," p. 250.

47. Allen, "Malory's Diptych *Distinctio*," p. 250; original emphasis.

48. Mahoney, "Truest and Holiest Tale," pp. 119–21.

49. For a careful analysis of Guinevere's religious rhetoric, see Jesmok's essay in this volume. For a less skeptical view of religious language in the *Morte*, see especially the essay by Hanks, also in this volume. In my opinion, the consistent rubrication of characters' names in the Winchester Manuscript reveals a telling pattern during this scene; for while *Lancelot*'s name in this scene is repeatedly rubricated, none of Guinevere's or Lancelot's uses of *God* or *Cryste* is so highlighted. See Malory, *Winchester Malory*, fol. 484r.

50. Cf. Lambert, *Malory: Style and Vision*, pp. 56–65. For reasons given in my discussion, I do not accept Atkinson's or Radulescu's arguments that the catalogue emphasizes the knights' sinful failures (Stephen Atkinson, "Malory's 'Healing of Sir Urry,'" pp. 344–46; Radulescu, "Malory's Lancelot and the Key to Salvation," p. 109.

51. Even in the black-and-white facsimile, many names stand out: see Malory, *Winchester Malory*, fols. 445v–448v. For color images of the manuscript see Takako Kato's www.maloryproject.com.

52. On the sense of sorrow accompanying the catalogue, see Cooper, "Book of Sir Tristram de Lyones," p. 188.

53. Archibald, "Malory's Ideal of Fellowship," p. 326. It is also, argues Lambert, "the most purely Malorian episode in *Le Morte Darthur*" (*Malory: Style and Vision*, p. 56).

54. This is not the same as Lumiansky's idea of Lancelot's "relief" at passing Arthur's test and so avoiding public confirmation of the adultery ("Tale of Launcelot and Guenevere," pp. 229–31). *Contra* Lumiansky, there is nothing to suggest that Arthur conceives of Urry's healing in this fashion.

55. For further details of the importance of fellowship in this scene, including a possible pun on the wholeness of the Round Table and the wholeness of Urry, see Lambert, *Malory: Style and Vision*, pp. 56–65.

56. Field, "Author, Scribe and Reader," pp. 87–88. Field adds that "the error may well be scribal."

57. Archibald, "Malory's Ideal of Fellowship," (quotation at p. 312); Kato, *Concordance to the Works of Sir Thomas Malory*, s.v. "felyshep," "felyship," "felyshipped," "felyshyp," "felyshyppe," "felyshyppyd," "felysship."

58. Larry D. Benson, *Malory's "Morte Darthur,"* p. 228.

59. On the originality of these scenes, see Vinaver's commentary in Malory, *Works*, 3:1589–90 and 1604.n. to 1092.9–1095.14; 3:1618–23 and 1659.n. to 1255.14–57.11. Note that Lancelot loves and laments both Arthur and Guinevere. Corey Olsen also discusses these two scenes in his essay in this volume. On the thematic and narrative importance of these speeches see further my "Love and Death," pp. 110–12.

60. C. David Benson, "Ending of the *Morte Darthur*," p. 225. Thus I cannot accept Field's argument that Elaine is admitting guilt for her excessive emotion ("Time and Elaine of Ascolat").

61. Larry D. Benson, *Malory's "Morte Darthur,"* p. 234.

62. Cf. C. David Benson, "Ending of the *Morte Darthur*," p. 237. See also my *Understanding Genre*, pp. 144–45.

63. Field, "Sir Thomas Malory's *Le Morte Darthur*," pp. 241 and 246.

64. Mahoney, "Truest and Holiest Tale," p. 111.

65. See further the essays by Jesmok and Tolhurst in this volume.

66. Deane, *Political and Social Ideas of St. Augustine*, p. 67.

67. Cf. Larry D. Benson, *Malory's "Morte Darthur,"* pp. 245–47.

68. Mahoney, "Truest and Holiest Tale," p. 111.

69. Mann, "Malory and the Grail Legend," p. 219.

70. See further 3:1203.29–4.1, a passage that observes that the sundering of fellowship will secure the destruction of the kingdom.

71. Archibald, "Malory's Ideal of Fellowship," pp. 325–26.

72. Tellingly, it is almost certainly based on Mordrede's speech over the fallen Gawayne in the alliterative *Morte*: a martial, not Christian, poem. See *Morte Arthure*, lines 3875–85. See further my *Understanding Genre*, pp. 106–8, and Archibald, "Malory's Lancelot and Guenevere," p. 324.

73. Twomey, "Voice of Aurality," pp. 112–14.

74. C. David Benson, "Ending of the *Morte Darthur*," p. 228.

75. C. David Benson, "Ending of the *Morte Darthur*," p. 237.

76. See Whetter, "Stanzaic *Morte Arthur*," pp. 87–111. Since the first version of this essay was submitted to the editors I have also produced a study of the significance of Malory's similar but more extensive tragic-romance genre. See my *Understanding Genre*, especially pp. 99–159.

77. Halliwell, "Plato's Repudiation of the Tragic," esp. (for the quotations) pp. 338–39.

78. Mahoney, "Truest and Holiest Tale," p. 115.

"In my harte I am [not] crystynde": What Can Malory Offer the Nonreligious Reader?

Felicia Nimue Ackerman

What can Malory offer the nonreligious reader? Part of the answer is splendidly obvious. Sir Thomas Malory's *Le Morte Darthur*[1] offers gorgeous language, thrilling episodes, and emotionally engaging and believable characters,[2] all in such abundance that it may seem the rankest greed to ask for more. But the greedy reader of Malory is rarely disappointed, and here I will discuss yet another way this is true.

Unlike most academic writers on Malory, I am a philosopher rather than a traditional literary scholar. So my discussion will be philosophical (in the sense of considering how the *Morte* sheds light on moral and philosophical issues that people face today) rather than literary (in the sense of considering the *Morte* in relation to other literary works or to literary theory). I am also a lifelong atheist, not the sort of atheist who engages in debates with theists but the sort who simply does not believe in God any more than she believes in Zeus. I will argue that some important elements of the *Morte*'s outlook and values have profound and startling relevance to present-day nonreligious readers that is independent of whatever Christian relevance they may also have. But some qualifications are in order at the outset.

The first qualification results from a fact widely acknowledged among Malory scholars: Malory's *Morte* has what D. S. Brewer calls "a rich inconsistency."[3] As Andrew Lynch says, "[w]e should not make a few speeches, whether by Malory's heroes or himself, into unbending rules for interpreting the whole narrative."[4] So when I discuss an element of the *Morte*, this element should not be assumed to be uniform throughout the *Morte*. Second, some of the *Morte*'s values obviously accord with the conventional wisdom of secular society nowadays. As Christina Hardyment says, "the *Morte* still has lessons to teach us: lessons about taking personal responsibility, being loyal and tolerant, defending the weak—the 'generosity of spirit' that Sir Walter Scott saw as the essence of chivalry."[5] The lessons I will argue that the *Morte* can teach us, however, go *against* conventional wisdom and hence offer a genuine alternative to some mainstream values of our society. Third and finally, in claiming that an element of the *Morte* has relevance to nonreligious readers, I am not denying that it may have a Christian underpinning. My aim is simply to show that the elements of the *Morte* that I discuss—attitudes toward death and toward lavish emotionality—have great import that is independent of religion, regardless of whether they have Christian import as well.

I will begin by discussing the *Morte*'s view of death, and I will focus my discussion on three aspects of this view. The first involves death in relation to honor and its opposite, shame. Shame is a state that Malory's characters often deem worse than death. For example, in a very early episode, Arthur tells Pellinore, "dethe ys wellcom to me whan hit commyth. But to yelde me unto the I woll nat!" (1:50.36–51.2). In Caxton, although not in Vinaver, Arthur explains, "I had leuer deye than to be soo shamed."[6] That Arthur is speaking literally is evident in the fact that he is acting on the literal sense of his statement—by risking his life in order to avoid shame. A similar point applies to Blamour's statement, "I had lever dye here with worshyp than lyve here with shame" (1:409.28–29) in support of his insistence that Tristram "sle me oute" (1:409.27) since Blamour refuses to yield to him. Likewise, in a very late episode, Guinevere tells Melleagaunt, "I had levir kut myne owne throte in twayne rather than thou sholde dishonoure me!" (3:1122.14–15). While proof of literalness is not available for Guinevere's remark, it hardly seems unreasonable to suppose that this noble queen values her honor as much as the noble men value theirs. Note also how Bors justifies his choice to rescue a maiden from rape rather than save his brother's life: "if I helpe nat the mayde she ys shamed, and shall lose hir virginité which she shall never gete agayne" (2:961.16–17).[7]

Arthur's and Blamour's attitude toward combat would find many dissenters nowadays. Moreover, few in our society hold that rape shames a woman, let alone that it shames her to the point where death is preferable. But these values, which may strike many present-day readers as archaic, can offer fresh perspectives on views of death, dying, and dignity that are widespread in America today.

Those perspectives become clearer once we examine the concepts of honor and shame in the *Morte* while also examining our own society's view of dignity. Dignity in our society's conventional wisdom is a default state: we are all assumed to have dignity unless deprived of it. Honor is a normally expected state in the *Morte*, but only for the aristocracy. Although honor among Malory's knights must be earned, "[p]rimarily . . . by fighting bravely in battle or tournament,"[8] the standard of honor extends to most knights who are central enough to be named in the narrative. As Lynch points out, "[p]articipation in the narrative is worship enough for all but a few."[9] The greatest honor, however, is accorded to the victors. Honor in Malory's world thus further differs from dignity in our world in that Malory's knights compete for degrees of honor, but people in our world do not compete for degrees of human dignity. Of course, our world, like Malory's, involves competition, with prestige for the winners. But our conventional wisdom does not hold that an unsuccessful competitor has less human dignity than a successful competitor.

An aristocrat can be shamed in the *Morte* for reasons that are the aristocrat's own fault, such as cowardice (as my examples illustrate) or depravity (as when ten knights warn Melleagaunt that his abduction of Guinevere is "aboute to jouparté thy worshyp to dishonoure" [3:1122.21–22]). An aristocrat can also be shamed in the *Morte* for reasons that are not the artistocrat's own fault, such as being raped or being cuckolded, as when Aggravaine avers that Arthur has been "shamed" by Lancelot's lying with Guinevere (3:1161.22–23).[10] (Although the speaker is the treacherous Aggravaine, his brothers on the scene do not contest his claim that Arthur has been shamed.)

Similarly, in our society's mainstream view, one can lose one's dignity for reasons that are one's own fault, such as cowardice or depravity, or for reasons that are as little one's own fault as being raped. Thus, although modern views of dignity may seem more generous and democratic than Malory's views of honor and shame, they are only partially so because both conceptions allow that people can fall into a stigmatized state through no fault of their own.

How can this occur in our society? Chiefly in the area of illness, disability, and dying. Our popular media often portray terminally ill or severely disabled people who want to die because, in the words of a twentieth-century philosophers' brief in favor of physician-assisted suicide, they "[believe] that further life means only degradation."[11] Our society does not generally use the words *honor* and *shame* in this context, but the word *dignity* is a staple of present-day discussions of end-of-life issues, where it frequently follows the words *death with*. People unfamiliar with such discussions might expect the phrase *death with dignity* to refer to a manner of dying—for example, a stately exit accompanied by ceremonial farewells. Instead, however, death with dignity is generally taken to mean to end or prevent a life without dignity, by which is meant a life degraded not by rape or by yielding in combat but by illness and disability. Of course, our society is hardly monolithic, and some people object to the view that illness and disability undermine one's dignity.[12] Yet a common present-day conception of dignity, like honor in Malory's world, relies heavily on the physical. The physical abilities that this conception of dignity requires include the ability to feed oneself and to control one's excretions. In Malory's world, a woman is shamed when penetrated by a rapist's penis; in our world, a sick person is often deemed to lose dignity when penetrated by a feeding tube. The parallel poses a challenge: if we think Malory's world is primitive in this respect, how is ours less so? If it is sexist to accord shame to a woman for being raped, why is it not equally bigoted to hold that physical disability degrades a person? Just as having impeccable moral character cannot keep a raped woman from being shamed in Malory's world, it does not keep an incontinent or feeding-tube-dependent person from often being deemed to lose dignity in ours. From a moral standpoint, both societies seem similarly inhumane in this regard. So here is an area where a philosophical approach to the *Morte* elucidates, for reasons completely independent of religion, the perspective that the *Morte* can provide on our own society. Since this perspective is independent of religion, it is part of what Malory can offer the nonreligious reader.

In Malory's world, death can be preferable to loss of honor, or shame, as we have seen. But the *Morte* offers another aspect of death, one involving Christianity and the afterlife, that is profoundly interesting for the atheist. As Kenneth Hodges has put it in conversation, such cases have a logic that illuminates secular values. "Logic" in this case stems from a simple assertion: I fear my own death and could never welcome it. Admittedly, this attitude is neither essential nor unique to atheists. Religious belief need not include belief in an afterlife (although Christian belief usually does), nor does belief in an afterlife preclude fear of death. Believers who are dying may, in spite of religious devotion, be reluctant to leave their familiar lives and loved ones, or they may fear an afterlife in hell. Conversely, some nonbelievers may consider their earthly lives, although the only lives they will ever have, as worse than no life at all. Perhaps such nonbelievers are (or expect shortly to be) in unbearable and intractable pain, or perhaps they accept our society's frequent disrespect toward the ill and the disabled. Moreover, some nonbelievers may be so self-abnegating as to be happy to end their lives, even if enjoyable, in order to serve some larger purpose. It is even possible (though atypical) for atheists to believe in an afterlife. Yet it is hardly surprising for atheists to dread their own deaths because to most of them their deaths mean, as the present-day philosopher Thomas Nagel puts it, "the unequivocal and permanent end of [their] existence."[13]

In contrast, consider Galahad. In Vinaver's book 6, Galahad's "joy of herte" (2:1032.21) in seeing "a parte of the adventures of the Sangreall" (2:1032.20) is so extreme that he later "felle on hys kneys and prayde longe tyme to Oure Lorde, that at what tyme that he asked, he myght passe oute of this worlde" (2:1032.10 –12), because of his anticipated "grete joy" (2:1032.23) at seeing "the Blyssed Trinité every day and the majesté of Oure Lorde Jesu Cryste" (2:1032.23-24) in the afterlife. And eventually he does request and joyfully receive his passage out of this world. Galahad's willingness—in fact, eagerness—to die is clearly grounded in his certainty of eternal bliss in the afterlife.

How can this convey a surprising lesson to the nonreligious reader? Precisely by highlighting the *Morte*'s profound insight that Galahad's ready acceptance of death relies on his belief that he is going to a better place. This provides a welcome contrast to our present-day culture which urges the old or terminally ill, regardless of whether they believe in an afterlife, to "accept" their own deaths, not just in the cognitive sense of realizing they have not long to live but also in the attitudinal sense of regarding their impending deaths with serenity, rather than fear or resentment, and reaching what one hospice official calls "a final stage [of] acceptance . . . not a resignation, but a real heartfelt feeling that what is happening is . . . not necessarily incorrect."[14] The hospice movement is surely the single most public response to death that our culture provides. Hospice counseling (which is urged upon, although not required of, patients receiving hospice care) aims to inculcate precisely such serene acceptance of death in the terminally ill. But while some hospices are religiously oriented and the National Hospice Organization's promotional material mentions that patients can "share their feelings" with "their own minister, priest, or rabbi [or] a chaplain who may be part of the hospice team,"[15] the present-day hospice movement *as such* is not officially religious, and many hospices seek to attract and care for nonbelievers as well as believers in an afterlife.

The paradox of nonreligious hospices can now be stated as follows. On the one hand, hospice care aims to make the lives of the dying comfortable, pleasant, and even meaningful. On the other hand, nonreligious hospice counseling is not predicated on belief in an afterlife. So why should we expect serene acceptance of death from those who believe their impending deaths will be the unequivocal and permanent end of their (comfortable, pleasant, and even meaningful) lives? Seen in the light of Galahad's attitude toward ascending into heaven, such a nonreligious hospice's expectation seems an attempt to import religiously grounded attitudes—attitudes that are reasonable on the assumption that the dying person will be going on to a desirable afterlife—into a context where the religious beliefs that ground these attitudes are lacking. It calls to mind G. K. Chesterton's aphorism, "[t]he modern world is full of the old Christian virtues gone mad."[16] As Nagel points out, for those of us who do not believe in an afterlife, "it can be said that [earthly] life is all we have and the loss of it is the greatest loss we can sustain."[17] Why, then, should we be expected to face this loss with serenity, as hospice suggests?

One popular present-day answer is that death is natural and, to quote a bestselling and award-winning book, "renewal requires that death precede it so that the weary may be replaced by the vigorous. This is what is meant by the cycles of nature."[18] If one is not weary of living or otherwise deeply dissatisfied with one's life, such a perspective on one's own death requires great self-abnegation. Many people reasonably find such self-abnegation hard to defend outside a religious context. Likewise problematic outside a religious context is the view that what is natural is good. Christians, as well as members of other faith traditions, may have reason to believe that what is natural is good, since they believe that God created the laws of nature. But it is unclear why a nonbeliever should consider something's naturalness as a point in its favor or as a reason to accept it serenely, rather than fear or resent it. As humanist philosopher John Stuart Mill points out, "[i]n sober truth, nearly all the things which men are hanged or imprisoned for doing to one another, are nature's every day performances. Killing, the most criminal act recognized by human laws, Nature does once to every being that lives; and in a large proportion of cases, after protracted tortures such as only the greatest monsters whom we read of ever purposely inflicted on their living fellow-creatures."[19] Thus, present-day readers who lack Galahad's belief in an afterlife can learn from Malory's acknowledgment that this belief is what underlies Galahad's attitude toward death. They can learn to ask, "Why should I regard the unequivocal and permanent end of my existence as welcomingly as Galahad regards the prospect of his eternal bliss?"

Another related aspect of death in the *Morte* also depends on Christianity, yet offers an underlying value that atheists can share. Consider Perceval's reaction to the death of his mother. Upon learning that his mother died of sorrow after his departure from her, Perceval says, "Hit sore forthynkith me; but all we muste change the lyff" (2:906.8). Then he immediately changes the subject to one that interests him more: "Now, fayre awnte, what ys that knyght? I deme hit be he that bare the rede armys on Whytsonday" (2:906.9–10). This reaction would be shockingly callous if Perceval regarded death as the unequivocal and permanent end of his mother's existence. But since he thinks death is literally "changing the life," his response, although perhaps callous about his mother's sorrow, is appropriate regarding her death, especially since he has prefaced it with "[n]ow God have mercy on hir soule!" (2:906.7). Perceval's response has dramatic relevance for nonreligious readers by indicating that his belief in the afterlife is what underlies his matter-of-fact acceptance of his mother's death. Our society's conventional wisdom also encourages people to accept the deaths of loved ones (or at least of elderly loved ones) with such bromides as "[w]e all must die." Perceval's attitude suggests the following challenge: in the absence of belief in an afterlife, what legitimate comfort can "[we] all must die" offer to the bereaved?

Perceval's reaction, though, is hardly typical of the bereaved in the *Morte*. More typical are weeping, swooning, and other manifestations of great dole. Such manifestations invite a question: why are these characters, Christian believers all, so devastated by the deaths of their loved ones? Why aren't the mourners rejoicing in—or at least comforted by— the thought that their loved ones have attained salvation? The answer differs in different cases, showing the complexity of Malory's world. I cannot discuss all the complexities here, so I single out a few.

In one sort of case, the mourner's self-interest is paramount: he laments being personally bereft of a loved one.[20] Thus, Arthur tells the dying Gawain, "in youre person and in sir Launcelot I moste had my joy and myne affyaunce. And now have I loste my joy of you bothe, wherefore all myne erthely joy ys gone fro me!" (3:1230.14–17). It is scarcely surprising that the thought of Gawain's salvation does not prevent Arthur's weeping, swooning, and generally making "greate sorow oute of mesure" (3:1230.5–8) over the dying Gawain. After all, Arthur objected to Gawain's instigation of the Grail Quest because "ye have berauffte me the fayryst and the trewyst of knyghthode that ever was sene togydir in ony realme of the worlde" (2:866.21–23). Consider also La Beale Isolde, who attempts suicide because she believes that Tristram is dead. Isolde bemoans her personal loss, saying, "I may nat lyve aftir the deth of sir Trystram de Lyones, for he was my firste love and shall be the laste!" (2:499.17–18). Perceval, by contrast, although he "dreme[s] of [his mother] muche in [his] slepe" (2:906.1–2) and is concerned enough about her to pray for God's mercy on her soul, seems to feel no such intense personal loss. As his aunt says, "synes ye departed from your modir ye wolde never se her, ye founde such felyship at the Table Rounde" (2:906.25–26).

One also finds sorrow for loss in Lancelot, whose reaction to Guinevere's death is so extreme that a hermit reproaches him, saying, "Ye be to blame, for ye dysplese God with suche maner of sorow-makyng" (3:1256.24–25). F. White-head's well-known comment that Lancelot's speech and "the inordinate emotion that he displays from this time onwards . . . are not in keeping with the monastic way of life he has adopted, and represent the introduction into the calm of the cloister of those worldly affections he is supposed to have renounced"[21] mentions two separate issues: "inordinate" emotion and worldly affections. From the stand-point of the hermit, worldly affections are presumably the real problem. It seems unlikely that the hermit would have objected if Lancelot had manifested intense emotion in the form of great joy at the prospect of seeing in the afterlife what Galahad calls "the Blyssed Trinité every day and the majesté of Oure Lorde Jesu Cryste" (2:1032.23–24). Lancelot's reply to the hermit, lamenting "how by my defaute and myn orgule and my pryde that [Arthur and Guinevere] were bothe layed ful lowe" (3:1256.33–34), introduces elements beyond self-interest into the mourning process. Guinevere's death brings home to Lancelot a devastating sense of his guilt in ending the glory of the reign of Arthur's kingdom on earth, a reign whose Christian dimension Lancelot acknowledges in saying that the king and queen "were pereles that ever was lyvyng of Cristen people" (3:1256.35). Not only does Lancelot follow Guinevere in entering into religious life ("But the [same] desteny that ye have takyn you to, I woll take me to" [3:1253.4–5]), he also follows her in entering into self-blame, repentance, suffering, and death. As Janet Jesmok points out in her essay in this volume, "As always, except when pursuing the Grail, Lancelot allows his queen to lead."[22]

Considering the manifestations of great dole upon the death of loved ones leads naturally to my discussion of the second area where the *Morte* offers a pow-erful lesson to the nonreligious reader. Such manifestations exemplify the lavish emotionality that pervades Malory's world. Although, as Eugène Vinaver says, Malory's knights are "men of action,"[23] they are men of unbridled emotion as well. Far from being strong, silent, stiff-upper-lip types, they are continually making great joy, making great dole, weeping, and swooning. Many present-day readers, accustomed to equating emotional strength with self-restraint, may be tempted to say that Malory's knights, although strong physically, are weak and childish emotionally, especially since Lancelot, for example, is once specifically described as weeping "as he had bene a chylde that had bene beatyn!" (3:1152.36).

In the *Morte*, though, lavish emotionality is not weakness. It is strength. Thus, consider Lynch's remark that a consequence of the Aristotelian view of pleasure is that "those with the greatest potential faculties experience the deepest pain or pleasure. . . . To be great, like any Malorian knight capable of surpassing deeds, is therefore to feel greatly."[24] Lynch adds a Christian cast to this when he says, "Thomas Aquinas held that Christ, perfect in his human nature, suffered more than any other person, because the sufferings were magnified by the sufferer's sensitivity. Similarly, Malory's noblest knights naturally have a deeper affective life."[25] Despite the Christian cast Lynch adds here, lavish emotionality has a value independent of religion. After all, religion is in no way a prerequisite for appreciating the emotional richness of Malory's world as contrasted with ours, where a "strong person" is conventionally taken to be one who is not overly emotional and who takes adversity in stride. By such present-day standards, Malory's knights would no doubt be said to need therapy to subdue their turbulent emotions—for example, grief therapy for Lancelot following Guinevere's death—and it is dismayingly easy to imagine what would be in store for Pelleas, whose impassioned pursuit of a woman who repeatedly rebuffs him makes most of my students dismiss him as a stalker. By the *Morte*'s emotionally rich standards—standards that are in principle independent of religion—the ideal embodied in the present-day therapeutic outlook seems hopelessly tepid and shallow.

Of course, as I have acknowledged in my discussion of dignity, present-day society is not monolithic. When the narrator in a twentieth-century short story by Kelly Cherry says, "[m]aturity is for people who don't have the good goddamn sense to tremble with terror every blessed moment of their existence, who don't recognize the enormity of the debt of gratitude we owe to God,"[26] she displays respect for lavish emotionality. As it stands, Cherry's remark contrasts a religious outlook with a therapeutic one; omit the words after *existence* and we get a contrast between a romantic outlook and a therapeutic one that would deem Lancelot's grief, Pelleas's pursuit of Ettard, and Elaine of Astolat's fatal reaction to Lancelot to be overemotional inappropriate affect.

Fervent respect for the romantic outlook is a paramount part of what Malory can offer the nonreligious reader. As Lynch says, "[t]he swoon is testimony to a disordered emotional situation, yet it may also be seen as an heroic deed in itself, 'proving' the great power of an individual's feeling."[27] I believe that something along these lines can be said even of madness in Malory's world. Consider the madness or near madness of La Beale Isolde, Tristram, and Lancelot in reaction to catastrophe in love. The *Morte* tells us that "whan quene Isode harde of thes tydyngis [of Tristram's death], she made such sorow that she was nyghe oute of hir mynde" (2:499.6–8), that "hit ys grete pité that ever so noble a knyght [Tristram]

sholde be so myscheved for the love of a lady" (2:497.6–8), that "for som har-
tely sorow that [Lancelot] hath takyn he ys fallyn madde" (2:819.6–7), and that
"all sir Launcelottys kynnesmen knew for whom he wente oute of hys mynde"
(2:833.3–5). Conventional opinion in our society would be that such derange-
ment indicates an underlying weakness in these characters. The *Morte* allows us to
believe it indicates the power and intensity of their love. Madness, like swooning,
is not an intrinsically desirable state in Malory's world, but it can be seen as a
richly intense emotional response to the death or defection of the loved one. This
passionate perspective, being independent of religion, is also part of what Malory
can offer the nonreligious reader.

In spite of the tidy arrangement of the above sections of my argument,
Malory's world does not fall into a simple little picture. As P. J. C. Field says, "few
generalisations about Malory are not subject to exceptions."[28] Elaine of Astolat's
love for Lancelot is hardly lacking in power and intensity, but she does not go mad
when he spurns it (2:1089–96).[29] By contrast, the callous Ettard comes to love
Pelleas "so sore that well-nyghe she was nere oute of hir mynde" (1:172.4). Arthur
is hardly lacking in emotional depth. But he does not go mad either from the
loss of his "fayre quene" (3:1184.3) or from what, notoriously, makes him "much
more . . . soryar" (3:1184.1–2)—the dissolution of the Round Table. However,
Elaine does not just "adjust," pick up the pieces, and walk away. Her love is so
deep that she dies of it, just as Lancelot later dies because, to quote Lynch, his
"heart exercises its potential for 'feeling' so strongly that his other life functions are
attacked."[30] Ettard's reaction is due to enchantment rather than to an intrinsically
passionate nature. And Arthur weeps and swoons. As a man of intense feeling, he
emotes greatly, rather than taking catastrophe in stride.

Not all Malory scholars see it this way. Despite acknowledging that
"Arthurian society was a superlative world"[31] and that characters in the *Morte* "display all the . . . superlative sentiments,"[32] Terence McCarthy disparages the idea
that "Arthurian knights regularly dissolve into tears as readily as any nineteenth
century heroine."[33] Instead, he claims, such "actual physical manifestations are a
metaphor"[34] and says, "Pamela yes, King Arthur no."[35] Here McCarthy reflects
the conventional present-day view that unbridled emotionality is a sign of weakness and unmanliness ill befitting a noble knight, let alone a king. On the contrary, recognition that extravagant emotional displays manifest a kind of strength,
excellence, and even nobility is one of the deepest values Malory can offer readers
regardless of religion.

In conclusion, Hardyment is right that the *Morte* still has lessons to teach
us. But some of these lessons are far more complex, surprising, and controversial
than those she mentions about taking personal responsibility, being loyal and
tolerant, and defending the weak. The fact that misfortune in Malory's world
can bring shame upon a morally impeccable victim can teach us to question

our society's tendency along such lines. Galahad's ready acceptance of his own death can teach us to question our society's promotion of this attitude even in the absence of the religious beliefs that ground it in Malory's world. The unbridled grief that many of the characters manifest at the deaths of their loved ones highlights the even greater basis for such reactions on the part of today's nonbelievers in an afterlife. And the *Morte*'s celebration of lavish emotionality offers a vibrant alternative to the mental health ethic of our society, which encourages people to scale down their passions rather than flourish their hearts. These last three lessons combine to show that it is altogether fitting and proper for a nonbeliever to rage openly against death—his own death or the death of loved ones—rather than accept death, as we are so often exhorted to do. How remarkable that a fifteenth-century Christian knight who was reactionary in his own time could have such an apt and subversive lesson to teach conventional "progressive" nonbelievers nowadays![36]

NOTES

1. Except where indicated, all quotations from Malory's text come from Malory, *Works*, 3rd rev. ed., and will be noted parenthetically by volume, page, and line numbers. The quotation in the title is from 2:666.26–27.

2. For defense of this claim about the *Morte*'s characters, see my "'Every Man of Worshyp'" and my *Ethics and Character*.

3. Brewer's introduction to *Morte Darthur, Parts Seven and Eight*, p. 26.

4. Lynch, *Malory's Book of Arms*, p. xvi.

5. Hardyment, *Malory*, p. 481.

6. Malory, *Caxton's Malory*, 1:58.34.

7. In Caxton, although not in Vinaver, Bors follows the word "shamed" with "foreuer" (Malory, *Caxton's Malory*, 1:472.29). See also the discussion in Cooper's edition (Malory, *Le Morte Darthur*, p. 553).

8. Brewer's introduction to *Morte Darthur, Parts Seven and Eight*, p. 25.

9. Lynch, *Malory's Book of Arms*, p. 39.

10. See the discussion in Brewer's introduction to *Morte Darthur, Parts Seven and Eight*, p. 29.

11. This formulation is from Dworkin et al., "Philosophers' Brief," p. 44.

12. See Ackerman, "Death, Dying."

13. Nagel, "Death," p. 1.

14. These are the words of hospice medical director Dr. Fred Schwartz in the documentary film *Letting Go: A Hospice Journey*, directed by Susan Froemke, Deborah Dickson, and Albert Maysles.

15. "About Hospice," p. 5.

16. Chesterton, *Orthodoxy*, p. 35.

17. Nagel, "Death," p. 1.

18. Nuland, *How We Die*, p. 58. (This book won the National Book Award in nonfiction.) For further criticism of Nuland's book, see my review, "No Exit."

19. Mill, "Nature," pp. 28–29. Of course it would be more accurate to say that nature kills every living being that does not die of some "unnatural" cause (such as homicide).

20. See the discussion in Brewer, "Death in Malory's *Le Morte Darthur*," which points out that "Malory does not invoke any hope of joining the beloved in heaven" (p. 49).

21. Whitehead, "Lancelot's Penance," p. 113.

22. Jesmok, "Rhetoric, Ritual," p. 98, in this volume. See her discussion of further complexities.

23. Vinaver, introduction to *King Arthur and His Knights*, p. xv.

24. Lynch, *Malory's Book of Arms*, p. 141

25. Lynch, *Malory's Book of Arms*, p. 142.

26. Cherry, "Covenant," p. 55.

27. Lynch, *Malory's Book of Arms*, p. 142.

28. Field, *Romance and Chronicle*, p. 119.

29. Madness in the *Morte* is often associated with disorientation, irrational violence, and/or running wild, as in the paradigm cases of Lancelot and Tristram. None of this is true of Elaine. She argues her case rationally and coherently to her confessor and composes a rational and coherent farewell letter to Lancelot. While it can be argued that rationality does not preclude madness and that Elaine simply turns her violence inward, Malory does not seem to regard Elaine's fatal reaction to Lancelot as indicating that she is mad. Although Malory readily tells readers when someone is mad, "wood," "oute of [one's] mynde," etc., he does not say this about Elaine when she prepares to die of love.

30. Lynch, *Malory's Book of Arms*, p. 146. As Jesmok points out, "Lancelot's death more closely resembles Elaine of Astolat's than Galahad's" (p. 100, in this volume).

31. McCarthy, *Introduction to Malory*, p. 107.

32. McCarthy, *Introduction to Malory*, p. 118.

33. McCarthy, *Introduction to Malory*, p. 109.

34. McCarthy, *Introduction to Malory*, p. 110.

35. McCarthy, *Introduction to Malory*, p. 110.

36. I thank D. Thomas Hanks, Jr., Kenneth Hodges, Janet Jesmok, Sara Ann Ketchum, and an anonymous reader for very helpful comments, criticisms, and suggestions.

Bibliography

Primary Sources

Abelard, Peter. "Historia Calamitatum." In *The Letters of Abelard and Heloise*, translated by Betty Radice, revised by M. T. Clanchy, pp. 3–43. London: Penguin Books, 2003.

Alliterative Morte Arthure. In *King Arthur's Death*, edited by Larry D. Benson, pp. 113–238. Exeter: Exeter University Press, 1986. First published 1974 by Bobbs-Merrill.

Aquinas, St. Thomas. *Summa Theologiae*. Blackfriar's edition. 61 vols. London: Eyre & Spottiswoode; New York: McGraw-Hill, 1964.

Ascham, Roger. *The Scholemaster*. London, 1570. On the World Wide Web at the University of Oregon's Renascence Editions (https://scholarsbank.uoregon.edu).

Athanasius. *Life of Anthony*. Translated by Evagrius of Antioch. In *Early Christian Lives*, edited and translated by Caroline White, pp. 7–70. London: Penguin Books, 1998.

Bartholomaeus Anglicus. *De Proprietatibus rerum*. 1601. Frankfurt: Minerva, 1964.

——— [trans. Jean Corbichon]. *Le Livre des propriétés des choses: Une encyclopédie au XIVe siècle*. Edited and translated by Bernard Ribémont. Paris: Stock, 1999.

Cassian, John. *The Conferences*. Translated by Boniface Ramsey. New York: Newman Press, 1997.

———. *Collationes XXIIII*. Edited by Michael Petschenig with supplements by Gottfried Kruez. CSEL (Corpus Scriptorum Ecclesiasticorum Latinorum) 13. Vienna: Verlag der Österreicheschen Akademie der Wissenschaften, 2004.

Caxton, William, ed. and trans. *The Golden Legend of Jacobus de Voragine*. Westminster: William Caxton, [1483]. London, British Library C. 11. d. 8. EEBO (Early English Books Online).

———. Preface to *Le Morte Darthur*. In *The Works of Sir Thomas Malory*, edited by Eugène Vinaver, revised by P. J. C. Field, 1:cxliii–cxlvii. 3rd ed. 3 vols. Oxford: Clarendon Press, 1990.

Charny, Geoffroi de. *The Book of Chivalry of Geoffroi de Charny: Text, Context, and Translation*. Edited and translated by Richard Kaeuper and Elspeth Kennedy. Philadelphia: University of Pennsylvania Press, 1996.

Chaucer, Geoffrey. *The Riverside Chaucer*. Edited by Larry D. Benson. 3rd ed. Boston: Houghton Mifflin, 1987.

Chesterton, G. K. *Orthodoxy*. San Francisco: Ignatius Press, 1995.

Colchester Deeds of the Fourteenth and Fifteenth Centuries. Edited by Richard Britnell. On the World Wide Web at http://www.dur.ac.uk/r.h.britnell/Colchester Deeds 1.htm.

Dugdale, William. *The Antiquities of Warwickshire*. 2nd ed. 2 vols. London, 1730. Facsimile edition, Didsbury: Morten, n.d.

Eliot, T. S. *The Waste Land*. Edited by Michael North. New York: W. W. Norton & Company, 2001.

L'Estoire del Saint Graal. Edited by Jean-Paul Ponceau. Paris: II. Champion, 1997.

Evagrius Ponticus. *Ad Monachos*. Edited and translated by Jeremy Driscoll. New York: Newman Press, 2003.

———. *The Praktikos and Chapters on Prayer*. Translated and introduced by John Eudes Bamberger. Preface by Jean LeClercq. Kalamazoo, MI: Cistercian Publications, 1981.

La Folie Lancelot: A Hitherto Unidentified Portion of the "Suite du Merlin" Contained in MSS B.N. fr. 112 and 12599. Edited by Fanni Bogdanow. Tübingen: Max Niemeyer, 1965.

The Hastings Hours: A 15th-Century Flemish Book of Hours. Preface and commentary by D. H. Turner. New York: Thames and Hudson, 1983.

Le Haut Livre du Graal: Perlesvaus. Edited by William A. Nitze and T. Atkinson Jenkins. 2 vols. Chicago: University of Chicago Press, 1932–37.

Heinrich von dem Türlin. *Diu Crône*. Edited by Gottlob Heinrich Friedrich Scholl. Litterarischer Verein in Stuttgart 27. Amsterdam: Editions Rodopi, 1966.

———. *The Crown: A Tale of Sir Gawein and King Arthur's Court [Diu Crône]*. Translated by John Wesley Thomas. Lincoln: University of Nebraska Press, 1989.

Hildegard of Bingen. *Symphonia*. Edited and translated by Barbara Newman. Ithaca, NY: Cornell University Press, 1988.

The Holy Bible. Douay-Rheims version. Rockford, IL: Tan Books, 1989.

The Holy Bible. Revised Standard Version. New York: Meridian, 1974.

Jacobus de Voragine. *The Golden Legend of Jacobus de Voragine*. Westminster: William Caxton, [1483]. London, British Library C. 11. d. 8. EEBO (Early English Books Online).

———. *The Golden Legend of Jacobus de Voragine*. Translated by Granger Ryan and Helmut Ripperger. 2 vols. New York: Longmans, Green and Co., 1941.

John of Glastonbury. *The Chronicle of Glastonbury Abbey: An Edition, Translation and Study of John of Glastonbury's "Cronica sive Antiquitates Glastoniensis Ecclesie."* Edited by James P. Carley and translated by David Townsend. Woodbridge: Boydell Press, 1985.

Julian of Norwich. *The Shewings of Julian of Norwich*. Edited by Georgia Ronan Crampton. Kalamazoo, MI: Medieval Institute Publications, 1993.

Kempe, Margery. *The Book of Margery Kempe*. Edited by Sanford Brown Meech and Hope Emily Allen. Oxford: Oxford University Press, 1940.

King Arthur's Death: The Middle English Stanzaic Morte Arthur and Alliterative Morte Arthure. Edited by Larry D. Benson. Exeter: Exeter University Press, 1986. First published 1974 by Bobbs-Merrill.

Lancelot-Grail: The Old French Arthurian Vulgate and Post-Vulgate in Translation. General editor Norris J. Lacy. 5 vols. New York: Garland Publishing, 1993–96.

Lancelot: Roman en Prose du XIIIème siècle. Edited by Alexandre Micha. 9 vols. Geneva: Droz, 1980.

Langland, William. *The Vision of Piers Plowman: A Critical Edition of the B-Text Based on Trinity College Cambridge MS B. 15.17*. Edited by A. V. C. Schmidt. 2nd ed. London: Everyman, 1995.

Layamon. *Selections from Layamon's "Brut."* Edited by G. L. Brook; revised by John Levitt. Exeter: University of Exeter Press, 1963, 1983.

Letting Go: A Hospice Journey. Film directed by Susan Froemke, Deborah Dickson, and Albert Maysles. New York: Home Box Office, 1996.

Llull, Ramon. *The Book of the Ordre of Chyvalry.* Translated and printed by William Caxton. Edited by Alfred T. P. Byles. EETS o.s. 168. London: Oxford University Press, 1926.

————. *The Book of the Ordre of Chyvalry or Knyghthode.* Westminster: William Caxton, 1484. Facsimile of the 1494 edition. Amsterdam: Walter J. Johnson, 1976.

Love, Nicholas. *The Mirror of the Blessed Life of Jesus Christ: A Reading Text.* Edited by Michael G. Sargent. Exeter: University of Exeter Press, 2004.

————. *Speculum vitae Christi* [*Meditations on the Life of Christ*]. Westminster: William Caxton, [1486]. Cambridge University Library, Class-mark Inc 4018, 3 J. 1.1. [3517]. EEBO (Early English Books Online).

Malory, Sir Thomas. *Caxton's Malory: A New Edition of Sir Thomas Malory's "Le Morte Darthur."* Edited by James W. Spisak. 2 vols. Berkeley: University of California Press, 1983.

————. *Sir Thomas Malory: Le Morte D'Arthur: Printed by William Caxton, 1485.* Reproduced in facsimile from the copy in the Pierpont Morgan Library, New York, with an introduction by Paul Needham. London: Scolar Press, 1976.

————. *Le Morte Darthur: The Winchester Manuscript.* Edited and abridged with an introduction by Helen Cooper. Oxford: Oxford University Press, 1998.

————. *The Winchester Malory: A Facsimile.* Introduction by N. R. Ker. London: Oxford University Press, 1976.

[————]. The Winchester Manuscript. British Library Additional MS. 59678.

————. *The Works of Sir Thomas Malory.* Ed. Eugène Vinaver. 3 vols. 1st ed., Oxford: Clarendon Press, 1947; 2nd ed., 1967; 3rd ed., revised by P. J. C. Field, 1990.

The Merlin Continuation. Translated by Martha Asher. Vol. 5 of *Lancelot-Grail: The Old French Arthurian Vulgate and Post-Vulgate in Translation.* New York: Garland Publishing, 1996.

The Middle English Dictionary. Edited by Hans Kurath. Ann Arbor: University of Michigan Press, 1952–2001.

Mill, John Stuart. "Nature." In *Three Essays on Religion*, pp. 3–65. London: Longmans Green & Co., 1923.

Mirk, John. *Liber festivalis.* Oxford: Theodoric Rood, 1486. Oxford, Bodleian Library, Arch. G. d. 34.

————. *Liber festivalis and Quattuor sermones.* Westminster: William Caxton, 1483. Oxford Bodleian Library, S. Selden d. 8.

————. *Mirk's Festial: A Collection of Homilies.* Edited by Theodor Erbe. EETS extra series 96. 1905. Reprint, Millwood, NY: Kraus, 1973.

Morte Arthure: A Critical Edition. [Alliterative]. Edited by Mary Hamel. New York: Garland Publishing, 1984.

Morte Arthur. [Stanzaic]. Edited by P. F. Hissiger. The Hague: Mouton, 1975.

La Mort le Roi Artu. Edited by Jean Frappier. Geneva: Librairie Droz, 1964.

The Paston Letters, 1422–1509. Edited by James H. Gairdner. 6 vols. 1903. Reprint, New York: AMS, 1965.

Paston Letters and Papers of the Fifteenth Century. Edited by Norman Davis. 2 vols. Oxford: Clarendon Press, 1971, 1976.

The Prologues and Epilogues of William Caxton. Edited by W. J. B. Crotch. 1928. Reprint, New York: Burt Franklin, 1971.

La Queste del Saint Graal: Roman du XIIIe Siècle. Edited by Albert Pauphilet. Paris: Librairie Ancienne Honoré Champion, 1923.

The Quest for the Holy Grail. Translated by E. Jane Burns. Vol. 4 of *Lancelot-Grail: The Old*

French Arthurian Vulgate and Post-Vulgate in Translation. New York: Garland Publishing, 1994.

The Quest of the Holy Grail. Translated by P. M. Matarasso. London: Penguin Books, 1969.

Religious Lyrics of the XVth Century. Edited by Carleton Brown. 1939. Reprint, Oxford: Clarendon Press, 1952.

Religious Pieces in Prose and Verse. Edited by G. G. Perry. EETS o.s. 26. London: N. Trübner and Co., 1867.

Riccoboni, Sister Bartolomea. *Life and Death in a Venetian Convent: The Chronicle and Necrology of Corpus Domini, 1395–1436.* Edited and translated by Daniel Bornstein. Chicago: University of Chicago Press, 2000.

Rolle, Richard, of Hampole. *The Pricke of Conscience (Stimulus Conscientiae): A Northumbrian Poem.* Edited by Richard Morris. 1863. New York: AMS Press, 1973.

Le Roman de Tristan en Prose. Edited by Renée L. Curtis. Woodbridge: D. S. Brewer, 1985.

Le Roman de Tristan en Prose. General editor Philippe Ménard. 9 vols. Textes littéraires français. Geneva: Droz, 1987–97.

The Sarum Missal Edited from Three Early Manuscripts. Edited by J. Wickham Legg. Oxford: Clarendon Press, 1916.

The Stanzaic Morte Arthur. In *King Arthur's Death*, edited by Larry D. Benson, pp. 1–111. Exeter: Exeter University Press, 1986. First published 1974 by Bobbs-Merrill.

La suite du roman de Merlin. Edited by Gilles Roussineau. 2 vols. Geneva: Librairie Droz, 1996.

Trevisa, John. *On the Properties of Things: John Trevisa's Translation of Bartholomaeus Anglicus, De proprietatibus rerum.* Edited by M. C. Seymour et al. 3 vols. Oxford: Clarendon Press, 1975–88.

Vitae Patrum. Edited by Heribert Rosweyde. Leiden, 1617. Patrologia Latina, online at http://pld.chadwyck.co.uk/, 73–74.

Vitas Patrum. Translated by William Caxton. Westminster: Wynkyn de Worde, 1495. Oxford, Bodleian Library, Arch. G. d .30.

Wace. *Roman de Brut: A History of the British.* Edited and translated by Judith Weiss. 1999. Revised edition, Exeter: University of Exeter Press, 2002.

William of Malmesbury's Chronicle of the Kings of England. Translated by John Sharpe. Edited by J. A. Giles. London, 1847.

Wolfram von Eschenbach. *Parzival.* Translated by A. T. Hatto. London: Penguin Books, 1980.

Yeats, William Butler. "The Second Coming." In *The Norton Anthology of English Literature*, edited by M. H. Abrams and Stephen Greenblatt, 2:2106–7. 7th ed. 2 vols. New York: W. W. Norton & Company, 2000.

Secondary Sources

"About Hospice." National Hospice Organization. Arlington, VA: National Hospice Organization, 1996.

Ackerman, Felicia Nimue. "Death, Dying, and Dignity." In *Ethics*, edited by Klaus Brinkmann, pp. 189–201. Vol. 1 of *Proceedings of the Twentieth World Congress of Philosophy*. Bowling Green, OH: Philosophy Documentation Center, 1999.

———. *Ethics and Character in Malory's "Le Morte Darthur."* New York: Palgrave Macmillan. Forthcoming.

———. "'Every Man of Worshyp': Emotion and Characterization in Malory's *Le Morte Darthur.*" *Arthuriana* 11.2 (2001): 32–42.

————. "'I may do no penaunce': Spiritual Sloth in Malory's *Morte*." *Arthuriana* 16.1 (2006): 47–53.

————. "No Exit." *American Scholar* 64.1 (1995): 131–35.

Allen, Judson B. "Malory's Diptych *Distinctio*: The Closing Books of His Work." In Spisak, *Studies in Malory*, pp. 237–55.

Anatolios, Khalid. *Athanasius*. London: Routledge, 2004.

Anderson, Earl R. "'Ein Kind wird geschlagen': The Meaning of Malory's Tale of the Healing of Sir Urry." *Literature and Psychology* 49.3 (2003): 45–74.

Archibald, Elizabeth. "Malory's Ideal of Fellowship." *Review of English Studies*, n.s. 43 (1992): 311–28.

————. "Malory's Lancelot and Guenevere." In Fulton, *Companion to Arthurian Literature*, pp. 312–25.

Archibald, Elizabeth, and A. S. G. Edwards, eds. *A Companion to Malory*. Cambridge: D. S. Brewer, 1996.

Armstrong, Dorsey. *Gender and the Chivalric Community in Malory's "Morte d'Arthur."* Gainesville: University of Florida Press, 2003.

————. "The (Non-)Christian Knight in Malory: A Contradiction in Terms?" *Arthuriana* 16.2 (2006): 30–34.

————. "Postcolonial Palomides: Malory's Saracen Knight and the Unmaking of the Arthurian Community." *Exemplaria* 18.1 (2006): 175–203.

Arnold-Forster, Frances. *Studies in Church Dedications, or England's Patron Saints*. 3 vols. London: Skeffington & Son, 1899.

Atkinson, David William, ed. *The English "Ars Moriendi."* New York: Peter Lang, 1992.

Atkinson, Stephen C. B. "Malory's 'Healing of Sir Urry': Lancelot, the Earthly Fellowship, and the World of the Grail." *Studies in Philology* 29 (1981): 341–52.

————. "Malory's Lancelot and the Quest of the Grail." In Spisak, *Studies in Malory*, pp. 129–52.

————. "'Now I Se and Undirstonde': The Grail Quest and the Education of Malory's Reader." In *The Arthurian Tradition: Essays in Convergence*, edited by Mary Flowers Braswell and John Bugge, pp. 90–108. Tuscaloosa: University of Alabama Press, 1988.

Barber, Richard. *The Holy Grail: Imagination and Belief*. Cambridge, MA: Harvard University Press, 2004.

Batt, Catherine. *Malory's "Morte Darthur": Remaking Arthurian Tradition*. New York: Palgrave, 2002.

Beaty, Nancy Lee. *The Craft of Dying: A Study in the Literary Tradition of the "Ars Moriendi" in England*. New Haven, CT: Yale University Press, 1970.

Bennett, H. S. *The Pastons and Their England*. 2nd ed. Cambridge: Cambridge University Press, 1951.

Bennett, J. A. W., ed. *Essays on Malory*. Oxford: Clarendon Press, 1963.

Benson, C. David. "The Ending of the *Morte Darthur*." In Archibald and Edwards, *Companion to Malory*, pp. 221–38.

Benson, Larry D. *Art and Tradition in "Sir Gawain and the Green Knight."* New Brunswick, NJ: Rutgers University Press, 1965.

————. *Malory's "Morte Darthur."* Cambridge, MA: Harvard University Press, 1976.

Boardman, Phillip C. "Grail and Quest in the Medieval English World of Arthur." In Lacy, *Grail, the Quest and the World of Arthur*, pp. 126–40.

Bogdanow, Fanni. "La chute du royaume d'Arthur: Évolution du thème." *Romania* 107 (1986): 504–19.

Boulanger, Jennifer. "Righting History: Redemptive Potential and the Written Word in Malory." *Arthuriana* 19.2 (2009): 27–41.

Brewer, D. S. "Death in Malory's *Le Morte Darthur.*" In *Zeit, Tod und Ewigkeit in der Renaissance Literatur*, 3:44–57. Analecta Cartusiana 117. Salzburg: Institut für Anglistik und Amerikanistik, Universität Salzburg, 1986–87.

———. "'[T]he hoole book.'" In J. A. W. Bennett, *Essays on Malory*, pp. 41–63.

———, ed. *"The Morte Darthur," Parts Seven and Eight by Sir Thomas Malory*. Evanston, IL: Northwestern University Press, 1974. First published 1968 by Edward Arnold.

Brown, Andrew D. *Popular Piety in Late Medieval England: The Diocese of Salisbury 1250–1550*. New York: Oxford University Press, 1995.

Brown, David. "The Trinity in Art." In *The Trinity: An Interdisciplinary Symposium on the Trinity*, edited by Stephen T. Davis, Daniel Kendall, and Gerald O'Collins, pp. 329–56. New York: Oxford University Press, 1999.

Burns, E. Jane. Introduction to *The Quest for the Holy Grail*. Translated by E. Jane Burns. Vol. 4 of *Lancelot-Grail: The Old French Arthurian Vulgate and Post-Vulgate in Translation*. New York: Garland Publishing, 1994.

Bynum, Caroline Walker. "Why All the Fuss about the Body? A Medievalist's Perspective." *Critical Inquiry* 22 (Autumn, 1995): 1–33.

Carpenter, Christine. "Religion." In *Gentry Culture and Late Medieval England*, edited by Raluca Radulescu and Alison Truelove, pp. 134–50. Manchester: Manchester University Press, 2005.

Chadwick, Henry. *The Early Church*. Rev. ed. London: Penguin Books, 1993.

Chambers, E. K. Review of *Sir Thomas Malory: His Turbulent Career*, by Edward Hicks. *Review of English Studies* 5.20 (1929): 465–67.

Cherewatuk, Karen. "Born-Again Virgins and Holy Bastards: Bors and Elyne and Lancelot and Galahad." *Arthuriana* 11.2 (2001): 52–64.

———. "Malory's Launcelot and the Language of Sin and Confession." *Arthuriana* 16.2 (2006): 68–71.

———. *Marriage, Adultery, and Inheritance in Malory's "Morte Darthur."* Cambridge: D. S. Brewer, 2006.

———. "The Saint's Life of Sir Launcelot: Hagiography and the Conclusion of Malory's *Morte Darthur.*" *Arthuriana* 5.1 (1995): 62–78.

Cherewatuk, Karen, and K. S. Whetter, eds. *The Arthurian Way of Death: The English Tradition*. Woodbridge: D. S. Brewer, 2009.

Cherry, Kelly. "Covenant." *Commentary* 51.5 (1971): 50–60.

Clanchy, M. T. *Abelard: A Medieval Life*. Oxford: Blackwell, 1997.

Cole, Harry E. "Forgiveness as Structure: 'The Book of Sir Launcelot and Queen Guinevere.'" *Chaucer Review* 31.1 (1996): 36–44.

Cooper, Helen. "The Book of Sir Tristram de Lyones." In Archibald and Edwards, *Companion to Malory*, pp. 183–201.

———. *The English Romance in Time: Transforming Motifs from Geoffrey of Monmouth to the Death of Shakespeare*. Oxford: Oxford University Press, 2004.

———. "God Grant Mercy! A Pun in Malory?" *Notes and Queries* 39 (1992): 24–25.

Davies, R. T. "The Worshipful Way in Malory." In *Patterns of Love and Courtesy: Essays in Honor of C. S. Lewis*, edited by John Lawlor, pp. 157–77. London: Edward Arnold, 1966.

de Weever, Jacqueline. "Introduction: The Saracen as Narrative Knot." *Arthuriana* 16.4 (2006): 4–9.

Deane, Herbert A. *The Political and Social Ideas of St. Augustine.* New York: Columbia University Press, 1963.

Dobyns, Ann. "Rhetoric of Character in Malory's *Morte Darthur.*" *Texas Studies in Language and Literature* 28 (1986): 339–52.

Dosanjh, Kate. "Rest in Peace: Launcelot's Spiritual Journey in *Le Morte Darthur.*" *Arthuriana* 16.2 (2006): 63–67.

Duffy, Eamon. *The Stripping of the Altars: Traditional Religion in England c. 1400–c. 1580.* 1992. 2nd ed. New Haven, CT: Yale University Press, 2005.

Dulin-Mallory, Nina H. "'Seven trewe bataylis for Jesus sake': The Long-Suffering Saracen Palomides." In *Western Views of Islam in Medieval and Early Modern Europe: Perception of Other,* edited by David R. Blanks and Michael Frassetto, pp. 165–72. New York: St. Martin's Press, 1999.

Dworkin, Ronald, Thomas Nagel, Robert Nozick, John Rawls, Thomas Scanlon, and Judith Jarvis Thomson. "The Philosophers' Brief." *New York Review of Books* 44.5 (1997): 41–47.

Edwards, Elizabeth. *The Genesis of Narrative in Malory's "Morte Darthur."* Cambridge: D. S. Brewer, 2001.

Evans, Murray J. "Camelot or Corbenic?: Malory's New Blend of Secular and Religious Chivalry in the 'Tale of the Holy Grail.'" *English Studies in Canada* 8 (1982): 249–61.

Eynon, Nadine Ruth. "The Use of Trial by Battle in the Work of Sir Thomas Malory." MA thesis, University of Saskatchewan, 1974.

Ferguson, Arthur B. *The Indian Summer of English Chivalry.* Durham, NC: Duke University Press, 1970.

Field, P. J. C. "Author, Scribe and Reader in Malory: The Case of Harleuse and Peryne." In *Malory: Texts and Sources,* pp. 72–88.

———. *Life and Times of Sir Thomas Malory.* Cambridge: D. S. Brewer, 1993, 1999.

———. *Malory: Texts and Sources.* Cambridge: D. S. Brewer, 1998.

———. "Malory and the Grail: The Importance of Detail." In Lacy, *Grail, the Quest and the World of Arthur,* pp. 141–55.

———. "The Malory Life Records." In Archibald and Edwards, *Companion to Malory,* pp. 115–30.

———. "Malory's Minor Sources." In *Malory: Texts and Sources,* pp. 27–31.

———. *Romance and Chronicle: A Study of Malory's Prose Style.* Bloomington: Indiana University Press, 1971.

———. "Sir Thomas Malory's *Le Morte Darthur.*" In *The Arthur of the English: The Arthurian Legend in Medieval English Life and Literature,* edited by W. R. J. Barron, pp. 225–46. Cardiff: University of Wales Press, 1999.

———. "Time and Elaine of Ascolat." In *Malory: Texts and Sources,* pp. 280–83.

Finke, Laurie A., and Martin B. Shichtman. "Introduction." *Arthuriana* 8.2 (1998): 3–9.

Fletcher, Alan J. "King Arthur's Passing in the *Morte D'Arthur.*" *English Language Notes* 31.4 (1994): 19–24.

Fries, Maureen. "Indiscreet Objects of Desire: Malory's 'Tristram' and the Necessity of Deceit." In Spisak, *Studies in Malory,* pp. 87–108.

———. "Malory's Tristram as Counter-Hero to the *Morte Darthur.*" *Neuphilologische Mitteilungen: Bulletin of the Modern Language Society* 76 (1975): 605–13.

Fry, Timothy. Introduction to *The Rule of St. Benedict in Latin and English with Notes,* pp. 1–151. Collegeville, MN: Liturgical Press, 1981.

Fulton, Helen, ed. *A Companion to Arthurian Literature.* Chichester: Wiley-Blackwell, 2009.

Goodrich, Peter. "Saracens and Islamic Alterity in Malory's *Le Morte Darthur*." *Arthuriana* 16.4 (2006): 10–28.

Grimm, Kevin. "Knightly Love and the Narrative Structure of Malory's Tale Seven." *Arthurian Interpretations* 3 (1989): 76–95.

———. "The Love and Envy of Sir Palomides." *Arthuriana* 11.2 (2001): 65–74.

———. "Sir Thomas Malory's Narrative of Faith." *Arthuriana* 16.2 (2006): 16–20.

Guerin, Wilfred. "'The Tale of the Death of Arthur': Catastrophe and Resolution." In Lumiansky, *Malory's Originality*, pp. 233–74.

Halliwell, Stephen. "Plato's Repudiation of the Tragic." In *Tragedy and the Tragic: Greek Theatre and Beyond*, edited by M. S. Silk, pp. 332–49. Oxford: Oxford University Press, 1996.

Hanks, D. Thomas, Jr. "Malory, the *Mort[e]*s, and the Confrontation in Guinevere's Chamber." In *Sir Thomas Malory: Views and Re-Views*, pp. 78–90. New York: AMS Press, 1992.

———. "Malory's *Book of Sir Tristram*: Focusing *Le Morte Darthur*." *Quondam et Futurus: A Journal of Arthurian Interpretations* 3.1 (Spring 1993): 14–31.

———. "T. H. White's Merlin: More than Malory Made Him." In *The Figure of Merlin in the Nineteenth and Twentieth Centuries*, edited by Maureen Fries and Jeanie Watson, pp. 101–20. Lewiston, NY: Edwin Mellin, 1989.

Hardyment, Christina. *Malory: The Life and Times of King Arthur's Chronicler*. New York: HarperCollins, 2005.

Harp, Richard L. "The Christian Poetic of the Search for the Holy Grail." *Christian Scholar's Review* 4 (1975): 300–310.

Hodges, Kenneth. *Forging Chivalric Communities in Malory's "Morte Darthur."* New York: Palgrave Macmillan, 2005.

———. "Haunting Pieties: Malory's Use of Chivalric Christian *Exempla* after the Grail." *Arthuriana* 17.2 (2007): 28–48.

———. "Making Arthur Protestant: Translating Malory's Grail Quest into Spenser's Book of Holiness." *Review of English Studies* n.s. 62 (2010): 193–211.

Hodnett, Edward. *English Woodcuts, 1480–1535*. 1935. Reprint, London: Bibliographical Society, 1973.

Hoffman, Donald L. "Assimilating Saracens: The Aliens in Malory's *Morte Darthur*." *Arthuriana* 16.4 (2006): 43–64.

———. "Perceval's Sister: Malory's Rejected Masculinities." *Arthuriana* 6.4 (1996): 72–83.

Hynes-Berry, Mary. "A Tale 'Breffly Drawyne Oute of Freynshe.'" In Takamiya and Brewer, *Aspects of Malory*, pp. 93–106.

Ihle, Sandra Ness. *Malory's Grail Quest: Invention and Adaptation in Medieval Prose Romance*. Madison: University of Wisconsin Press, 1983.

Jesmok, Janet. "The Double Life of Malory's Lancelot du Lake." *Arthuriana* 17.4 (2007): 81–92.

———. "Malory's 'Knight of the Cart.'" *Michigan Academician* 13.1 (1980): 107–15.

Kato, Tomomi. *A Concordance to the Works of Sir Thomas Malory*. Tokyo: University of Tokyo Press, 1974.

Kaeuper, Richard. *Chivalry and Violence in Medieval Europe*. Oxford: Oxford University Press, 1999.

Kaeuper, Richard W., and Montgomery Bohna. "War and Chivalry." In *A Companion to Medieval English Literature and Culture c.1350–c.1500*, edited by Peter Brown, pp. 273–91. Malden, MA: Blackwell, 2007.

Keen, Maurice. *Chivalry*. New Haven, CT: Yale University Press, 1984.

Kelly, J. N. D. *The Athanasian Creed*. New York: Harper and Row, 1964.

———. *Early Christian Creeds*. 3rd ed. Harlow: Longman, 1972.

———. *Early Christian Doctrines*. 5th rev. ed. London: Continuum, 2004.

Kelly, Robert L. "Wounds, Healing, and Knighthood in Malory's Tale of Lancelot and Guenevere." In Spisak, *Studies in Malory*, pp. 173–97.

Kennedy, Beverly. *Knighthood in the "Morte Darthur."* 2nd ed. Woodbridge: D. S. Brewer, 1992.

———. "Malory's Lancelot: 'Trewest Lover, of a Synful Man.'" *Viator* 12 (1981): 409–56.

Kennedy, Edward Donald. "Malory's Guenevere: 'A Woman Who Had Grown a Soul.'" *Arthuriana* 9.2 (1999): 37–45. Reprinted in *On Arthurian Women: Essays in Memory of Maureen Fries*, ed. Bonnie Wheeler and Fiona Tolhurst, pp. 35–44. Dallas: Scriptorium Press, 2001.

———. "Malory's *Morte Darthur*: A Politically Neutral English Adaptation of the Arthurian Story." *Arthurian Literature* 20 (2003): 145–69.

Kraemer, Alfred Robert. *Malory's Grail Seekers and Fifteenth-Century English Hagiography*. New York: Peter Lang, 1999.

Lacy, Norris J. "From Medieval to Post-Modern: The Arthurian Quest in France." *South Atlantic Review* 65.2 (2000): 114–33.

———, ed. *The Grail, the Quest and the World of Arthur*. Arthurian Studies 62. Woodbridge: D. S. Brewer, 2008.

Laing, Lloyd, and Jennifer Laing. *Medieval Britain: The Age of Chivalry*. New York: St. Martin's Press, 1996.

Lambert, Mark. *Malory: Style and Vision in "Le Morte Darthur."* New Haven, CT: Yale University Press, 1975.

Le Clercq, Jean. Preface to Evagrius Ponticus. *The Praktikos and Chapters on Prayer*, ed. John Eudes Bamberger, pp. vii–xxii. Kalamazoo, MI: Cistercian Publications, 1981.

Leitch, Megan G. "Speaking (of) Treason in Malory's *Morte Darthur*." *Arthurian Literature* 27 (2010): 103–34.

Lewis, C. S. "The English Prose *Morte*." In J. A. W. Bennett, *Essays on Malory*, pp. 7–28.

Lumiansky, R. M., ed. *Malory's Originality: A Critical Study of "Le Morte Darthur."* Baltimore: Johns Hopkins University Press, 1964.

———. "'The Tale of Launcelot and Guenevere': Suspense." In *Malory's Originality*, pp. 205–32.

Lundie, R. S. "Divided Allegiance in the Last Two Books of Malory." *Theoria* 26 (1966): 93–111.

Lynch, Andrew. *Malory's Book of Arms: The Narrative of Combat in "Le Morte Darthur."* Woodbridge: D. S. Brewer, 1997.

Mahoney, Dhira B., ed. *The Grail: A Casebook*. New York: Garland Publishing, 2000.

———. "Hermits in Malory's *Morte Darthur*: The Fiction and the Reality." *Arthurian Interpretations* 2.1 (Fall 1987): 1–26.

———. "The Truest and Holiest Tale: Malory's Transformation of *La Queste del Saint Graal*." In Spisak, *Studies in Malory*, pp. 109–28. Reprinted in *The Grail: A Casebook*, pp. 379–96.

Mann, Jill. "Malory and the Grail Legend." In Archibald and Edwards, *Companion to Malory*, pp. 203–20.

Marenbon, John. *The Philosophy of Peter Abelard*. Cambridge: Cambridge University Press, 1997.

McCarthy, Terence. *An Introduction to Malory: Reading the "Morte Darthur."* Woodbridge: D. S. Brewer, 1988, 2002.

―――. "Malory and His Sources." In Archibald and Edwards, *Companion to Malory*, pp. 75–95.

―――. "The Sequence of Malory's Tales." In Takamiya and Brewer, *Aspects of Malory*, pp. 107–24.

McDonald, J. Ian H. *The Crucible of Christian Morality.* London: Routledge, 1998.

McEntire, Sandra. *The Doctrine of Compunction in Medieval England: Holy Tears.* Lewiston, NY: Edwin Mellen, 1990.

McGrath, Alister E. *The Future of Christianity.* Oxford: Blackwell, 2002.

Mongan, Olga Burakov. "Between Knights: Triangular Desire and Sir Palomides in Sir Thomas Malory's *The Book of Sir Tristram de Lyones*." *Arthuriana* 12.4 (2002): 74–89.

Moorman, Charles. "'The Tale of the Sankgreall': Human Frailty." In Lumiansky, *Malory's Originality*, pp. 184–204.

Morris, Celia. "From Malory to Tennyson: Spiritual Triumph to Spiritual Defeat." *Mosaic* 7.3 (1974): 87–98.

Nagel, Thomas. "Death." In *Mortal Questions*, pp. 1–10. Cambridge: Cambridge University Press, 1996.

Nuland, Sherwin B. *How We Die: Reflections on Life's Final Chapter.* New York: Knopf, 1994.

Oakeshott, W. F. "The Finding of the Manuscript." In J. A. W. Bennett, *Essays on Malory*, pp. 1–6.

Owen, Nancy H., and Lewis J. Owen. "The Tristram in the *Morte Darthur*: Structure and Function." *Tristania: A Journal Devoted to Tristan Studies* 3.2 (1978): 4–21.

Painter, George D. *William Caxton: A Quincentenary Biography of England's First Printer.* London: Chatto and Windus, 1976.

Parins, Marylyn Jackson. *Malory: The Critical Heritage.* London: Routledge, 1995.

Parry, Joseph D. "Following Malory out of Arthur's World." *Modern Philology* 95.2 (1997): 147–69.

Pearsall, Derek. *Arthurian Romance.* Oxford: Blackwell, 2003.

Plummer, John F. "Tunc se Coeperunt non Intelligere: The Image of Language in Malory's Last Books." In Spisak, *Studies in Malory*, pp. 153–72.

Pochoda, Elizabeth. *Arthurian Propaganda: "Le Morte Darthur" as an Historical Ideal of Life.* Chapel Hill: University of North Carolina Press, 1971.

Radulescu, Raluca L. "Malory and the Quest for the Holy Grail." In Fulton, *Companion to Arthurian Literature*, pp. 326–39.

―――. "Malory's Lancelot and the Key to Salvation." *Arthurian Literature* 25 (2008): 93–118.

―――. "'Now I take uppon me the adventures to seke of holy thynges': Lancelot and the Crisis of Arthurian Knighthood." In *Arthurian Studies in Honour of P. J. C. Field*, edited by Bonnie Wheeler, pp. 285–95. Woodbridge: D. S. Brewer, 2004.

Reynolds, Rebecca. "Elaine of Ascolat's Death and the *Ars Moriendi*." *Arthuriana* 16.2 (2006): 35–39.

Richmond, Colin. "Religion and the Fifteenth-Century English Gentleman." In *The Church, Politics, and Patronage in Fifteenth-Century England*, edited by R. B. Dobson, pp. 193–208. Gloucester: Sutton, 1984.

―――. "The Visual Culture of Fifteenth-Century England." In *The Wars of the Roses*, edited by A. J. Pollard, pp. 186–209. London: Macmillan Press, 1995.

Rickert, Margaret. *Painting in Britain: The Middle Ages.* 2nd ed. London: Penguin Books, 1965.

Riddy, Felicity. "Chivalric Nationalism and the Holy Grail in John Hardyng's *Chronicle*." In Mahoney, *The Grail: A Casebook*, pp. 397–414.

———. *Sir Thomas Malory.* Leiden: E. J. Brill, 1987.

———. "Structure and Meaning in Malory's 'The Fair Maid of Astolat.'" *Forum for Modern Language Studies* 12 (1976): 354–66.

Robeson, Lisa. "Women's Worship: Female Versions of Chivalric Honour." In Whetter and Radulescu, *Re-Viewing "Le Morte Darthur,"* pp. 107–18.

Roland, Meg. "Arthur and the Turks." *Arthuriana* 16.4 (2006): 29–42.

Rumble, Thomas C. "'The Tale of Tristram': Development by Analogy." In Lumiansky, *Malory's Originality*, pp. 118–83.

Ryrie, Alec. "Britain and Ireland." In *Palgrave Advances in the European Reformations*, pp. 124–46. New York: Palgrave Macmillan, 2006.

Shichtman, Martin B. "Percival's Sister: Genealogy, Virginity, and Blood." *Arthuriana* 9.2 (1999): 11–20.

Southern, R. W. *The Making of the Middle Ages.* New Haven, CT: Yale University Press, 1953.

Spisak, James W., ed. *Studies in Malory.* Kalamazoo, MI: Medieval Institute Publications, 1985.

Starr, Nathan C. "The Moral Problem in Malory." *Dalhousie Review* 47 (1967–68): 467–74.

Stuhmiller, Jacqueline. "*Iudicium Dei, iudicium fortunae*: Trial by Combat in Malory's *Le Morte Darthur*." *Speculum* 81.2 (2006): 427–62.

Sutton, Anne. "Malory in Newgate: A New Document." *Library*, 7th series, 1.3 (2000): 243–62.

Swanson, Keith. "'God Woll Have a Stroke': Judicial Combat in the *Morte Darthur*." *Bulletin of the John Rylands University Library of Manchester* 74 (1992): 155–73.

Sweeney, Michelle. "Divine Love or Loving Divinely?: The Ending of Malory's *Morte Darthur*." *Arthuriana* 16.2 (2006): 73–77.

Takamiya, Toshiyuki, and Derek Brewer, eds. *Aspects of Malory.* Woodbridge: D. S. Brewer, 1981. Reprinted with a revised bibliography, Totowa, NJ: Rowman & Littlefield, 1986.

Thompson, John J. *Robert Thornton and the London Thornton Manuscript.* Cambridge: D. S. Brewer, 1987.

Tolhurst, Fiona. "The Once and Future Queen: The Development of Guenevere from Geoffrey of Monmouth to Malory." *Bibliographical Bulletin of the International Arthurian Society* 50 (1998): 272–308.

———. "Why Every Knight Needs His Lady: Re-viewing Questions of Genre and 'Cohesion' in Malory's *Le Morte Darthur*." In Whetter and Radulescu, *Re-Viewing "Le Morte Darthur,"* pp. 133–47.

Tucker, P. E. "Chivalry in the *Morte*." In J. A. W. Bennett, *Essays on Malory*, pp. 64–103.

———. "A Source for 'The Healing of Sir Urry' in the *Morte Darthur*." *Modern Language Review* 50 (1955): 490–92.

Twomey, Michael D. "'Hadet with an aluisch mon' and 'britned to noȝt': *Sir Gawain and the Green Knight*, Death, and the Devil." In Cherewatuk and Whetter, *Arthurian Way of Death*, pp. 73–93.

———. "The Voice of Aurality in the *Morte Darthur*." *Arthuriana* 13.4 (Winter 2003): 103–18.

Unwin, George. *The Gilds and Companies of London.* 4th ed. New York: Barnes and Noble, 1964.

Van Engen, John. "The Christian Middle Ages as an Historiographical Problem." *American Historical Review* 91.3 (1986): 519–52. On the World Wide Web through JSTOR.

Vinaver, Eugène. *King Arthur and His Knights: Selected Tales by Sir Thomas Malory*. Oxford: Oxford University Press, 1975.

———. *Malory*. Oxford: Clarendon Press, 1929.

———. "A Note on Malory's Prose." In Takamiya and Brewer, *Aspects of Malory*, pp. 9–15.

———. "On Art and Nature." In J. A. W. Bennett, *Essays on Malory*, pp. 29–40.

Virgoe, Roger. *Private Life in the Fifteenth Century*. New York: Weidenfeld & Nicolson, 1989.

Weston, David W. V. *Carlisle Cathedral History*. Carlisle, UK: Carlisle Bookcase, 2000.

Wheeler, Bonnie. "Grief in Avalon: Sir Palomydes' Psychic Pain." In *Grief and Gender: 700–1700*, edited by Jennifer C. Vaught with Lynne Dickson Bruckner, pp. 65–80. New York: Palgrave Macmillan, 2003.

Whetter, K. S. "Love and Death in Arthurian Romance." In Cherewatuk and Whetter, *Arthurian Way of Death*, pp. 94–114.

———. "The Stanzaic *Morte Arthur* and Medieval Tragedy." *Reading Medieval Studies* 28 (2002): 87–111.

———. *Understanding Genre and Medieval Romance*. Aldershot: Ashgate, 2008.

———. "Warfare and Combat in *Le Morte Darthur*." In *Writing War: Medieval Literary Responses to Warfare*, edited by Corinne Saunders, Françoise Le Saux, and Neil Thomas, pp. 169–86. Cambridge: D. S. Brewer, 2004.

Whetter, K. S., and Raluca L. Radulescu, eds. *Re-Viewing "Le Morte Darthur": Texts and Contexts, Characters and Themes*. Cambridge: D. S. Brewer, 2005.

Whitaker, Muriel. *Arthur's Kingdom of Adventure: The World of Malory's "Morte Darthur."* Cambridge: D. S. Brewer; Totowa, NJ: Barnes and Noble, 1984.

Whitehead, F. "Lancelot's Penance." In J. A. W. Bennett, *Essays on Malory*, pp. 104–13.

Wood, Juliette. "The Holy Grail: From Romance Motif to Modern Genre." *Folklore* 111 (2000): 169–90.

Wright, Thomas L. "'The Tale of King Arthur': Beginnings and Foreshadowings." In Lumiansky, *Malory's Originality*, pp. 9–66.

Contributors

FELICIA NIMUE ACKERMAN is professor of philosophy at Brown University. Much of her research deals with how analytic philosophy can enrich Malory scholarship and vice versa. Her publications dealing with Malory include essays, book reviews, short stories, light verse, and op-ed columns. Her most recent piece in *Arthuriana* is "'Your charge is to me a plesure': Manipulation, Gareth, Lynet, and Malory," *Arthuriana* 19.3 (2009). Her book *Ethics and Character in Malory's "Le Morte D'Arthur"* is forthcoming in the Palgrave series Studies in Arthurian and Courtly Cultures.

DORSEY ARMSTRONG is associate professor of English at Purdue University, where she teaches courses on Old and Middle English, the medieval world, history of the English language, and Arthurian literature. Her research focuses primarily on Sir Thomas Malory—her book *Gender and the Chivalric Community in Sir Thomas Malory's "Morte d'Arthur"* (University Press of Florida) appeared in 2003 and her modern English translation—*Sir Thomas Malory's "Morte Darthur": A New English Translation Based on the Winchester Manuscript* (Parlor Press) appeared in 2009. Currently she serves as editor-in-chief of the academic journal *Arthuriana* and is working on a book entitled *Mapping Malory's Morte* (co-authored with Kenneth Hodges) due to appear from Palgrave Macmillan in 2014.

KAREN CHEREWATUK, professor of English at St. Olaf College, Northfield, MN, has always been fascinated by the intersection of literature and the cultural context that produces it. Malory's attention to the details of funeral rituals served as the catalyst to the article in this collection, while her book *Marriage, Adultery and Inheritance in Malory's Morte Darthur* (Arthurian Studies, D. S. Brewer, 2006) explores late medieval ideas about marriage (as opposed to adultery) that undergird the *Morte Darthur*. With Ulrike Wiethaus, she edited *Dear Sister: Medieval Women and the Epistolary Genre* (Univ. of Pennsylvania Press, 1993) and with K. S. Whetter *The Arthurian Way of Death* (Arthurian Studies, 2009). Cherewatuk's scholarship aims to help modern readers understand something of the assumptions with which medieval audiences approached a text.

D. Thomas Hanks, Jr., has been at Baylor University for thirty-five years. His teaching and research focus on stylistic and manuscript issues in Malory's *Morte Darthur*, on Chaucer's *Canterbury Tales*, and on classics of children's literature. He has published in *Arthuriana*, the Arthurian Studies series, *The Arthurian Yearbook*, *The Chaucer Review, ELN, The Children's Literature Journal*, and in various edited volumes of studies on Chaucer or Malory. He has also recorded in several Chaucerian or Malorian roles with the Chaucer Studio.

Sue Ellen Holbrook is professor of English at Southern Connecticut State University, specializing in composition/rhetoric and medieval literature. She has published essays and book reviews in various venues, including "Nymue, the Chief Lady of the Lake, in Malory's *Le Morte D'Arthur*" in *Arthurian Women* (Garland, 1996), revised in *On Arthurian Women: Essays in Memory of Maureen Fries*, in which she also published an essay on a biographical review of Helaine Scudder. She regularly presents papers at national and international conferences on medieval literature.

Janet Jesmok retired Emerita in 2001 from the Honors College of the University of Wisconsin–Milwaukee, where she taught courses in epic and romance, Arthurian literature, Chaucer, and academic writing. She has been involved in Malory studies since the late 1970s, when she wrote her dissertation on Malory's women. She has been a frequent presenter at the annual International Congress on Medieval Studies at Western Michigan University and participated in Reading Malory Aloud for several years. Her essays, often focusing on issues of language, women and gender, heroism, and the psychology of knighthood, have appeared most recently in *Arthuriana*.

Corey Olsen is president of Signum University and founder of the Mythgard Institute, an online teaching center for the study of Tolkien and other works of imaginative literature. He received his PhD in medieval literature from Columbia University, and his research interests include Malory, Chaucer, and Tolkien. His first book, *Exploring J.R.R. Tolkien's The Hobbit*, was published by Houghton Mifflin Harcourt in 2012.

Fiona Tolhurst is maître assistante in medieval and early modern English at the University of Geneva. Her previous publications in the field of Arthurian studies include two monographs: *Geoffrey of Monmouth and the Feminist Origins of the Arthurian Legend* (Palgrave Macmillan, 2012) and *Geoffrey of Monmouth and the Translation of Female Kingship* (Palgrave Macmillan, 2013). Her articles have appeared in journals such as *Arthuriana*, *The Bibliographical Bulletin of the International Arthurian Society*, and *Historical Reflections/Réflections Historiques* as well as in *Eleanor of Aquitaine: Lord and Lady* (Palgrave Macmillan, 2003) and *Reviewing Le Morte Darthur: Texts and Contexts, Characters and Themes* (Boydell and Brewer, 2005). She is also the editor of a special issue of *Arthuriana* on theoretical approaches to Geoffrey of Monmouth (1998) and co-editor with Bonnie Wheeler of *On Arthurian Women: Essays in Memory of Maureen Fries* (Scriptorium, 2001). In two recent contributions to *Arthuriana*, she studies the presentation of female heroism in contemporary Arthurian novels for young adults and C. S. Lewis as a writer and reader of Arthurian literature.

K. S. WHETTER is professor of English at Acadia University, Nova Scotia, where his teaching duties include courses on Arthurian and medieval literature. His principal research areas are medieval romance and Malory's *Morte Darthur*. He is especially interested in Malory's presentation of character, combat, and tragedy, interests which have been explored in part in his monograph *Understanding Genre and Medieval Romance* (Ashgate, 2008). His chapter in *Malory and Christianity* reflects his current interests in romance and religion, as well as in the interconnections between the lexical and bibliographic texts of the *Morte Darthur*.

Index

Typeset in 10/13 Adobe Caslon Pro
Composed by Tom Krol
Manufactured by Cushing-Malloy, Inc.

Medieval Institute Publications
College of Arts and Sciences
Western Michigan University
1903 W. Michigan Avenue
Kalamazoo, MI 49008-5432
http://www.wmich.edu/medieval/mip

WESTERN MICHIGAN UNIVERSITY